PAUL LOGOTHETIS

TOE BLAKE

Winning is Everything

ECW

Get the eBook free!*
*proof of purchase required

Purchase the print edition
and receive the eBook free.
For details, go to ecwpress.com/eBook.

Copyright © Paul Logothetis, 2020

Published by ECW Press
665 Gerrard Street East
Toronto, Ontario, Canada M4M 1Y2
416-694-3348 / info@ecwpress.com

All rights reserved. No part of this publication may be reproduced, stored in a retrieval system, or transmitted in any form by any process — electronic, mechanical, photocopying, recording, or otherwise — without the prior written permission of the copyright owners and ECW Press. The scanning, uploading, and distribution of this book via the Internet or via any other means without the permission of the publisher is illegal and punishable by law. Please purchase only authorized electronic editions, and do not participate in or encourage electronic piracy of copyrighted materials. Your support of the author's rights is appreciated.

Editor for the Press: Michael Holmes
Cover design: David A. Gee
Front cover photograph © Le Studio du Hockey/Hockey Hall of Fame
All photos are from the collection of Bruce Blake.

LIBRARY AND ARCHIVES CANADA CATALOGUING IN PUBLICATION

Title: Toe Blake : winning is everything / Paul Logothetis.

Names: Logothetis, Paul, author.

Identifiers: Canadiana (print) 20200166514
Canadiana (ebook) 20200166522

ISBN 978-1-77041-490-7 (softcover)
ISBN 978-1-77305-483-4 (PDF)
ISBN 978-1-77305-482-7 (EPUB)

Subjects: LCSH: Blake, Toe, 1912-1995. | LCSH: Hockey players—Canada—Biography. | LCSH: Hockey coaches—Canada—Biography. | LCGFT: Biographies.

Classification: LCC GV848.5.B54 L64 2020
DDC 796.962092—dc23

The publication of *Toe Blake* has been funded in part by the Government of Canada. *Ce livre est financé en partie par le gouvernement du Canada.* We also acknowledge the contribution of the Government of Ontario through the Ontario Book Publishing Tax Credit, and through Ontario Creates for the marketing of this book.

ONTARIO CREATES

Canada

PRINTED AND BOUND IN CANADA

PRINTING: FRIESENS 5 4 3 2 1

MIX
Paper from responsible sources
FSC® C016245
FSC www.fsc.org

To Jacqueline, Jorgia, and
Montreal Canadiens fans everywhere.

CONTENTS

FOREWORD
BY SCOTTY BOWMAN

TOE BLAKE HAD SUCH a formidable influence on my coaching career that it can feel very difficult to put my thoughts into words. Although I did not have a first-hand perspective of seeing Toe during his playing career, I did have an in-depth view of his coaching career from the early Fifties when he took charge of the Valleyfield Braves of the Quebec Senior League. Coaching a small market team in that league was quite a challenge, but Toe always accepted challenges. His work with Valleyfield meant he often competed against Punch Imlach and his Quebec Aces Senior team, which included a young center named Jean Beliveau, and the experience paved the way for Toe to be so successful coaching the Montreal Canadiens to eight Stanley Cup wins in his 13 years in charge. This remarkable feat will go down in NHL history as unmatched. Watching Toe win the Stanley Cup in his first five seasons (from 1956 to 1961) leading the Canadiens inspired me to be a coach, and I started my junior coaching career at this same time with the Ottawa Junior Canadiens.

I next got to meet Toe in 1964 when I became coach of the Jr. Canadiens in Montreal. It was then that he became my mentor and good friend. With the expansion of the NHL in 1967, I was hired as the coach of the St. Louis Blues and eventually lost to Toe Blake's Canadiens team in the 1968 Stanley Cup Final, which was his eighth and last Stanley Cup win. When I returned to Montreal as coach in 1971, Toe was an advisor with the Canadiens and we had so many great times and visits as we won five Cups in eight years. His strong attributes became the footprint of my lengthy coaching career. Accountability, honesty and practice were the hallmark habits that made Toe, and he passed them on to me. They are also the qualities I have always referred to as why Toe Blake should be regarded as the most successful NHL coach in history.

His playing career in Montreal briefly included a stint with the Montreal Maroons followed by a stellar career with the Montreal Canadiens, where he was a member of the famous Punch Line with Elmer Lach and Maurice Richard, and he was named "The Old Lamplighter" in reference to his goal-scoring ability. Rightfully so, Toe is an honored member of the Hockey Hall of Fame and it is truly unique that his playing career and coaching career were so successful. I am truly blessed to have known Toe Blake as my mentor and good friend.

Regards,
Scotty Bowman, January 2020

AUTHOR'S NOTE & ACKNOWLEDGEMENTS

THE IDEA OF A biography of Toe Blake had been simmering in my mind for years. I was afforded the opportunity to meet Toe as a child through his son Bruce. I was in my early teens and I had just returned from the Doug Crossman hockey camp to find Toe visiting Bruce and the family one summer day. Toe spoke to me about hockey and offered to test out the goalie skills I'd picked up. Suddenly, goalie pads were strapped on to my legs and a glove and blocker emerged and Toe grabbed a hockey stick and started firing shots at me. A moment of nostalgia that remains burned into the memory. Why was that? Because I was lucky enough to understand who Toe was, what he stood for and what that meant to the Montreal Canadiens franchise.

Toe evoked the championship pedigree of Stanley Cups, record runs and winning. I relish having had the opportunity to see this firsthand with the Stanley Cup triumphs of 1986 and '93. I know that Toe was involved with the 1986 Cup run, traveling with the team to Calgary for the Final and offering encouragement to the team behind the scenes. The contrast to today's Montreal

Canadiens group is astounding; when I mentioned Toe Blake's name to one leading player during interviews for this book it only evoked a vacant stare. This, despite Toe's image being painted right above us on the locker room alongside other Habs greats. Has hockey forgotten Toe? It feels like it. The Montreal Canadiens take such great pride in celebrating their illustrious past and the greats who made a mark on the franchise, and yet Toe is rarely honoured. A visit to the Bell Centre offers little by way of homage except for a plaque that blends in with the others. Nothing more to remind us that winning was the only thing that mattered—not making the playoffs and then seeing what happened. Such a strategy would have made Toe's blood boil. Everything you did, every action you took had one single outcome: victory. A glance up to the rafters at the Bell Centre displays retired jerseys that hang as generational reminders, and yet nothing reminds us of Toe. His Punch Line teammates Maurice Richard and Elmer Lach both have their jerseys retired, but not Blake's No. 6. I hope this maiden biography about one of old-time hockey's greatest influences can help remind us of his influence and contributions to the club.

Having worked for over a decade in Europe and followed the daily narrative that is world soccer, I always admired how knowledgeable the fans were of the historic greats of their sport, regardless of tribal connections. You could travel to a remote village in Spain and mention the name of Alex Ferguson, identified by many as one of the greatest soccer managers of our time, and no one would bat an eye; every soccer fan would know the Manchester United figure and his exploits. Even if he coached in another league, country, or continent – the game honours him. I could not comprehend how no biography about the greatest coach in NHL history had never been written. Not only that, but one of the 100 greatest players in NHL history.

Researching this book was a combination of archival research and interviews with former players, acquaintances and family members. In those instances when you are with Toe and his thoughts, these are observations and quotes from Toe that have been paraphrased to reflect the moment, as he has described it. It was impossible to be inside of Toe's head but the research, his own words from interviews and memories from those who knew him helped construct this aspect of the narrative. I thank Toe's son Bruce for giving me his blessing to move forward on the project and for providing valuable family insight. Many of the anecdotes and memories date to over 40 years ago so I thank everyone who was so patient with my repetitive questions, especially former players and colleagues of Toe's. There was a lot of microfiche loaded and scrolled through, radio and TV clips reviewed, and all kinds of genealogy documents consulted. I thank the people at Radio-Canada, Archives Canada, The Hockey News and the Hockey Hall of Fame for all of their assistance in digging up documents for me, as well as sites like Ancestry.ca and Newspapers.com for providing me access to their own library of records.

I must also thank my family for their support, especially my wife Kimberly who put up with so many hours and weekends of me away writing or doing research in the library to take care of our girls, Jacqueline and Jorgia. My mother Revilla has always been one of my biggest supporters and I also have to thank Carol and Alex for letting me borrow their cottage for a few days to put the final touches on the manuscript.

I'd also like to thank ECW Press for taking a chance on a first-time author and for showing genuine excitement on this project from the start. My editor Michael Holmes has worked diligently with me to get this book done, just like everyone who calls the office on Gerrard Street East home. It has been a long, winding process, but it is something that I have taken great joy and purpose in doing. Now, I hope you, the reader, can enjoy a portrait of Toe's remarkable and eventful life and his influence on one of professional sport's proudest franchises.

PAUL LOGOTHETIS, JANUARY 2020

CHAPTER 1

GAME DAY

THERE IS LITTLE TO hold your eye as you glance around Bruce Blake's dining room. But the view to the lake is captivating, giving the cedar walls and close confines a breath of fresh air. Bruce sits at the table with a cigarette in hand, watching the snow trickle down and emitting a terse cough between drags. Ash dangles off the tray onto the thick plastic cover draping the table. Bruce is gaunt and pale, and his breath wheezes with excitement when an incredulous moment or personal anecdote about his father comes to mind. Their relationship was turbulent: Bruce, the lone son to a father who found himself the middle member of a family of 13 scraping through the Great Depression.

In his small cottage on the lake, Bruce might be able to forget about the explosive family dinners, the wild locker room celebrations, the lonely nights in an empty home, the inexplicable, tragic curse that seems to follow his family. Though it's likely easier in the summer months, over beers with long-time friends who are up at the cottage for the season, or by pulling out his long, slender walking stick and stepping out for a stroll amid the evergreen, oak, cedar and birch trees that populate the surrounding woods. These are the months when Montreal and its fan base exhales, when the Canadiens take a break and Bruce can, too.

Winter, meanwhile, is another story.

Every period in an 82-game NHL schedule provides a flashback to the past.

His father would have never juggled the lines like this coach, says Bruce; he would be strongly against it, saying the team should work together, make the line work. A giveaway deep in the zone and the resulting goal bring back the agony his father lived out behind the bench on a nightly basis, when players had to restrain him from jumping on the ice to chase after an official or watch on in disbelief as he banged his head against the glass partition separating him from the first row of seats. A blown call costs the Canadiens a point and irks Bruce — until his father's words from a similar moment, years past, long after leaving his rinkside post, ultimately calm him. "It's only a game, Bruce," Toe Blake would say from the comfort of his La-Z-Boy, with a scotch and water in hand.

Luckily, with Toe behind the bench, most nights ended in victory. But these days, Bruce must wait for the occasional Saturday night thrill for the Bell Centre to come alive and the golden memories to come flooding back, of when the Forum was a fortress and the Montreal Canadiens the lords of the league.

Bruce knows he was lucky to grow up during a special time, watching as his father guided the Canadiens to eight Stanley Cups over 13 seasons. Winning was not only routine but expected. Bruce was left puzzled in 1961, when Toe did not bring the Cup back to the Blake home as he had the previous five straight springs. Today, a glance around the Blake home reveals no relation to Toe. There are a couple of photographs, but they are not obvious. Bruce has to butt out his cigarette and get up to fetch them.

He brings out one framed picture and another loose one, both black-and-white. The framed photograph is of his parents on their wedding day, in 1934. Toe, 22, was playing for the Hamilton Tigers when he met Betty Marianne Walters, daughter to a Winona, Ontario, fruit dealer, and—fittingly—the Peach Queen of Niagara Falls. Toe looks the picture of a strapping young man—no hulk, but a frame filled in enough to merit his reputation as a physical, gritty player boys admired while their mothers tried to shutter their ears to keep his foul-mouthed tirades from seeping in.

The other picture features Toe in the Montreal Forum alongside Jacques Plante and Maurice Richard at some time in the 1950s. All are standing behind children who appear to be their sons. But is it Bruce whose shoulders welcome Toe's hands? The kid sports a Canadiens jersey with the No. 8 on it while Toe wore No. 6 for the Habs.

Bruce has one more item to show. He slides over a small, green case that flips open to reveal the Order of Canada medal his father received in 1982. This is the one of the few tangible pieces of silverware Bruce has left to show from Toe's illustrious Hall of Fame career.

Toe won three Stanley Cups as a player with the Montreal Maroons and Canadiens. Captain of the Canadiens for eight seasons, he won the 1939 Hart Trophy as the league's most valuable player, on a last-place team. He cleaned up his act to win the Lady Byng Trophy as the league's most sportsmanlike player seven years later, amassing a head-scratching two penalty minutes. Toe was a three-time First Team All-Star and a Second Team pick twice. There was a Memorial Cup victory with the Sudbury Wolves before all of that, a triumph that spawned his reputation as a gritty, all-round team guy. And then, as coach of the Canadiens, another eight Stanley Cup rings.

Yet none of the rings or silverware associated with these triumphs can be found in Bruce Blake's Laurentian-area home.

Nor can one spot the diamond ring, the silver tray, the near-life-size bust or the key to the city of Sudbury his father was awarded during his playing days. The player caricatures that famously hung on the walls inside his tavern on St. Catherine Street West are also nowhere to be seen.

Everything disappeared over the years, bungled into burlap sacks during midnight robberies, packed away deep in cardboard boxes that were hauled away to Goodwill, or scavenged by neighbors or friendly vultures shortly after his death. The rest was left out on the corner with the trash.

"Things get lost over time. If I had known I'd be left with nothing, I would have kept one of his goddamn fedoras at least," Bruce says.

But not all has been lost—a ring to commemorate the record five straight Stanley Cup triumphs between 1956 and '60 did survive all that carelessness. Bruce's son Brent has it in his home, in front of a small shrine constructed of the few precious mementos from his grandfather's glory days. The Montreal Canadiens displayed the ring for some time before shuttering the team museum inside the Bell Centre in 2014.

For Bruce, the ring is the only remaining memento of his father's legacy of success with the Montreal Canadiens franchise. Still, Bruce prefers not to be reminded of a past he has spent so long forgetting. That's why, after his father's death, he left all trophies, pictures and memorabilia in his father's home, and took only the tools.

• • •

A teenaged Bruce Blake awoke to the aroma of eggs and bacon. It was enough to prod him from bed and down the stairs to the kitchen, where his father, Toe, was sitting, sipping on coffee with the newspaper at hand as Betty served him a plate of breakfast. As Bruce took his seat, Toe wasted little time jabbing at him, taking issue with his long hair and the chores he had yet to complete. Bruce was still only rubbing his eyes, but the rituals of game day had already begun.

Game days were more manageable inside the large Sheraton Drive home in Montreal West than they had been when the entire family lived in a duplex at 5259 Ponsard Street. There, Toe would send everyone out of the house for the afternoon to ensure his rest. On Sheraton, it was only Betty, Bruce and Mrs. Salter, the housekeeper, in the home. Bruce's sisters, Joan and Betty, were both married and living in homes of their own. Toe always tried to stay occupied on game days to avoid falling into an unnecessary analysis of his team, that night's opponent, his history with the referee—any number of subjects. The Canadiens may have won three games in a row, but that wouldn't keep him from reflecting on the last defeat and trying to figure out what had gone wrong. Blake's obsessive fear of losing harkened back to his teenage years in Coniston, Ontario, where he grew up fighting for every little advantage for fear everything could collapse. That sentiment continued over the years as his duties grew, from Canadiens captain to coach.

After a steak lunch, "the Bear" would retreat to his bedroom for an afternoon nap. Outside Toe's door, Bruce would tiptoe down the stairs, pulling on his boots and jacket, and get out to the park. Bruce knew it was best to scram with the house on lockdown and Toe sequestered inside his room, locked up in a jail cell of his own making. Toe would lie on the bed, staring up at the ceiling, feeling overwhelmed by the image of Gordie Howe or Bobby Hull breaking through his defense untouched to score on goaltenders Gump Worsley or Charlie Hodge.

"I had to quit," Toe explained following his retirement in 1968. "It's not that I had no new worlds to conquer. Every game, every season is a new challenge. But I'd been meeting these challenges as coach of the Canadiens for 13 years . . . The pressure was getting to be unbearable. On the day of the game I was getting to be unbearable. The afternoons were the worst. All the thinking. And then the waiting, waiting, waiting. I was no good to anyone, not even my family . . . I had to quit."

Only Betty was privy to the turmoil Toe endured on those afternoons. Betty knew all about the stress the job commanded and the toll it took on Toe and the family. She often had to talk Toe down for hours into the night after a defeat, or when his nerves began to take over on game day. Bruce knew little of this at the time. He was a teenager looking forward to the Saturday night hockey game at the Forum. Bruce loved the Saturday routine. Toe would be in the family Buick and rolling out of the garage by 6 p.m.

"If you're in the car, you're coming to the game. If not . . ." he would trail off, his right foot already pressing on the gas pedal.

Once they arrived, Bruce and Betty would separate from Toe and make their way to the Forum coffee shop. There, Bruce would tuck into french fries with gravy while Betty sipped on a gin gimlet and enjoyed laughs and chatter with Worsley's wife, Doreen. Toe, meanwhile, descended the Forum steps into his own personal inferno. He made his way to the dressing room—the heart of the Montreal Forum—his hands in his pockets, slowing his pace to crack a comment or shake a hand along the way. He saluted Forum employees and staff with smiles and positive talk about that night's opponent and breezed into the dressing room looking confident. Blake was not one for small talk, but he greeted all he passed along his path. The players halted their conversations and preparations to salute their leader as he walked through to his office. Toe commanded respect in the dressing room because of his success as a player and coach, but fear was an integral part of his profile. Still, it ate at him to play the role of the despot, terrorizing his troops, threatening their livelihoods with the whisper of a benching. And Toe felt his influence was slipping the longer the team continued without a Stanley Cup win. This fear and frustration would manifest itself one intermission inside the dressing room when he took a hockey stick to a medicine cabinet with the fury of an axe felling a tree. Once the cabinet was in pieces, Toe dropped the stick onto the mangled mess, slicked his hair back into place, picked up his fedora and placed it on his head. Not a word was spoken, but the message was clear as he exited the dressing room. That time it worked . . . but Toe worried his techniques were losing effectiveness, that his players were becoming complacent. An old dog without new tricks.

The stress had been building since back-to-back 3–0 playoff losses to Chicago had ended the record run of five straight Stanley Cups in 1961. Montreal had failed to get past the semifinals of the six-team league for four straight seasons. The Toronto Maple Leafs had muscled them out of the playoffs the past two seasons, with the Leafs rallying from a 3–2 deficit to eliminate the Canadiens in seven games in the latest exit.

Toronto looked the favorite again before the start of the 1964–65 campaign. Ken Reardon, Blake's closest ally among the executive suits and the man most responsible for getting him the job, had resigned before the start of the season. General manager Frank Selke was out, replaced by Sam Pollock. David Molson had moved up from vice-president to president. The changes and mood within the organization were palpable. Suddenly, the stakes were higher, and Toe could feel it. So, too, could the beat writers covering the team. Some of the hockey press labelled Toe a caretaker coach who had coasted to success on the backs of All-Stars like Jean Beliveau, Maurice "Rocket" Richard and Jacques Plante during the record run. It was impossible not to let those words get to him. And it was happening at a time when, off the ice, Betty Blake had been diagnosed with cancer, leaving Toe watching from the middle as his two loves suffered. The ensuing years were a seesaw battle within Toe's own mind. He was devoted to leading his beloved Canadiens, which compromised his ability to attend to the needs of his wife. On the road, Toe would pace his hotel room, wondering, *Why am I doing this? We're not winning, my wife is sick . . .* Betty began a seven-year run in and out of hospitals.

Toe was sad, frustrated, agitated. By 1968, he had reached a boiling point, as summarized by captain Jean Beliveau during the playoff run of what proved to be Toe's final season:

> When I entered his room, I found him pacing back and forth like a caged bear. "Jean, I don't know what's wrong with me. Something is going to snap here." He clutched his head with both hands and repeated, "Something's going to snap." I was probably the only person he could talk to besides Betty. Thirteen years of performance pressure must have finally overwhelmed him. We sat and talked for a couple of hours until he finally calmed down. For years Toe had been the man most responsible for our Stanley Cup successes. Blake was the real cornerstone of the Canadiens' dynasty, and we simply followed his lead.

Bruce had little inkling his father was dealing with these pressures as he took his seat, his tummy full of marshmallow ice cream, which he was proud to have kept entirely off his suit and tie. The seats were magnificent—just a few rows up off the ice in the corner of the reds. Toe also owned season tickets further up in the blues, but those were normally left for friends or other family. A wide grin enveloped Bruce's face every time he sat down on the cold wooden plank of his seat to watch his treasured Habitants at the Forum instead of at home alongside Mrs. Salter and her baloney sandwiches.

But Bruce did wince occasionally after a goal was scored on the home team, not for himself but for the reaction it elicited from his father. "Holy Dirty Dora!" Toe would exclaim, slapping his hands against his sides in frustration. He would then turn in circles behind the bench, chomping on his gum like a jackhammer while yelling instructions out loud for the entire team to hear, but sometimes the tirade was really destined for those players at fault for the goal and they knew it.

Luckily, the Canadiens won most Saturday nights, and Bruce would get to visit the dressing room afterward, where he would mingle with his heroes. There was a young forward, John Ferguson, who was one of the toughest players in the league and had instantly taken to Bruce, who felt like the luckiest kid in the world. Bruce would even join Toe and Betty in the directors' room a little later, where executives, suits and VIPs rubbed shoulders while Bruce picked at the sandwiches.

The game over and a glass of rye in his hand, Toe was finally able to loosen up. He was a warm, generous man who shared a joke as often as he laughed at one, but rarely at anyone's expense. Inside the walls of the Forum, Bruce could see how happy his parents were. He could only wonder why it was so different at home.

CHAPTER 2

CHILDHOOD

"I was lucky, I knew what I wanted to do from the first minute I was born. I wanted to play hockey."

ON AUGUST 21, 1912, the ground below was moving when Wilmer Blake welcomed his son Joseph Hector into the world.

The ninth child conceived by Wilmer and his wife, Arzélie Filion, Hector was one of the lucky 11 who would survive beyond birth. His arrival was cause for celebration, even if Wilmer knew this moment of joy would soon be disrupted.

Wilmer clutched his pipe with one hand and stroked his handlebar moustache with the other, his gaze turning toward the children who had gathered around to inspect their newest sibling. They poked, prodded and petted their little brother while Arzélie, exhausted, looked on. Hector's birth had blessed their home—number 6 on the south side of No. 3 Street in Victoria Mines—but Wilmer knew this place would remain but a memory for the family. The mine was closing, and there was no choice but to move on.

Originally known as Denison or McConnell mine, the Victoria mine was one of the key cogs in Mond Nickel Company's operations in the Sudbury area at the turn of the century. Dr. Alfred Mond established operations at the Victoria mine following its purchase in 1899, naming it after either Queen Victoria or a French woman named Victoria who lived in the town. The mine would churn out the bulk of the company's ore over the next decade.

Mineral deposits are what brought many families like the Blakes to Ontario. Wilmer and Arzélie had married in Angers, Quebec, in 1898, before picking up and moving west for work—as many Quebecers did at the time—to Sudbury's Nickel Belt region. They first settled in Copper Cliff. Come 1901, when operations at the mine had begun, they found themselves in nearby Creighton with their two sons, Tom and Leonard.

Wilmer was one of 200 employees working at the smelter, which sat two miles to the south of the Victoria mine. The smelter handled the ore from the Victoria mine and nearby Garson and Worthington as well as some from the Canadian Copper Company.

Mond had recently announced it was closing the smelter and moving those operations to Coniston, a farming town 21 miles west and closer to Sudbury. Coniston offered more desirable conditions, including proximity to other mines, plus two crucial factors that led Dr. Mond to sign off on the move.

Coniston sat on the junction of three railway lines: it was on the main lines of the Canadian Pacific Railway and the Canadian Northern Railway, and it also accessed the CNR's Toronto-Romford line. The Coniston smelter would have easy access to a national rail line that could deliver ore to Montreal, from which it would be shipped on to Swansea, Wales, to be refined. Furthermore, the Victoria mine site was not deemed suitable for expansion: it was sinking.

For Wilmer, the signs that Victoria Mines would be a ghost town within a year were clear. The Ukrainians living in the row houses across the street were normally reluctant to emerge from their dwellings. Now their constant public appearances indicated they were preparing for a forthcoming move. Suddenly, they were no longer hidden within their homes but moving freely—and a little frantically—between them. The Jolicoeurs—"Jim" Blake's neighbors at number 7—were considering sawing their home into sections to be moved to Coniston, as was normal practice at the time.

The Coniston smelter was nearing completion. Blake's job as a shaft sinker—a member of the crew that dug the initial holes in the mud—was about to disappear.

Mond had already begun construction of the new town at Coniston. The company had elected a relatively modern grid-style format, with streets, sidewalks, drainage, a water distribution system and fire protection all part of the plans. Homes may not have been equipped with bathrooms—there was a communal outhouse at the end of each block—but there was electricity. The town's wood sidewalks offered reprieve from the mud and dirt and offered easy access to Main Street's general stores, churches, schools, police station and clubhouse.

Owing to the location of the railway lines, Coniston's remote location carried with it an oddly isolated feel. The bare landscape surrounding the town was the result of years of intense logging. It started with the lumber demands related to the rebuild of Chicago following the great fire of 1871 and followed with the establishment of Coniston. People were coming from across Canada and Europe to settle here due to the certainty of work.

By the time Hector was crawling, the Blakes were on the move. Wilmer packed up a horse-pulled wagon with the family's belongings and set off for this new destination with Arzélie, Hector and two-year-old Denis at his side while his other children—Tom, Leonard, Aldege, Irene and Rose—followed alongside on foot.

• • •

The Blakes settled into a very modest three-bedroom home on Third Avenue. It was one of the many rented out by the Mond Nickel Company to its workers for five dollars per month.

The outside was constructed with white pine boards. Inside, the shiplap walls of plank pine boards were insulated with wood shavings hauled in from the lumber mill. The house was heated by a cookstove that Arzélie used to prepare family meals during the cold winter months. The kitchen became a cold storage during the winter, the room piled high with wood.

Wilmer was born to Eustache Blake and Christiana Osbourne in Massachusetts in 1874 and most likely came to Canada around the time of Eustache's death on June 28, 1896. Wilmer's father was buried two days later at La Paroisse De L'Ange-Gardien de Angers. Wilmer was a tall, handsome man of English and Irish descent, naturally pensive and quiet with an adventurous spirit. It may have been a result of his wanderlust English roots, said to be traceable to the famous Somersetshire sea-dog Admiral Blake who swept England's enemies from the seas. Despite so many mouths to feed, he would impulsively quit work at the smelter and go prospecting on occasion.

When his prospects were low, Wilmer worked at the Dennie Fur Farm, on a nearby creek where beavers swam. Wilmer's swashbuckling spirit ran in the family—Hector's older brother Leonard would quit the Mond mine at age 27 after 10 years as a converter skimmer, moving his wife Irene Giroux and their family to Detroit to work on the General Motors assembly line. But, like Wilmer, Leonard would ultimately return to Mond and Coniston, settling in at the Frood mine in 1929. He worked as pipe fitter, pump man, powder man and warehouse worker before eventually retiring in 1965. Hector and his younger brother George, who also enjoyed a professional hockey career but never reached the NHL, were the only members of the family to move away from Coniston.

Wilmer would return to work at the smelter as a crane operator. But one day, while moving some of the melted ore, he was seriously burned. The accident disabled Wilmer, and he was moved to the new position of motor man on the charge floor, where he worked until his retirement in 1942. He earned a full-service pension.

Inside the Blake household, Wilmer spoke English and Arzélie spoke French. Both parents were bilingual, but Arzélie refused to bend on her mother tongue, even when speaking to her Italian neighbor. The pair of women would be rambling on in their own languages to each other as they hung up the laundry. Questions over Hector's heritage would come when he joined the Montreal Canadiens, with the club pushing Blake to use the surname Blass, Blais or Blace to appeal to the francophone fan. But Hector, who was always at ease with the French language, was adamant he was a descendent of the Blakes.

"I speak French pretty well despite being raised in an English environment like Ontario. That's because we spoke French inside the family home, all 11 kids," Blake said. Arzélie enjoyed French roots, with the first mention of her family in Quebec dating to the 17th century. Rene Feuillon and Mathurine Nicou were likely the first immigrants from her family to reach Nouvelle-France, with Michelle Feuillon marrying in Batiscan, Quebec, in 1668. The family name changed to Fillion in 1740 and, at some point, the family surname settled on Filion. Arzélie would be the eighth child born to Francois Filion and Adeline D'Aoust on July 7, 1877 in Buckingham, Quebec.

Arzélie was proudly French and did all she could to ensure her children spoke her native language. She was hot to Wilmer's cold. Her features were haunting: piercing blue eyes below snow-white hair, and a frown that commanded attention. She was likely to "chew the rag" about the banks (which she did not trust), the Italians, the Polish—there was always something that irked her—while Wilmer rocked in his chair, listening on without offering a word. Liquor brought as a gift to Wilmer in his later years often found itself poured down the sink by Arzélie.

"She didn't smile much," her granddaughter Claudette Dumontelle remembers. "She never dressed up, she always wore a house dress. She always had something to say about people. Nowadays, grandmothers don't look old; she looked old."

As soon as Hector was old enough, he was expected to contribute to the family. The Blake boys would look for odd jobs around town, from home repair to woodcutting to general field work. The girls, meanwhile, were paid up to 50 cents a day to tend to domestic chores that included baking, laundry and helping sickly women or those recovering from childbirth. The Blake home was an industrious one, with all 11 children known for having a strong work ethic. Part of that ethic translated to sports, too. Wilmer raised his boys to be athletic, and he played on ball teams with many of his sons, including Hector.

When Hector wasn't working, he was like any other child, exploring his surroundings and playing with the neighborhood kids. There was a constant stream of trains coming and going to marvel at from atop one of the nearby hills. Coniston's landscape may have become more and more desolate, but there were rolling hills to explore. Children would often clamber up and get lost in their own adventures amid the wintergreens, whose leaves were sprouting tender and tasty plants they could snack on. This was preferable to the bitter winter snack of rotten wood root, which was collected and stored for those winter months to keep vitamin A deficiency or anemia at bay, with vegetables and fruit not always available. Hector enjoyed frolicking among the remaining evergreens, birch, maple and alder in the woods, even as these joys were being eradicated by pollution from the smelter.

The roast yard—where the ore would burn for up to three months so the iron and ore content could oxidize—was one mile from the Coniston plant. The ore was received in side-bottom dump cars, which swung onto one side and then the other, dumping the ore into a ditch between two tracks of rails laid at 20-foot centers. After one side had been dumped, the car was switched to the other track to prevent its other side falling into the ditch. Wilmer operated one of the 15-ton locomotive cranes in the roast yard, which ultimately led to the accident that would force him onto the Coniston plant floor. The sulfuric fumes and ashes permeated the air and killed the trees, leaving bare branches akin to skeletons with piles of dry, fallen leaves gathering below for Hector and his friends to run among in the summer months.

Out on the baseball diamond, Hector would gasp whenever the wind picked up and blew sulfuric gas into town, leaving a burning sensation in his eyes, nose and throat. "The gas was so strong and thick, we could no longer see the smelter," remembered one resident. "The vegetation on the mountainside and the grass in the fields would turn yellow. The leaves on the trees would wither and die and then the leaves would fall off the trees in the middle of July. When the wind was blowing from the south, it would change the atmosphere to a medium blue haze and make breathing difficult and adding to the air pollution was the sand that was used in the smelting process. When the wind was blowing hard enough, the sand would cover the ground and in winter, would turn the snow a yellow-ochre shade." Little survived in these conditions, yet the townspeople soldiered on. Hector knew no different.

Maurice "Rocket" Richard was privy to Coniston's "moonscape" during his own playing days. Richard and his wife, Lucille, stopped off in Blake's hometown during one trip west on the suggestion of his "Punch Line" teammate Blake. Toe sent the Rocket to the home of his boyhood friend and Sudbury Wolves teammate Larry Lafrance.

"Maurice knocked on Larry's door, and when my grandfather opened the door, he asked, incredulously, 'What are you doing here, Rocket?'" Lafrance's grandson Brian Tuuri recounts. "Richard told my grandfather, 'Toe always talked about Coniston, its giant oak trees and open land, so I promised him I would stop in on one of my trips.' But Coniston was a wasteland from all the smeltering. So my grandfather brought Maurice out and showed him around. It didn't take long for the Rocket to figure things out, looking around at a scene that looked more like the moon than a postcard. My grandfather said Maurice just muttered, 'That goddamn Toe.'"

• • •

As sport began to consume his life, Coniston began to call Hector "Toe."

Newspaper clipping after clipping, books, anecdotes and even his son, Bruce, and his grandson Kenny credit Toe's younger sister Margaret with creating his lifelong moniker. The story goes that Margaret could not properly pronounce his name as a child, instead referring to him as "Hec-Toe."

But Toe himself, when being honored at the President Hotel in Sudbury in July 1983, suggested his brother Lionel—two years his junior, compared to Margaret's seven years—was the true culprit. "It's rare that people call me Hector. I got the nickname 'Toe' as a youngster. My little brother, attempting to pronounce 'Hector,' came up with something like 'Hec-toe,'" Blake explained on a night when he was "roasted and toasted" by the Sudbury community for his hockey achievements.

Another belief was that Hector had earned the nickname because of his playing style. Toe seemed to carry the puck between his legs and near his toes like the powerful Montreal Maroons center Nels Stewart.

Whichever sibling is to be thanked, they provided Toe with a unique title just as hockey was becoming a popular pastime for the 1,000-plus residents of Coniston. The oldest hockey-related photograph dates to sometime in 1914 or '15, with seven players (teams played seven a-side then) dressed in striped shirts with a large *C* in the center. They all look sternly into the camera, with two referees sitting alongside them dressed in suits.

Coniston has produced an impressive list of reputable NHL players despite its small size. Randy Boyd, Jim Fox and Noel Price all played at the highest professional level, while Toe's younger brother George managed a short career in the AHL. Blake isn't the only Hall of Fame coach to emerge from the Sudbury region, either. New York Islanders great Al Arbour is a local, as well as former fellow Toronto Maple Leafs players George Armstrong and Eddie Shack.

While Fox and Boyd honed their trade at the Coniston Community Centre/Arena—renamed the Toe Blake Memorial Arena in 2011—there were no such indoor luxuries for Toe. He and his teammates had only the outdoor ice surface in the center of town to play on. Toe would pass it every day on his way to school, trudging through several feet of snow, dreaming up what could be. He imagined directing a pass from Howie Morenz past the opposing goalie for the game winner, with the crowd rising to its feet and the Montreal Canadiens legend jumping into his arms in celebration.

"I was always a Canadiens fan, even when I was eight years old in Coniston," said Toe, whose earliest ambition was to be the next Morenz. "I was very young when I heard about the famous Howie Morenz. It's rare to find an athlete in Ontario who hasn't heard about the feats of Morenz and hasn't adopted him as their idol with the dream of being his equal, one day."

Blake already understood what his destiny was by the age of 10. "My ambition was to play in the National Hockey League and not baseball," Toe told *The Hockey News* in 1960. "I guess I'd figured out that a kid born in Canada didn't have much chance to be a major league ball player. If I'd been born in the United States, I'd probably have thought differently. But I saw all those Canadians playing in the NHL and I felt I had a chance to make it."

School may not always provide children with excitement, but for Toe it was a great outlet for his growing appetite for sports. At the Coniston Separate School, it was mandatory for boys to play sports at recess, the period Toe looked forward to with glee from the moment he awoke every day.

With his lunch rolled up in a newspaper, Toe left home each morning in bitterly cold conditions thanks to a north wind, trudging in what felt like slow motion past men shoveling the snow. The worst storms saw the white stuff piled as high as telegraph wires, and sometimes it took days to clear the roads. The wooden sidewalks weren't plowed, so once enough snow was cleared for a horse-drawn cutter to get moving, Toe could walk behind it or follow the already laid track to make the journey that little bit easier. The bitter cold was biting, and the cotton or wool garments the children wore never seemed to completely keep it out. Once they arrived at school, they would often linger in the basement close to the steam room, which heated the building, to warm up.

Coniston's outdoor ice rink—the only playing surface in town—was near the school, which meant Toe could be in goal within minutes of the recess bell. Toe would wolf down the salted pork lunch that was the norm in winter unless it was a day when beef drippings on bread were served (which delayed his exit to the rink, as he took a little more time to savor the unexpected treat).

At first Toe played goalie—because he could not afford skates. He was happy to be out on the ice, where he found joy despite his mother's negative attitude toward hockey. She was adamantly opposed to his participation "in such foolishness as hockey." She hoped Toe would get a nice, steady job working in the mines. She was unwavering in her strictness, and without remorse—qualities that Toe resented in her.

Unlike Arzélie, Wilmer did not frown on Toe's love of hockey. Wilmer himself was a sportsman and took time to ensure all the boys were physically active. He coached the boys' baseball team in the summer, and Toe acted as the batboy for some of the older teams when he wasn't playing. It is said Toe's distaste for officials was not sparked on the ice but from these early days around the baseball diamond.

There was no disposable income for skates in the Blake home, where nails served as coat hangers. So Toe worked and saved up. He held a part-time job delivering bread, and at age 12 he got a job with Palm Dairy, hitching horses and delivering before school.

Meanwhile, Toe found ingenious ways to borrow blades. When a player, before entering the wood shack, deposited his skates by the stove to warm up, Toe would snatch them, regardless of the size, so he could get out and take real strides on the ice. It sure beat playing goalie.

Toe finally began playing competitive, organized hockey in 1927, at age 15, suiting up as goalie for the Coniston Boy Scout League alongside his brother Dennis and his friend Larry Lafrance. Equipment was rudimentary, with the pucks cut from birch trees. The Eaton's catalog from inside the outhouse often went missing so players could cut out homemade pads. Still unable to afford his own skates, Toe played goalie; lacking the canvas- and cloth-covered padding with wood slats that came with pads, he would stuff telephone books or catalogs down his socks to protect his legs. The pucks stung thanks to their three-sided shape, which was sometimes a result of wear. Sticks, normally made of heavy woods such as ash or yellow birch, were often handed down or around, unless someone was lucky enough to get their hands on a Hespeler (the first company to manufacture the two-piece wood stick). Toe found himself sharing the ice with Italian, Polish, Ukrainian and Finnish children, plus the Canadian kids whose parents had immigrated to the Nickel Belt region with the promise of work.

Toe increased his savings by taking a milk route, where his generosity sometimes set his savings back. "I can still see the tweed cap he was wearing, with a hole burnt on the right side," Lorenzo Lalonde writes in his memoir *When a Nickel was Worth a Nickel*, "as clearly as if it was yesterday. As a milkman, Toe supplied milk to many people in Coniston. If there wasn't a bottle on the steps, Toe would leave a full bottle, and he must have been short a lot of money at the end of the month."

Toe hung on to that route for some years, and it wasn't long before the young teen was able to afford his first pair of skates. Toe and his classmates wore the colors of their favorite teams and kept their skates inside the classroom. In high school, Blake would put his skates on at eight every morning, and they wouldn't come off until 9 p.m.

"That year did more for my skating than any other years put together," said Toe, who spent his weekends skating on the frozen rivers nearby, when he wasn't working. "Recess was too short to change from regular boots to skates, so I solved the problem by skating to and from school all the time. I was always fully equipped for a turn on the ice. That's why my legs are so strong."

Even when delivering milk, Toe was devising ways to get on the ice as quickly as possible once his route was completed. His leather-top boots were never laced higher than his ankles, allowing him to strap on his skates even quicker.

Toe wasn't the only one embracing hockey—the entire town of Coniston was caught up in a sport that was growing in popularity. And with workers flooding into the region for work, more men were itching for something to do once their shift at the mine was done for the day. Toe would soon be one of them, too, wading through the rubble before landing on a Memorial Cup–winning team and embarking on a professional career in the NHL.

CHAPTER 3

SUDBURY

THE OPPORTUNITY WAS THERE, and Toe would be damned if he let that son of a bitch get away without delivering a message . . . Larry Lafrance had the little bastard wrapped up and was guiding him right toward Toe. Blake dug his blade into the crisp ice and pushed off, exploding toward his marker. The opponent in his sights had earlier taken a run at Sudbury Wolves teammate and top scorer Larry Lafrance. Lafrance and Blake had known each other since their teen years, when they scrambled past one another to reach that free pair of ice skates first so they could get out on the ice. Lafrance recognized the look in his friend's eyes, the grin on his face and the determination in his stride. Lafrance corralled his opponent into the path of Blake, who met the unsuspecting victim just as Larry was driving him in the other direction. Snap! The player fell to the ice, pain shooting through him as he clutched what would ultimately be a broken leg. Blake made his way back to the Wolves bench, unrepentant and reveling in the moment. A skirmish on the ice was sure to ensue. *There is no place I would rather be,* Blake thought to himself before jumping back over the boards to join the fracas.

• • •

Like most area teens of the time, Toe Blake worked the mines and played hockey.

In the early-morning hours, he found himself suiting up among children and men, slipping protective wear over a single long-sleeved cotton undershirt. Men puffed on cigarettes and pipes as they picked out protective tin hats and lanterns to strap on. Toe slowly shuffled alongside the scrum of men to the ladder to make his way down into the mine. If he was lucky, he could get a ride down on the skip. The skip submerged into drifts—or passages—that led underground to cramped and dangerous spaces where drills and dynamite perforating the nickel copper ore provided constant ringing in the ears. Toe's frame filled in quickly as he shoveled piles of nickel and budged slabs of stone. He kept an eye out for the occasional errant rock, which could prove debilitating and end his hockey aspirations. Toe and his cohorts shoveled two tons of rock into carts and then rolled them toward the loading pocket, a great bin cut 50 feet deep in the stone. Toe had already inherited his mother's tough, plainspoken character, which was further nurtured below the earth's surface.

"I really think Toe was a product of his upbringing," former teammate Kenny Reardon told Michael Ulmer, author of *Canadiens Captains*. "He came from mining country, he worked in the mines when he was younger and that showed through. He had a very dogged personality."

Toe's demeanor changed when the afternoon bell rang out at the end of his work shift. He raced back up to the earth's surface to the outdoor rink, where he could breathe fresh air and dust himself off with a skate. The 1920s were boom years for the region as the nickel market rebounded following a drop after the end of the First World War. Nickel was used to manufacture automobiles, mining machinery and household appliances, and it would be instrumental in construction in the war effort some years later.

This boom led to a housing expansion in Coniston. Such a large influx of people arrived that boardinghouses couldn't keep up with the demand and "hot bedding" became a reality, with men sleeping in shifts. By 16, Toe was right alongside these men, earning his keep and contributing to the family income inside the mines. Coniston was stable thanks to the smelter, where workers were paid an average wage of 45 cents per hour.

Mond Nickel wasn't the only major industry keeping the Sudbury region churning. Canadian Industries Limited (CIL), Canadian Pacific Rail, the Falconbridge mine—these businesses kept people employed, fueled the region's expansion and fostered hockey.

They were the impetus behind the founding of the Nickel Belt Hockey League in 1926. The NBHL provided locals with a league championship to follow and teams to cheer for and fed the regional junior clubs with talent. It was a competitive entity, with up to eight teams fighting for the title every season, populated by the men who worked in those industries. Each town already had a local league for young players, and the next logical step in their hockey career was tied to the reality of their personal lives and professional careers. The Coniston town league was made up of three teams from the smelter and one from the shops. There was extra incentive to impress here: the best players from all four teams could be cherry-picked by regional junior teams such as the Sudbury Wolves for the playoffs—referred to as "playdowns"—in the spring.

But by 1928, Coniston's stability under Mond began to slip away as discussion of a merger with the International Nickel Company of Canada took shape. The rival companies had discovered a vast ore deposit across their properties. To avoid costly duplication and competition, they merged to form Inco, which now controlled 90 percent of the world's nickel. Mond became a subsidiary of Inco, leaving the residents of Coniston concerned after Copper Cliff became the company's Canadian headquarters. The arrival of the Great Depression took its toll as layoffs followed a production decrease and Inco laid off a large number of workers in Coniston. But Toe managed to keep his job at the Falconbridge mine even as the smelter closed in 1930 and Copper Cliff became the new center of operation. Nickel remained in demand, and production numbers continued to rise. The mine was resilient, and the fluctuating fortunes of the area were represented in the tale of mining prospector and inventor Thomas Edison. Edison was credited with the original discovery of the Falconbridge ore body in 1901, a site, to his chagrin, he gave up on by abandoning his mining claim two years later. He would be reminded of this failure with his greatest success, as nickel and cobalt deposits were used in his production of his electrical bulbs.

The Blake household seemed to weather the Great Depression well enough: the family stayed together while other families were forced to rely on welfare—or relief, as it was known. Young men over 16 were discouraged from living at home and were forced out of the family dwelling since they jeopardized their family's ability to receive relief if they stayed. The Great Depression ushered in desperate times for many, but for Toe it marked the start of a promising junior hockey career.

As his body grew lean, Toe's footing on the ice improved. The 17-year-old Toe played his first organized league game—beyond the Boy Scouts—over the course of the 1929–30 season. At 5-foot-10 and 165 pounds, he featured in seven games for the Cochrane Dunlops of the Northern Ontario Junior Hockey Association.

Despite living in a time of obstacles, Toe Blake was finally playing the game he loved on a regular basis and making a living during a time of crisis. But that still wasn't enough in the eyes of Arzélie.

"When I got home and it was discovered I had been playing hockey, the forbidden sport, I got many a tanning with the family strap," Toe revealed, adding he would later be forced to "run away from home" to join the Hamilton Tigers without his family's knowledge. "My mother was dead set against me playing hockey. But after I made good with the Canadiens she changed completely. She became a real hockey bug. I have a younger brother, George, and my mother practically drove him into hockey. She bought him skates, and did everything to make him a player of big-league caliber."

By December 1930, Toe was no longer stuck on defense but playing forward, splitting his time between Falconbridge and CIL, and getting noticed. The Sudbury Wolves coach was scouting the young talent that would be at the disposal to the junior club in the coming years and was excited by the plethora of forward prospects emerging from Coniston: Bob and Jack McInnes, Lafrance and Blake. Toe was given a tryout with the Wolves on the left wing prior to Christmas.

In the new year, Blake made an impression playing on the left side for CIL—burning up the already soft ice alongside Lafrance and center George Roque in a 3–0 win over CPR. The line's speed left the "railroaders" lagging, and the trio's smart combinations ultimately allowed Blake to bulge the twine for what was likely his first semi-professional goal. The "turnstile troops," as the *Sudbury Star* called them, displayed smart team play and excellent individual skills during a "shout-raising" contest. Blake's reputation for physical play was already developing. The victory included a "free-for-all scrap that ended only when the police entered into the contest."

Blake could skate with anyone and was versatile, filling in at center when need be. Positions did not matter to Toe; the only important thing was being on the ice. Blake could take it as hard as he could give it, playing on after receiving a check "that jarred his teeth." In his first season with CIL, Blake scored seven goals with one assist in eight games and added one goal and one assist in the playoffs. He led the team with 10 penalty minutes over the regular season. His endless stamina, tireless back-checking and strong defensive qualities won him admirers and caught the attention of former Montreal Maroons player and Falconbridge coach Sammy Rothschild. Rothschild had returned to his native Sudbury as a Seagram's liquor company sales representative and had also agreed to take over as coach of the Sudbury Wolves in his spare time. Rothschild had played on the 1919 Wolves before making the jump to the professionals a few years later. The NHL's first Jewish player had played three seasons for the Maroons, winning a Stanley Cup in 1926 before moving on to Pittsburgh and the New York Americans, where a knee injury ended his career.

Rothschild immediately took to Blake and recruited him for the Cub Wolves, the senior B team. Rothschild didn't expect immediate results, sensing the experience would be the biggest benefit to Blake. Local expectations began to rise, however, for the team with the youthful additions, considering the Wolves had been winless away from home for three years and counting. Blake filled in wherever needed, and this led to even more playing time with the Wolves, plus Falconbridge whenever his CIL team would allow it.

Toe quickly improved. His stickhandling was starting to befuddle opponents, his untiring work ethic ran them ragged, and his speed was noticeable. Toe's shot was errant, but he still managed to bulge the twine to the tune of a point per game. His physical play also maintained an average of about one penalty per game. He combined marvellously with fellow Coniston boy Lafrance, who was also playing for the Cub Wolves. Blake's rise coincided with the improving fortunes of the Nickel Belt Hockey League, which was keen to wrestle the McNamara Cup away from Northern Ontario Junior Hockey League (NOHA) champion Sault Ste. Marie. It wasn't to be for Rothschild's young nucleus in 1931, however, as the Greyhounds won a fourth straight northern title.

The Wolves now had their sights on the Allan Cup. At the Dominion Championship playoffs at Toronto's Arena Gardens, their youthful vigor and fearlessness won over neutral fans. Blake led this spectacular brand of team play constructed by Rothschild, enjoying a three-point night in the first game, scoring two first-period goals in an 8–3 victory over the intermediate Ontario Hockey Association (OHA) champion Cadets from Kingston's Royal Military College. The Wolves immediately took to the larger ice surface, especially the sensational Blake, who eluded markers and checks and drew applause with every touch of the puck. His play gained the attention of Frank Selke, then-coach of Toronto's Marlboro Junior Hockey Club and future general manager of the Canadiens. Selke said the Toronto club even reached out to Blake in a bid to bring him to Toronto before negotiations were dropped.

Blake's coming-out was short-lived, as the Wolves lost 2–1 to Hamilton to exit, but the experience was valuable, and he notched the team's lone goal in the second period. The Wolves returned home with experience, and Rothschild was encouraged enough to welcome expectations for the next run, in a year's time—this time for the Memorial Cup.

• • •

Toe Blake relished climbing down into the mine for the start of his shift on December 3, 1931. The sooner his workday was over, the sooner he could lace up the skates for the first time that season. A mild start to the winter had left the NOHA impatiently waiting for a cold spell to flood the outdoor rinks and begin the season. That finally arrived on the night of December 2. Hopes were high for the Wolves, thanks to the experienced and "outstanding forward line that brings a lot of adjectives from the coach," as the *Star* described it.

Weather played havoc with the hockey season as Northern Ontario enjoyed a green Christmas, with bright blue skies, clear air and temperatures hovering around the zero mark. The majority of the skating rinks were closed.

Meanwhile, the sports pages offered up hockey reports. In Montreal, Canadiens owner Leo Dandurand was plotting a move away from the Forum to build the city's $3 million "new hockey palace." Blake might have made the sign of the cross while imagining playing in front of 18,000 fans in a building slated to be built facing St. Patrick's Basilica, at the corner of Dorchester and St. Alexander Streets.

Falconbridge was the favorite to win the Nickel Belt Hockey League. Blake, Lafrance and Bennett did not disappoint in the home-opening 5–1 win over CPR in front of a record 1,000 fans at the Palace Rink. Blake set up Lafrance for the winner as the Nickel Belt teams displayed "a brand of hockey that merits support." The support was there, too, despite the soft ice from the unpredictable mild spells, which had already led to postponements.

The Wolves' opening game of the southern NOHA group match with the Sault Ste. Marie Junior Greyhounds was one of those affected. There was no ice in Sault Ste. Marie, forcing a two-week postponement. The Greyhounds got the odd skate on Blind River, but no rink was up and running by January 9. That afforded the Wolves extra leeway with Nickel Belt Hockey League officials, who weren't exactly overjoyed by the prospect of losing their top performers during Sudbury's Memorial Cup run. In the meantime, Blake and his fellow Wolves continued playing for their Nickel Belt teams.

The delay also meant Rothschild could spend less time in the company of Wolves owner Max Silverman, a smooth-talking, cigar-chomping son of downtown merchants and tireless local sports booster. Silverman had worked his way through the Wolves organization, starting out as a water boy in 1919 before becoming manager and coach by 1930. Silverman respected Rothschild's professional experience and the job he had done at Falconbridge. He decided to step back and let a well-qualified professional take charge of the Wolves. He had seen how Rothschild had already built an incredible rapport with these teens, imparting his experience and turning the group into a potential champion. Silverman and Rothschild would feud when the latter left the team after this season, but for now, with their eyes on the prize, their determination superseded any ego.

Anthony "Ant" Healy of Owen Sound started in goal, his ability to "sidestep as neatly as a tap dancer" proving invaluable that season. Healy would be a sought-after goalie following his Memorial Cup displays, but he spurned offers from the International League to retire from hockey altogether and attend the University of Toronto. He would not attempt to make varsity there, either. On defense, the Wolves counted on captain Esmer "Red" Porter, a burly native of Iroquois Falls who had moved to Sudbury at 17 to work the mines. He was a fan favorite for his aggressive end-to-end rushes. He and his partner, Bob McInnes, were fierce checkers "known for applying the sandwich." Sudbury's top line was led by NHL prospect Dalton "Nakina" Smith, who took his name from his hometown, a small railroad stop north of Thunder Bay. Rothschild alerted the Montreal Maroons to the youngster, who could "slide through an air hole in a brick wall and have nothing more than his hair ruffled." Smith's only crack at the NHL in a 15-year minor league career would be 10 games for the Detroit Red Wings in 1943–44; he went on to raise horses in California. Smith centered a line that featured Adelard Lafrance and Jack McInnes on his wing. Lawrence, the son of a prominent Sudbury fur merchant, went on to play three games for the Montreal Canadiens. Blake anchored the second line alongside a pair of familiar faces: Maxie Bennett and boyhood friend Larry Lafrance, whose career continued to advance alongside Blake's.

Blake's play for Falconbridge assured his place on the Wolves. He scored four times in a 5–2 win over High School on January 23. It was the perfect warm-up for Blake ahead of the upcoming tilt with Sault Ste. Marie, the four-time defending champions. But the Pups' prospects were dim, since they had no ice to practice on due to the warm winter. Sault Ste. Marie coach George Westman predicted a 12–1 defeat. Blake scored a hat trick in the 11–2 triumph.

"They sifted through the Sault whenever they pleased. It wasn't a hockey game; it was simply a slaughter of the innocents," the *Sudbury Star* summarized, paying particular attention to Blake—as did the 1,100 spectators. "This boy Blake, alternating on the wing, went as if he was all wound up and wondered how long his spring would last. On a lone sortie, he stickhandled through the entire Sault team and laid the rubber to rest right in the old igloo for the Woofers' third marker."

Blake's influence on the team grew with each game, as he scored twice in the 5–2 return-leg win that clinched the Southern championship. The victory meant the Wolves moved on to play Monteith Academy for the NOHA Championship. A 5–0 victory away made a 3–2 defeat on the thawing and soggy surface of the Palace Rink moot. The Wolves' first defeat of the season was labeled the "Frog Pond Fracas." It resembled an old-time shinny performance, as a Florida-like climate engulfed the region, leaving enormous slush puddles in the rink corners.

The triumph propelled Sudbury into the OHA final against the Toronto Marlboros, who had once again tried to sign Blake during the season to no avail. "He refused to leave the Sudbury club because of a series of kindnesses they had conferred on him," Frank Selke wrote in a 1946 Montreal Forum program. "Even at that early age Blake was loyal to the core, an attribute which had stood him in good stead in all the years during which he steadily climbed the ladder of hockey success." Blake and his teammates boarded a train destined for the Queen City on March 10, set to begin a month-long odyssey with the Memorial Cup the objective. The 18-year-old Blake and the "husky-looking squad" impressed local newspapermen in their first workouts at the Gardens, even if bookies offered them little chance.

"The boys are in first-class condition. Sudbury will put up a real showing and we aren't a bit afraid," Silverman said. "We're as good as the best of them."

The Marlboros would have taken one look across the ice at their opponents and seen boys wearing mismatched gloves and socks, who did well to hide the weight of the moment, of playing on artificial ice for the first time. From the bench, Sudbury Wolves trainer Morris Dabous found his gaze stuck on his own players as the two teams lined the ice. In their tattered green-and-white uniforms and socks with holes, they looked more like a group of boys taking on men.

While Silverman enjoyed touting ideas that may have been too good to be true, he was not wrong with his prediction. The "fresh and frisky" Wolves surprised and breezed around the Marlboros with their blazing speed, launching blistering attacks while checking—and double-checking—their bewildered opponent in a 3–0 upset in front of 4,046 fans. The self-belief Rothschild had instilled in his players crafted them into a brainy group that worked hard and responded to his demands.

"A coach does not make a team, but a good team makes a coach," said Rothschild, who never tired of parlaying all the credit to his players and never spun the focus in his own direction. Rothschild's philosophy left the first imprint of a model that would influence Toe's accomplished coaching career.

The Wolves had dominated the opening minutes of the two-legged series, with Blake's speed and ability launching him through the defense. His active involvement ultimately helped net the opening—and winning—goal at 14:15 of the opening frame. Confidence was high in Sudbury's camp after taking a sizable advantage in the two-legged playdown on their opponent's home ice.

"There are a lot of you smart fellows who said we couldn't beat the Marlboros. Well, we did; now laugh that off," Silverman said ahead of the second leg. "We're going to win tonight, too, and I'm not boasting. We've got the stuff, pal, we've got the stuff."

The Arena Gardens was filled for the second game, including 600 fans from the Nickel City who had come on two special trains. The Wolves were making a splash with Toronto hockey fans curious about this team of ragtag kids from the mining country. They were rewarded in the return leg.

"There will be hockey games and there will be hockey games, but never there was, and there never will be a hockey game surpassing Wednesday night's affair at the Maple Leaf Gardens," James Y. Nichol wrote in the *Sudbury Star*. "Almost 13,000 fans filled the palatial Gardens to witness the epic encounter, and they were strung to piano wire tension. So were the teams."

The Marlies were ready for the fast-skating, close-checking Wolves this time around, and a fast start threw the contest wide open, leaving spectators in a daze. Back-to-back penalties to Blake and Smith gave the hosts all the momentum they needed as they notched three goals in 26 seconds for a 3–0 first period lead.

"For a moment it looked as if the Woofers were going to crumble," wrote Nichol, "as if they would fold up and fall flatter than the fish's fin in Finland of which mention had been made . . . But they didn't crack."

The Wolves managed to dig in and hold Toronto at bay, with Blake gaining a number of opportunities, only for his wayward shooting to let him down. The frantic crowd erupted 45 seconds into the third period, when the hosts scored to lead 4–0, and 4–3 on aggregate. The green-and-white shirts of Sudbury did not relent, however, even though the Marlies picked up their physical defensive play. Blake went to the corner of Toronto's end to collect the puck during a mad scramble, poking it toward goal. Lafrance seized it, pulled up short and fired past the goaltender to level the series at 4–4 with 15 minutes to play. Soon, 13,000 hysterical fans watched as the whistle was blown to signal overtime, when the suspense only grew despite tentative starts by both clubs. Blake had been a constant worry to the opposition despite his errant touch in front of goal. But he made up for that with his physical presence and defensive responsibility.

With over seven minutes played in the 10-minute overtime period, Maxie Bennett picked up the puck in his own end and skated right up the middle and through a pair of Toronto checks into the opponent's zone, where he released a high-rising shot. Goalie Joey Worters stopped it from reaching the top left corner but couldn't contain it as the puck dropped into his skates and trickled toward the goal line. It seemed like a year before the red goal light came on as the disc inched over the line. The goal set off a howl of celebration by Sudbury supporters, whose enthusiasm to mimic their mascot left them hoarse or voiceless by morning. Game programs flew up in the air and newspapers soon littered the ice as Sudbury's players mobbed Bennett, who had been pulled from the game in the first period after being knocked out by a check into the boards. He had returned to play with tape plastered across his forehead, which he eventually removed because of the discomfort. There still remained 2:25 to play in the overtime period, but the Marlies could not conjure up a response, and when referee William Duncan blew the final whistle, Toronto's players rushed at the referee, attempting to trip him and cross-check him to the ice. One player even attempted to connect a swinging punch to his jaw. Silverman and another Wolves official named Joey Ironstone both flew over the boards to come to Duncan's defense, with the pair taking their own pokes at opposing players. Ironstone even landed two shots to the face of future Toronto Maple Leafs center Jack Shill, who had initially swung at Duncan. Police officers rushed onto the ice as spectators began swarming the rink to add to the fist-swinging melee before hockey officials and the authorities managed to squash the ruckus.

The Green Shirts' Herculean upset was acknowledged by fans as the team retreated to their dressing room, with the unlikely result already elevated to classic status as a demonstration of "Northern spunk," especially since the roster was replete with local Sudbury lads. The *Toronto Star* heaped praise on the victors:

> From goal out it was impossible to find a weak spot: The Wolves had terrific speed, an effective short passing game that was a treat to watch and a powerful, hard hitting rearguard. They came down here with the reputation of being regular greyhounds on skates. Bull terriers would have suited them better for they clung to their checks like glue and covered up like pros. The most difficult task of the night was to pick out of the Sudbury stars. Every player fitted into a perfect machine wielded by coach Sammy Rothschild who deserves unstinted praise for the masterful play of his team. They are one of the finest coached aggregations to take the ice in these parts for a long while.

Blake had always felt Rothschild had perfected a system that maximized the qualities of his men and tapped into their fundamental skills. "It was my first real taste of competitive hockey," Blake said. "It's something I keep remembering time and time again, how our club beat a couple of high-scoring teams by putting the checking part into the game."

The win propelled them into the semifinals of the Eastern Final against the equally green-shirted Ottawa Shamrocks.

Since Sudbury had no covered rink, the team was forced to play its home games at Toronto's Arena Gardens, which naturally elevated costs. Silverman put a front-page public appeal for funds from fans in the *Sudbury Star*, announcing the team was short on cash after factoring in costs of railway tickets and hotel rooms and asking fans to wire them money. Sudbury Mayor Peter Fenton collected $180 to send on to the team. The public appeal wasn't a bad idea—the thirst for Wolves hockey was growing the further they advanced toward the Memorial Cup. The *Sudbury Star* newspaper took out a temporary broadcast license so it could carry the games live on 1200 AM, and the city's legion halls charged 50 cents for the right to listen. Ticket holders at the Grand Theatre were also treated to the second and third periods following that night's film screening. The phones at the *Star*'s offices were manned between 8:30 and 11:30 p.m. on game nights to provide updates to hundreds of callers.

Sudbury scored an emphatic 2–0 victory to open the two-legged series in Toronto, where Sudbury was forced to wear Marlboro colors to prevent a clash of green uniforms. The Wolves' superior puck-handling skills and speed caught out the visitors, while goalie Ant Healy starred. Still, the Shamrocks felt positive about their chances in the return game. They had begun the season as Memorial Cup prospects and that goal was still within reach as the action moved to the nation's capital.

There was a festive atmosphere inside the Auditorium in Ottawa. Fifteen members from the Sudbury Legion and a brass band were among the 300 traveling Sudbury fans who brought the attendance to 8,000. The Shamrocks were kitted in red-and-blue stripes while the Wolves were back in their classic green-and-white kits. The Montreal Amateur Athletics Association (MAAA) awaited the victor in the Eastern Dominion Final. The home crowd's energy propelled Ottawa from the start, with the locals tying the series 2–2 on aggregate thanks to a pair of goals inside seven minutes. But the Wolves slowly began to show signs of life following the early letup. The crowd came to its feet as Shamrocks goalie Rick Perley made a dashing save on Blake, who had released a powerful shot from inside the Ottawa blue line. Sudbury's stamina quickly recovered after weathering the early storm. An injury to Perley halted the game and proved to be a turning point. Sudbury emerged from the first break to score a pair of goals, with Smith's second of the game in the third period icing the series. Once again, another finale was marred by violence, as Ottawa's opening-goal scorer, Stan Pratt, bodychecked Jack McInnes into the boards. McInnes replied by slashing Pratt in the head, sparking a fight between the two players.

The team had little time to savor 3–2 triumph and 5–2 aggregate win, as the club quickly made its way to Montreal for the first of the home-and-away series. The trip made an impression on the players, including Blake, who enjoyed his first-ever skate on Montreal Forum ice on March 25. Because Rothschild was the Seagram's representative for Northern Ontario, Seagram's president Samuel Bronfman held a luncheon for the team at company headquarters, in the heart of Canada's largest metropolis. But the long slog of being on the road, with several players reportedly battling the flu, looked to be taking its toll. The Woofers enjoyed more of the play in a 1–1 draw, but they looked stale, lacking the attitude that had carried them this far. Their reputation had preceded them, with some coining Smith "a budding Howie Morenz," and reports suggested Blake would get his first professional offer in Montreal. Blake had good spells in this opening match—which was broadcast to Sudbury, with Foster Hewitt at the helm, via a special signal—but his poor finishing continued to let him down. "I started talking to myself, and I said, 'Blake, you must be getting awfully old,'" Blake later joked about his first performance in Montreal.

The players boarded the return train to Toronto for the home leg, with some added incentive coming from a short stop at 5 a.m. in Sudbury, where 500 fans were waiting to cheer them on. Meanwhile, the Saskatoon Wesleys led the Winnipeg Monarchs 1–0 after the first leg of the Western Final.

Blake's focus throughout the playoffs had been unwavering, with the Coniston lad unmoved by the public attention his team was suddenly receiving. *Sports Illustrated* reported that when Rothschild walked by Blake's room at night and spotted light emerging from under his door, "he would step in and find Toe desperately trying to fill an inside straight when he should have been in bed."

Blake had alternated between left wing and center throughout the playoffs, but against MAAA, Rothschild decided to leave him in the middle. His perseverance inspired his teammates, and Rothschild knew Blake would never skirt his defensive duties. The Wolves roared back to life in a rougher return game, Blake assisting on McInnes's goal in a 3–0 win that gave Sudbury a 4–1 aggregate victory and a place in the Memorial Cup Final. The Monarchs handled Saskatoon out west, securing a 3–1 win to reach the best-of-three final series for the first time. Winnipeg dressed three players who had been part of the Winnipeg Elmwoods Millionaires' national-title-winning campaign a year earlier. The Wolves would be traveling to Winnipeg for Game 1 as heavy underdogs. The team's CPR train made another early-morning stop in Sudbury as it lurched westward for one final public appearance before the series began; again, 500 locals, including mayor Pete Fenton, filled the train platforms to wave them on. At a time when the world was wrapped up in thoughts about breadlines and the Lindbergh kidnapping, the Wolves offered rosier sentiments. Silverman, who had sprained one of his fingers ordering Blake to bed that evening as the team continued to revel in its Eastern Final win, emerged in slippers while Rothschild stayed snug in his green pajamas and the confines of his berth, peeking through the blinds of his window. The team did welcome one addition to their group:

Father Dufresne of Blind River, who would accompany the lads as "spiritual advisor" for the series.

Sudbury arrived in Winnipeg for the opening game to an atmosphere of smug confidence from the locals. Winnipeg's players were physically superior in size and hyped as a superior outfit to the Elmwoods team that had triumphed one year earlier. As the players settled in for the night at the Royal Alexandra Hotel, Rothschild sipped on a Seagram's rye and looked over the final touches to the game plan he had constructed. Rothschild had identified a strategy that he believed would keep Sudbury's opponents flustered and unable to settle into their own game plan. It was a tactic that causes much consternation in hockey circles today: the trap.

Rothschild instructed his players to back-check fiercely and not allow the Monarchs to dump the puck into the Sudbury zone to set up play. This frustrating tactic initially worked, and the Wolves went into the first break leading 1–0. Blake's sore wrists limited his already wayward shooting, so he had them taped up to play through the pain. But the sacrifice was for naught, as Winnipeg scored three unanswered goals to lead 3–1 after two periods. In the third, trailing 4–2, Rothschild decided to drop Blake back onto defense so his utility player could step up into the attack. The gamble worked: Sudbury cut the lead to 4–3, but that was as close as they would get. Despite the setback, Rothschild saw in Blake an all-round player prepared to contribute whatever necessary for the benefit of the team. His scoring was not excellent, but the rest of his 200-foot game made up for those droughts. Sudbury had played comeback spoiler before, against Toronto, and he was confident the best-of-three series was far from over.

"Tell everyone in Sudbury we'll win by 4–1, and you just watch and see if I'm right," Silverman boasted before Game 2. "If this Winnipeg team think they can send their forwards to toss around behind our goal like they did in the first game, we'll show them. We can play that kind of game ourselves, and we can beat them at it, too. If they try the same sort of stuff tonight, we'll make them look foolish and I'm not kidding, either."

Rothschild had already devised a better plan than trying to match force with more of the same. He wanted to switch the lines around, putting Blake at center between Larry Lafrance and Jack McInnes as the team's first line. "Blake has been going great guns on his rushes though his wrists are sore and his shooting is a trifle off," as the *Star* described it. "The Monarchs have yet to find a player that can make him quit. He is one of the most valuable play carriers in the Woofers line-up."

Almost 6,000 spectators crammed into the Amphitheatre for Game 2 of the best-of-three series, with the title on the line. One woman fainted outside the box office amid all the jostling, pushing and shoving in the scramble for tickets. The frenzied atmosphere transferred into the stadium and onto the ice as players on both teams put on a combination boxing and wrestling tournament. In the second period, Silverman ran onto the ice and took a poke at a Winnipeg player before both benches cleared. It took the emergence of half a dozen police officers to usher the hotheaded Silverman off the ice and the players back into the game at hand. Silverman lost his hat during the disturbance.

Before the melee, Blake had helped manufacture the Wolves' opener, carrying the puck end to end before putting it on the stick of Gordon Grant, who scored from a distance just as Blake was checked out of the play in the Winnipeg zone. But the Monarchs tied it up late in the third period to force overtime. Adelard Lafrance scored the overtime winner to keep Sudbury in the hunt.

Blake had proven the real hero of this hockey classic after stepping in to replace the injured Nakina Smith at center on the top line. Smith suffered a broken cheekbone, and Blake was called on to play increased minutes: 60 out of the 70 minutes of the second game.

"Just after the second period got under way he was called upon to fill the difficult role of center ice player for injured Smith. He went up against Norman Yellowlees, star of the Monarchs. Blake back-checked this player into submission, camping on his trail at every turn, and he was a constant source of worry to the Winnipeg goalie with his brilliant rushes. He played almost entirely during the third period without a substitute and all of the overtime. The Coniston lad proved to be a regular iron man," Nichol wrote in the *Star*.

Blake's work rate would diminish only slightly in the title-clinching match: he was on the ice for 50 of the 60 minutes played in the final game. It was a true revelation of the character of Blake, the player, who was unrelenting in the face of adversity with everything on the line. Blake would go through a wall for Rothschild if he asked. And he practically did against the Monarchs, sticking to Monarch star and towering centerman Yellowlees. Smith returned despite the broken cheekbone to play a pivotal role in the third game, scoring just 1:50 into the series decider as the plucky Nickelbackers caught their opponents out early with their guard down. It proved the game winner. Sudbury lifted the Memorial Cup as Dominion champions for the first time in club history thanks to the 1–0 triumph. Sudbury simply adhered to Rothschild's game plan, sticking to their men and closing down the neutral zone, with Blake completely marking Yellowlees out of the contest. The Wolves team was simply stronger, a more cohesive unit in which each player understood his role and the importance it played.

"He was all guts. He was all heart and he was always out to win," Renaldo Olivier, a childhood friend of Blake's, told the *Sudbury Star*. "That guy, with the effort and stamina he had, practically won the Memorial Cup himself."

A *Star* editorial following the championship read: "Never has Northern Ontario, even the whole of Canada, seen such a spectacular display of outstanding talent and wonderful performance.

The unanimous outburst of applause and enthusiasm, reminiscent of Armistice Day, 1918, that greeted the final results of the last game played Monday in Winnipeg, was a manifest evidence of the true spirit that prevailed in the city."

Celebrations erupted in Sudbury as thousands poured into the city's streets amid the uninterrupted sounds of automobile horns and men and women—perfect strangers—embraced. Every corner trash can was set ablaze. At the corner of Elm and Durham Streets, mattresses and other inflammables were heaped high and doused with coal oil ready to be lit, but no soul was brave enough to strike the match. The streets cleared out by 3 a.m., with the odd fender, mattress and truckload of bottles left behind.

The team was cheered on by hockey fans at train stations along its route home to Sudbury, where 20,000 waited at the station to hail the Memorial Cup champions. There were reports of people "suffering either from palsy or the effects of the Monday night celebration." The streets were clogged with cars honking their horns, and the town band frantically tried to keep up with the pace of the celebration. The players rode in the back of a truck through the jammed streets to a reception at the Nickel Range Hotel, where they received pocket watches and the key to the city from Mayor Fenton. It was the largest civic banquet a hockey team had ever known. Three hundred and eighty-four attended as the four trophies won on the run—the Memorial Cup, the Copeland Cup, the McNamara Cup and the maiden Richardson Cup—were presented. The Honorable W.H. Price, K.C., the attorney general of Ontario, brought congratulations on behalf of the provincial government, stating that the Wolves' "gumption typifies the best in Canadian life."

The simmering tension between Rothschild and Silverman took a back seat for one last occasion as the Sudbury coach lauded his charges: "Most of them are high school boys. Only two or three of them had ever played on artificial ice; they were in a strange land, before strange crowds, and on a strange ice and few teams have ever been faced with such heartbreaking handicaps and come through. Winnipeg was the hardest series we played. They were a bigger team, the crowd was unfavorable, and it seemed at times the referees were not giving the boys a break. The conduct of the boys off-ice was exceptional."

Following this triumph, Blake signed with the Hamilton Tigers of the Ontario Hockey Association. It was certain: hockey was now his career.

CHAPTER 4

MONTREAL

TOE DIDN'T FEEL THE sweat streaming down his face, back and chest. Perspiration and dirt mixed before ultimately collecting in his stained shirt. It was nothing he wasn't used to: this was a pleasure compared to those long days working the mines deep below the earth's surface. Here he was above ground. He was still inside the confines of a factory, but here you felt alive thanks to the heat of the sun coming through the window. There was none of the cold dampness of rock that makes your body recoil. The summer of 1934 was a particularly warm summer, one of the hottest on record. Toe had this job at National Steel Car thanks to the Hamilton Tigers of the Ontario Hockey Association (OHA), where he had recently wrapped his second full season.

He'd enjoyed a strong sophomore season with the Tigers, finishing second in league scoring. NHL clubs had taken notice. But the budding prospect preferred to stay on in Steel City despite the growing interest from the professional ranks. It was the first time Blake had allowed a matter of the heart to sway his next hockey move. Betty Marion Walters was suddenly in the picture.

Betty, 23, was the youngest of Edward McKay Walters and Lena Bell Shephard's five children. She was born Bessie Marion Walters in Beamsville, Ontario, before the family farm ended up at the corner of Kelson and Winston Roads in Winona, on the outskirts of Hamilton. The family home remains today, even if the property was divided by the arrival of the Queen Elizabeth Highway. "Bett" or "Betsy," as she was also called by friends and family, was a vivacious, outgoing girl, often looking to distinguish herself from her siblings, Harry, Nell (Nelly), Gertrude (Gert or Gerti) and Violet (Vi). The farm ran right up to the shores of Lake Ontario, giving the Walters children ample space to let their imaginations run wild when they weren't helping their father attend to the fruit. Edward grew grapes, sweet cherries, raspberries, peaches and a few other items on his fair-sized farm, which also included a few animals such as horses, pigs and chickens.

"In those days you didn't need to have a big farm to make a living. The work wasn't too difficult, picking fruit was probably the hardest part," says Howard Walters, son of Harry and nephew to Betty.

Betty didn't work much on the farm and, looking to expand her horizons, left for Hamilton with Gerti. There she worked at Eaton's and took a job sewing at the Eaton Knitting Mill undergarment factory.

"Betty was very musical," Howard recalls. "My grandfather played the violin. She played the piano and sang. She was a very lively personality—that's probably how they met."

Betty and her sister lived in the apartment downstairs from Toe and Maxie Bennett, his teammate from Sudbury, who had also made the move to the Hamilton Tigers. Toe found himself immediately enamored with his neighbor.

"Betty and Gerti had a lot of fun. Being independent, self-sufficient, I'm sure they went to a lot of hockey games. They were definitely big fans," says Margaret McKie, Gerti's daughter and Betty's niece. "I guess it was love at first sight, from what I've heard. They were devoted to each other."

The pair were married on November 24, 1934, with Bennett acting as the best man. Blake elected to forgo a tryout with the Canadiens in October but did reportedly turn up at a Boston Bruins camp in Quebec City later in the month after signing a tryout contract, according to reports at the time. "During my time in Hamilton I received offers to turn professional, but it was a matter of the heart that kept me in Hamilton," Blake told *Le Petit Journal* in 1937. "It's near there where I met the woman who would go on to become Mrs. Hector Blake."

Toe's impact with the yellow-and-gold-clad Tigers was near immediate. In his first season at the Barton Street Arena, Hamilton reached the OHA final before succumbing to Niagara Falls. Toe had shown his value, and Tigers coach George Redding quickly gave his hard-nosed recruit a prominent role, making him a permanent fixture at left wing alongside center Maxie Bennett and right winger Steve Conick. Blake's shooting remained errant, but he still managed to stand out on this responsible trio, which took a lot of pressure off the defense. They led the attack but never backed down from a challenge, either, including some reported fiery melees with the Port Colborne Sailors. The trio—nicknamed the "Three Musketeers"—led Hamilton to the OHA title and finishing the scoring race 1-2-3. It was the second consecutive season Blake had finished second in scoring. After winning the OHA, the club reached the Eastern Canada Final of the Allan Cup, where it bowed out to the Moncton Hawks.

People were taking notice of Blake: one headline screamed, "Fame Beckons," adding, "The pot of gold is already beckoning." The story went on to say that "without (the Three Musketeers), the Tigers would hardly be in the first flight of the leading teams in the country but with them the yellow-and-black striped gentry are justly rated as the team to beat for the provincial championship."

Such was the trio's standing that NHL scouts from Montreal began to take notice. In January 1935, Montreal Maroons president James Strachan signaled Blake had been placed on the team's negotiation list. Blake then enjoyed the first of several failed flirtations with the Montreal Canadiens. Valentine's Day was a special one for Blake: he shared it with his future wife *and* his future hockey club.

Leo Dandurand and Howie Morenz traveled to Hamilton to meet owner Percy Thompson to register their interest in Blake and Bennett on behalf of the Canadiens. Maroons coach Eddie Gerard then decided his team needed Blake and boarded a train to Hamilton. Gerard was swayed by Blake's teammate Herbie Cain's play, and he returned to the Forum with Cain's signature instead of Blake's. Cain would rise to stardom on a line with Bob Gracie and Gus Marker. The Toronto Maple Leafs were also actively chasing Blake and might have signed him if not for an unintentional slight by owner Conn Smythe during a playoff game in March. Smythe had sent Blake a contract offer outlining salary conditions. Toe didn't respond until appearing on Smythe's doorstep at Maple Leaf Gardens with the Leafs trailing a playoff game 1–0.

"Mr. Smythe was pacing up and down the hall, his head bowed, and his hands behind his back. I stopped in front of him, and said: 'Hello, Mr. Smythe, I'm here,'" Blake told the *Montreal Herald* years later. "Smythe stopped in his tracks, looked me straight in the eye for fully 20 seconds, then dropped his head and paced on without a word. I guess I picked the worst possible time to meet him. But it was a good break. If I had met him with Leafs ahead, I might have become a Leaf. Maybe I would have settled in Toronto. I like it better here."

Blake was forced to publicly tame the Tigers' fears that he had any intention to leave. Club officials were nervous after learning Blake had traveled to Toronto to meet Montreal Maroons officials. The Canadiens focus, meanwhile, seemed to have switched to Bennett, "the little chunk of dynamite," allowing the Maroons full reign over Blake. Blake had in fact traveled to the "Queen City" to meet with Maroons general manager Tommy Gorman, but reports suggested the Maroons' offer was not generous enough to coax Blake out of his sweetheart's hometown. But the Maroons persevered, and Art Cayford, secretary-treasurer of the Maroons, traveled to Detroit in February to finally seal Blake's signature.

Blake's decision to jump into the professional ranks was met with disbelief in Hamilton, where the Tigers leader was labeled a "deserter." The Canadian Amateur Hockey Association attempted to pass a rule that would keep professional clubs from taking prospects away from junior teams. "The brilliant left-winger has been one of the leading factors in the success achieved by the Bengals . . . and his absence will mean a definite lessening of their effectiveness," one newspaper wrote. "One player does not make a team but without Blake the Tigers cannot feel as optimistic to their chances of winning the O.H.A. title, going on to Allan Cup and with a win there having the chance to represent Canada at Olympics (in a year from now)."

But Toe was unconcerned with the noise as he and Betty moved to Montreal to join the Maroons. He was called on to fill in for the injured Dave Trottier, making his professional debut in front of 5,500 fans in a 4–0 victory in St. Louis against the last-place Eagles.

"All through the game I was in a daze. The players kept whizzing past me, and I couldn't figure out what it was all about. But I got over that and it never came back to me! It was a debut that didn't announce much about my potential. But from the second shift I found my feet and that was all in the past," Blake said.

Toe, sporting the No. 8 jersey, ended up playing in eight regular-season games without registering a point or a penalty minute. He fit into the tight-checking team and managed to get into one playoff game that season. When the Maroons beat the Toronto Maple Leafs 4–1 on April 9, 1935, for a 3–0 Stanley Cup Final sweep, his name was inscribed on the Cup for the very first of 11 times. Only Henri Richard has his name on the trophy as many times as Blake.

That summer began an annual tradition for the Blakes of heading west to Coniston to work in the mines or to Hamilton and National Steel Car and the Walters fruit farm. After their first daughter, Joan Isabelle Blake, was born on July 2, 1936, at the Moyer Nursing Home in Grimsby, Ontario, the Blakes appeared to spend more time in Hamilton during the summers. With Betty and Joan at his side, Toe drove from Montreal to Winona in a mobile home and parked it at the bottom of Betty's uncle Howard's farm by the lake. Lena ensured Toe ate well those summer months, baking her special chicken pot pies and fruit pies that left Toe returning to camp a few pounds overweight, as he liked it. As the years passed, those summer nights left lasting memories. The adults played euchre and the kids had sing-alongs at evening parties in the steady breeze coming up off Lake Ontario.

"We looked up to him as a real good athlete," Howard Walters recalls. "His history with the Canadiens was a plus for our family. He was well known around Winona. He came here for the summers and also played ball at nights with the local team. He was a good ball player, too."

Toe played baseball for the Winona team and eventually played for a semi-professional team out of Hamilton. He was friendly with everyone, an ordinary guy who could be found eating dinner at the Pines restaurant at Lake Avenue and 8th after the game. It was one of the few restaurants in Winona where honeydew melon was an exotic starter: cantaloupes, not green melons, were native to the area. Toe was obsessed with off-season conditioning, something that dated back to the start of his career, and he did all he could to ensure extending his playing career for as long as he could, however he could. Toe took construction jobs with this in mind and scoffed at those who looked down on him.

"I didn't take any soft spots, none of this material clerking, or expediting stuff, no time-keeping. None of that," he told *The Hockey News*.

> I'd work as a common day laborer. I'd be pushing a wheelbarrow, swinging a pick, and a shovel in turn, carrying heavy loads, timber, stones or bricks on my shoulder. It's the kind of work they often given to uneducated men, or foreigners. And many of my friends, at least they thought they were my friends, used to sniff and sneer. They thought it unbecoming of a guy who made good money in the wintertime playing hockey, working at such menial tasks. Why, some white-collar guys openly snubbed me on the street.
>
> But I don't care, I knew what I was doing. For me that kind of work did many things. First of all, I was keeping in the best of shape. I was giving my body that case-hardening you never can get by playing individual games or working out in the gym. The discipline was important, too. There was always that seven o'clock whistle, or that alarm clock. With that in mind I had neither the inclination nor the incentive to play around at nights. Anyway, I was too tired. And what's more I was saving my money. I was so busy in the daytime that I had no time to spend any of the dough I might have banked during the winter, and that's where my playoff and Stanley Cup cheques went,

> too. And I was paying my way in the summertime out of the money I earned as a hunkie or whatever you care to call the members of the gang I happened to be working with on these various occasions.

While Blake was busy keeping in playing shape, back in Montreal there were rumblings that one of the city's two NHL outfits wouldn't be around for much longer. The Canadiens came out of the 1934–35 season with $40,000 in operating losses following a season spent with a $30,000 deficit. The idea—or ploy—of moving Les Tricolores to Cleveland surfaced.

"Montreal is obviously losing interest in professional hockey. The game here has passed its peak of popularity. The city is too small to support two clubs," said Canadiens owner Joe Cattarinich, who looked to force the hand of the Canadian Arena Company—owner of the Forum—by suggesting there was a $200,000 offer on the table. The Canadian Arena Company—a syndicate headed by J. Ernest Savard and Maurice Forget—ultimately bought the Canadiens for $165,000 to keep them in Montreal. Toe didn't pay too much attention to these developments from Winnipeg, the site of the Maroons' pre-season camp. His focus was on making an impact in his upcoming debut full NHL campaign. Cracking the Maroons roster would be no easy task. The reigning champions, coached by "miracle man" Tommy Gorman, were expected to finish top of the Canadian Division again. Gorman had delivered a Stanley Cup to Chicago before joining the Maroons and earning immediate success.

But Blake would not be at the November 16 season-opening 1–0 win over Boston, when the Maroons raised their first ever Stanley Cup pennant inside the famed Forum. Gorman felt Blake needed more grooming. The Maroons manager preferred Blake start the 1935–36 season with one of the club's affiliate teams in the Canadian–American League. Gorman gave Providence Reds coach Albert Leduc the opportunity to choose: Did he want Blake or Sammy McManus, a sprite winger hailing from Belfast? Leduc chose wisely, recruiting Blake and lending McManus to New York Rangers farm club the Philadelphia Ramblers. While McManus had won a pair of Allan Cups and was also listed on the Stanley Cup alongside Blake, "Twinkle Toes" did not last long in the NHL, playing just 25 games for the Maroons.

Blake, meanwhile, reluctantly joined the Reds. He had signed with the Maroons to play at the Forum, not the Rhode Island Auditorium. Blake was starting to regret his decision to sign with the NHL champions. This newfound regret fueled his desire to get back to the NHL. Blake had had a small taste of pro hockey, and now he wanted to drink it all in.

• • •

The 6,500 attendees at the Eastern States Coliseum were giving it to Blake. But one Springfield Indians fan's goading stood out to the Providence Reds left winger, who wasted no time and charged. Blake jumped the boards, his stick dangling from his hand, chasing after the ticket holder. Springfield's Ted Saunders raced toward Blake, enticing him to leave the spectator and return to the ice for another melee between the pair. The game was barely a period old, but Blake was right in the middle of the free-for-all.

Blake's antics appeared to help on this day—the Reds' 6–4 victory moved them into second place in the league. But barely one week later, Springfield reclaimed second place with a 1–0 win at the Auditorium. Blake and Saunders squared off again as the bad blood remained, bubbling up in Blake's veins. In Providence, Blake was allowed to tap into a natural mean streak fueled by the desire to show up the Maroons for their decision to stick him back in the minors. Albert "Battleship" Leduc did not rein Blake in—Toe was second only to the player-coach in penalty minutes over the 1935–36 season. Since his arrival in Providence, Blake had shown why several NHL clubs were interested in him. Playing alongside Red Conn and Gus Rivers on the top line, Blake was fifth in Can–Am scoring by the end of January, eventually finishing with 12 goals and 23 points alongside 65 penalty minutes. Blake didn't stay in Providence long, but it was clear Leduc had gambled wisely. Blake repaid his confidence with two goals in a 5–3 win over Philadelphia in late January. Blake always credited Leduc with being one of the biggest influences of his career, helping him adapt his style of play to the professional ranks.

But the Maroons brass, unable to look past Blake's aggressive behavior, failed to see his improved shooting, skating and stickhandling. They were not even swayed when some reporters labeled him an "all-around wizard" for his complete game, which included his value as a penalty killer. "He is adept at keeping the puck away from the opposition . . . if he can overcome a habit of going into opposing players with stick held too high" wrote one.

Leduc knew Blake was primed for the NHL and had relayed this information to Gorman. But Gorman showed little urgency in bringing Blake into the fold, with the Maroons on top of the league standings. Luckily for Blake, Leduc had tipped off Montreal Canadiens scout Billy Boucher, who had the ear of coach Sylvio Mantha. Bringing Blake to the team was perhaps Mantha's best move during a doomed season that saw him relieved of his duties in the spring. The Canadiens shipped Vezina Trophy–winning goalie Lorne Chabot to the Maroons for Blake and Bill Miller. Some reports suggested both deals were loans, others that it was a swap. *La Patrie* newspaper referred to the newcomer as "Tow Blake" in its headline of February 11, 1936—the day Blake made his Montreal Canadiens debut in front of 5,000 Forum fans in a 1–1 draw with the New York Rangers. *La Patrie* said Blake "played with honour" and that if the club did have an option to buy the husky forward, "they had a steal on their hands." The *Montreal Star* said Blake showed good energy but found his "surroundings a trifle strange."

Blake did enough in the draw to stay with the team, with *L'Illustration* stating Blake played hockey of the "first order. Blake has all the tools to succeed: stature, speed and a shot." Blake's first NHL goal came on February 22 at the Forum, the winner in Montreal's 1–0 victory over the New York Americans. At 17:39 of the second period, Blake managed to turn and lift a backhanded shot past Americans goalie Roy Worters from a sprawled position along the ice. Now that he had bagged his first goal, Blake could finally exhale. His arrival was part of the Canadiens' retooling. Blake had realized he could not allow his temper to become a hindrance in his quest to make it in the NHL. But it took a vicious duel with Detroit's Ebbie Goodfellow to remind him of this.

"God-damn right he was tough, he had fingers like hot dogs," Kenny Reardon recalled to *Canadiens Captains* author Michael Ulmer. "One time he took on the whole Detroit team. They all came after him and he stood there at centre ice swinging his stick saying, 'which one of you bastards wants it first?' It was like a bunch of dogs trying to get at him."

It all started when Blake and Goodfellow traded punches. With less than two minutes to play in a 3–1 Canadiens loss at Detroit, Goodfellow charged Blake, knocking him to the ground and jumping on him to deliver a pummeling. Blake managed to land a few blows himself before the players were separated and guided to the penalty boxes, the screams of 12,000 bloodthirsty hockey fans filling the Olympia's frame. Goodfellow—with his back to Blake—was on his way to the penalty box when "Blake, in a sudden rage, swung his stick down hard at the Detroit player's head at terrific speed," *Le Devoir* reported.

Herb Lewis deflected the blow onto his teammate's shoulder. Goodfellow charged Blake, who in the ensuing melee decided to include Detroit right winger Hec Kilrea in the festivities. The referees looked to have finally parted Blake from the fuss before he pounced on Doug Young.

By the time Blake was hustled off the ice, the fans were attempting to get a lick at him, and Blake was obliging. The incident led the NHL to adopt a new rule: fines of $100 for using your stick as a weapon and $50 for leaving the bench during a brawl.

When the two teams met again later in the season, there were no scores settled. Blake had made his point, and now he wanted to get down to the business of hockey.

• • •

Come summer, the Canadiens organization had to move quickly to lock in Blake to its roster. Dandurand had reportedly put Blake on the Canadiens reserve list following his trip to Hamilton alongside Morenz, before allowing the Maroons to sign him on the condition he be returned upon request. Now the Canadiens were exercising that option as interest in Blake grew, with three NHL clubs weighing their options at prying him away from the Habs. "We are trying to build up our team and we certainly cannot start disposing of our young players at this stage," said incoming manager Cecil Hart.

Blake spent the summer at the Walters fruit farm, focused on the Canadiens, who were already making major roster changes. Cecil Hart returned as coach after a three-year absence and the club re-signed Howie Morenz.

"I was very anxious to make good. When I realized that I would be playing with my childhood idol, Howie Morenz, you can bet that I was a pretty happy fellow!" Blake said. "Now I'm with Les Canadiens I'm happy and I feel sure that I will be able to help them toward a Stanley Cup."

Blake signed a new deal with the club on October 8 as the players returned for training camp at the Palestre Nationale. After scoring a magnificent overtime winner against the Rangers, it was clear Blake would be a permanent fixture on the second line, playing alongside center Pit Lepine and right winger Joffre Desilets. He wore No. 16 because the No. 6 shirt was worn by goalie Wilf Cude. Led by the top line of Morenz, Joliat and Gagnon, the Canadiens quickly put last season's misery behind them, and Blake was one of the reasons why. "Toe Blake is a sturdy fellow who fears no one," wrote *La Presse*, "and a player no one can do harm. He's as hard as stone and you'll just hurt yourself if you come up against him."

Blake's temper was under control—he would rack up only 12 penalty minutes in 43 games—despite the occasional slipup, such as when Blake and Walter "Happy" Harnott staged what one reporter called "the Battle of Gettysburg on the ice" in a 2–1 loss at Boston on November 15. Blake was consistent at home or on the road, fighting for every puck, digging into the corners and finishing every check. His scoring finish continued to be the lone weak spot.

"Our team, as it is presently composed, is one of the most powerful and resilient in the NHL and, barring any injuries, our players will be featuring in the playoffs and might even have a great chance of winning the title," Hart said.

But the Canadiens' success was rubbing Maroons general manager Gorman wrong, especially with Blake playing an important part in it. The Canadiens announced the suspension of all business with their crosstown rivals following the Maroons' use of Paul Runge in a December 12 game. Gorman defended the use of Runge on the basis that Blake had not been returned to his team at the end of the previous season: "We loaned Bill Miller and Toe Blake and had arrived at a gentleman's agreement the pair would be returned to the Maroons at season's end. This agreement was violated by Mr. Savard with the result being we lost Miller and Blake, for who we had already refused large offers for last April. If we had taken the right precautions with the Miller-Blake deal they would still both be Maroons players today."

Canadiens owner Ernest Savard penned a long retort that was published in several newspapers. "Toe Blake was in Providence," he wrote. "Mr. Gorman, who always believes his club is the best in the league so he doesn't have to worry, without a doubt forgot Toe Blake was a player with a lot of promise. The great malaise that Mr. Gorman presently feels is from . . . his inability to endure seeing the Canadiens atop the standings and his club in danger of sitting last after tonight's game."

"I don't want to say anything on the subject of the Maroons," said Blake, stuck in the middle of this tug-of-war of words but pleased to have switched from maroon to Canadiens red. "They were a great group of teammates, but the Canadiens players are famous."

With the Maroons squarely in the rearview mirror, Blake continued to cement his stake in his new club in the 1936–37 season. He contributed a spurt of goals in late January and early February as the Canadiens moved further ahead of the Maroons on top of the Canadian Division. Blake, who was now wearing No. 21 after having worn 18 earlier in the campaign, was getting recognized around town. His emergence came just as the team lost Morenz to a broken leg in a 6–5 win over Chicago. It would be Blake's last game alongside Morenz, who never recovered from the injury, which ultimately took his life on March 8. On the eve of Morenz's death, Blake looked lost for the season after fracturing his right hand when crashing hard along the boards. Blake hadn't realized the hand was fractured until he was sitting in the dressing room during the first intermission.

Against the odds, Blake returned from the injury two weeks later in a 3–1 loss to the Rangers in New York. The fragile hand did not deter Blake, who exchanged slashes with Ott Heller as the pair nearly came to blows. Heller tripped Blake as the pair came out of the penalty box, and Hart—sensing his left winger was on the cusp of a meltdown—removed Blake from the game. Blake, who had tallied just 12 penalty minutes, ended the 1936–37 season with 22 points, including 10 goals.

The Canadiens finished on top of the Canadian Division to set up a playoff matchup with American Division winner Detroit. Montreal promptly fell behind 2–0 before Blake redirected Babe Siebert's shot into goal for the opening score of a 3–1 win in front of 13,000 at the Forum. The Canadiens eventually tied the series at 2–2, but their poor playoff run stretched to six straight playoff series defeats when they dropped the deciding fifth game 2–1 in triple overtime. According to the *Montreal Gazette*, it was an unruly, raucous affair at the "smoke-hazy" Forum right from the start, with fans littering the ice with debris at one point, and a woman aiming her lipstick at officials. Montreal tied it up with just over five minutes to play, but in the third overtime, Hec Kilrea was well-positioned when an errant shot took a friendly rebound off the boards and landed on his stick in front of the goal.

Afterward, Savard and Hart spoke of a minor shake-up being needed for the next season, with three of four more players coming in. There was no mention of reinforcing left wing, just right wing and center.

• • •

"I could never let up. Others could, but I had to drive myself," Blake told *Sports Illustrated* in 1965. If anyone needed proof, they only had to glance at the scoreline of the Canadiens' 25–6 exhibition win over the Sydney Telephones, the champions of Cape Breton. Blake scored 20 goals in the victory. While the Telephones were far from an NHL-caliber team, the scoreline spoke to Blake's competitive nature. His tenacity fed off his boiling character, which knew no fear. Toe quickly turned into a model player—fighting for every puck, throwing himself into every corner and defending teammates whenever challenged. Even in an exhibition game.

Blake was no average player. While many might figure him to be the third wheel on the legendary Punch Line, Toe "was right up there—he wasn't at the very top in the class of a Howie Morenz but he was very good," hockey historian Stan Fischler recalled. "He was maybe not an idol, but he was a superior player. There's a top banana and a bottom banana—he was in the second tier under the top."

Blake played at a time when hockey was pure—or so historians like Fischler remember, through the fog of nostalgia. There were no helmets or goalie masks—it was league of men making a living playing a pure game. Blake was, in fact, a pure hockey man.

After Morenz's death, Blake swapped No. 16 for 6 and began to take a leading role with the Canadiens from the 1937–38 campaign. After a 33-point season with 17 goals in 43 games, he was named a Second Team All-Star. Blake's temper continued to rear up in dramatic fashion at least once a season. Blake earned 12 of his 33 penalty minutes, and three points, in a 3–3 tie at Toronto. Blake fumed after referee Ag Smith struck away a goal, which he ruled came after the whistle. Blake's protest was made in vain. When play resumed, Blake—still fuming—swung his stick at Dave Trottier while trying to trap the puck, which sent the Leaf into a tailspin as he was simultaneously hit by Walter Buswell. Blake saw a 10-minute misconduct added to his two-minute penalty for calling Smith "everything from Haitebury to Halifax."

Toe's influence inside the locker room was growing—no one could dispute his intensity or work ethic. The team was made up of good, spirited two-way players who, Babe Siebert told the *Gazette*, "cuss and bawl each other out on the ice, but that just makes us mad enough to play harder and fight harder. After the game, anything that's been said out there is forgotten—as it should be." Toe's style of play was no different—he was "a throwback. When Toe scores a goal it is often engraved in the spectator's mind for some time."

The team was riding high in December following a lukewarm start. Superstition played an important part in the run. Wilf Cude wore a blue shirt to the rink for each game of a five-game unbeaten run, keeping it out of the laundry: "I'm going to keep on wearing it—if I can keep it away from my wife," he told the *Gazette.*

Toe, Betty and Joan—now a toddler—settled into their lives in the working-class district of the Plateau-Mont-Royal, at 823 St. Joseph Boulevard at the corner of St. André. Buswell was a neighbor and drinking companion; Toe enjoyed a bottle of beer after every game "to help soothe his nerves."

The NHL was moving toward a single division, and 1937–38 was the last season featuring separate Canadian and American Divisions. The Canadiens finished the season third in the Canadian, setting up a best-of-three series with the Blackhawks. Chicago had finished third in the American Division, squeaking into the playoffs ahead of Detroit, and closing out the regular season with three straight losses. They dropped their fourth straight to trail 1–0 in the series. But they bounced back to win the next two games of the best-of-three series, en route to an unlikely Stanley Cup title. Montreal had been less than 90 seconds away from advancing before Earl Seibert tied it up with a long, floating shot. The Blackhawks prevailed in overtime. Blake's three goals and four points left him tied for the playoff scoring lead after one round.

That off-season promised plenty of changes to the roster, with Pit Lepine and Aurel Joliat among the departed. Manager Cecil Hart also announced after the game that the Canadiens and Red Wings—both eliminated—would travel to Europe for six weeks to play a series of exhibition matches in London and Paris. Blake went, despite having played the close of the season with injured rib ligaments, which had kept him out of several games but not the playoffs.

The players arrived in London on April 19 and, two nights

later, Blake netted the first NHL game winner outside of North America, in front of 8,000 on the sticky ice at Earls Court, in a 5–4 victory. Blake managed to rile up the Brighton locals in the subsequent 5–5 tie by exchanging blows with Pete Bessoni, a local favorite who had played amateur hockey in England and France. The games moved on to Paris, where the Prince of Wales Cup was contested at the Palais des Sports. The Canadiens played tourist, taking in the sights and enjoying champagne lunches at honorary banquets. As in London, the teams played to large crowds—a reported 8,500—with the Canadiens ultimately winning five of the nine games, with one tie. Toe received $250 for the exhibition tour, which was the closest thing to a vacation he had ever had.

That summer turned into a springboard for Blake's career year in 1938–39, when he won the Hart Trophy as the league's top player.

Blake started the season on the third line, but his superior play quickly moved him up the team pecking order. "Speedball Hurling Hector," as one newspaper writer dubbed him, clinched the scoring title with a game to spare, three points better than Sweeney Schriner of the Americans. Blake's feats were expanding, as typified in a 5–1 win over Chicago in which, as the *Montreal Herald* described it, he "raced in from the right, pirouetted once and then let fly for the far corner of the cage, a slicing shot which fanned Karakas as he lunged . . . a dazzling bit of legerdemain with puck and stick." The "chunky" Canadiens winger finished with 47 points from 24 goals and 23 assists, plus 10 penalty minutes, to be named a unanimous First Team All-Star and claim the Hart Trophy.

The award led to further acclaim and money on top of the $6,000 salary he earned from the Canadiens that season. His hometown of Coniston honored his accomplishment with a diamond ring. Betty watched with excitement at the public ceremony as mayor E.T. Austin presented the glittering honor before Morris Dubé, Toe's nephew, presented Betty with a bouquet of flowers. Blake appeared in national newspapers flogging six-cent bars of Odex soap. The Maple Leafs offered the Canadiens seven regular NHL players in exchange for Blake's contract, including Nick Metz, Reggie Hamilton and Jack Church. Savard pondered the trade for a week before ultimately rejecting the offer.

Despite the accolades, Blake still made his trip to Coniston a working one as he continued to toil in the mines—a job that he was growing to hate but needed both to keep him honest and also to allow him to keep playing hockey and avoid conscription. The company he kept also helped, as he spent his free time talking hockey with former Sudbury Wolves coach Sammy Rothschild at former NHL player Charlie Langlois's brasserie, where local store owner Red Green would occasionally join in. Toe might have spent his summers toiling underground, but it afforded him the opportunity to return home to see "Mame" and most of the family, as the majority had stayed on in Coniston. "The family—they were a riot all together," niece Claudette Dumontelle remembers.

Blake's rising fame affected his dealings with the Canadiens going into the 1939–40 season. He held out from training camp for a raise, feeling he deserved the league limit of $7,500 after winning league MVP on a penultimate-placed team. Canadiens management was in turmoil. Recently retired former Hart Trophy winner Babe Siebert, who was set to coach the club, drowned off the shores of his parent's cottage on Lake Huron in August, forcing Pit Lepine to be drafted in as coach. Blake's absence from the entire camp—he only signed his contract on the eve of the season—did not help, even if the club got off to a hot start. It was perhaps the lone moment of his career where Blake's selfishness cost the club and provided an excuse for his poor start to the season. He led the Canadiens in scoring again, but his 17-goal, 36-point season was a disappointment.

"The main stumbling block to the boys hitting the (20-goal) mark now is the fact that each club has gone out of its way in the past few years to build up three good forward lines. Back awhile, a team probably had one good line and that line played possibly 30 or 40 minutes in a game," Blake reasoned. "But with hockey streamlined as it is now, a line goes out for three or four minutes at a time and you might get only 15 or 20 minutes of play in a game. I'm not worried about winning the scoring title as long as we can keep on winning."

Unfortunately, there was little winning throughout the season—including a losing streak of nine straight games. The losing irked Blake, but not enough to stop him being a regular at Langlois's tavern the ensuing summer.

• • •

Dick Irvin Sr. nestled himself into the stiff wooden seat as best he could, extending one arm across the neighboring seatback before hoisting his leg up on the chair in front of him. The cramped seats weren't designed for Irvin's outstretched limbs, or general warmth or comfort, but Irvin felt at ease in the stands, watching over the horde of bodies on the ice below. Perhaps the distance between himself and his charges helped. Irvin hardly knew a player skating below. There was a slew of rookies from across Canada to make up for the loss of players signing up to the war effort and the general house-clearing the Canadiens had performed in the off-season. Irvin wanted to give himself a better view at how this bunch could skate, shoot, pass. It felt like none of them could do it. Down on that sheet of ice was a miserable bunch. An awful team. He recognized only a few of the men's faces. And he preferred it that way. They were the only worthy talents on the team. How could he have promised a playoff spot come spring with this crop?

Thank Christ we still have Blake, Irvin must have thought: Toe's spirited voice was one of the few commanding attention from those stands. Irvin had deputized Blake to lead practices when he wasn't on the ice or at the bench so he could get a different look at what was on the ice below. Knowing the habits of this team, Irvin thought the players might think it was a chance to lollygag. Irvin knew he could count on Blake, who led by example with everything he did. Every drill Blake led was performed with gamelike intensity because the Canadiens captain would have it no other way. Irvin shook his head thinking about how the Canadiens had been ready to ship Blake to Toronto in exchange for wingers Red Horner and Gordon Drillon, the Leafs' scoring leader.

"One thing about Toe was the way he practised. Boy, how he would work," Elmer Lach recounted in Dick Irvin Jr.'s *The Habs: An Oral History of the Montreal Canadiens*. "He always said the way you practised was the way you played. He never fooled around in a practice. That's what made him successful."

"My dad," Dick Irvin Jr. recalled, "liked to think about his players in different ways and, once, I asked him: Of the hundreds of players he had coached, which one liked the life of a hockey player the best? His answer: Toe Blake."

Men were fighting a war across the ocean, which made the men here the luckiest in the world, or so Blake figured. They were earning their way playing hockey. There was no reason not to put every ounce of your effort into each shot, check or puck chase. Blake took satisfaction in Irvin's trust. Here he was, leading the Montreal Canadiens' practice, when just a few years ago the Maroons predicted he wouldn't be able to skate at the NHL level. He might miss suiting up before the city derby against the Maroons, and how it made his blood boil, but their absence from the league made no impact on him beyond that. His temper was seen as a liability by the "hoity-toity" Maroons, and Blake had managed to turn that aggression into "not showy hockey, nor brilliant nor spectacular hockey—but a hockey player's hockey player, a guy who works hard, fights every inch of the way, goes plunging into every play," as Elmer Ferguson wrote in the *Montreal Herald.* He had to stop himself from smiling whenever he thought about the Maroons and their assessment of a player they had worked so hard to sign.

Blake's ability to push his teammates afforded Irvin a frank opportunity to judge his players. It was clear who responded to Blake's cries, who possessed talent. And those who didn't. Talent was a figurative term for this bunch going into the 1940–41 season.

The Canadiens had languished in—or near—the cellar the past two seasons, and it would be another two before they finally emerged as Stanley Cup contenders. The process of changing this began with Irvin's appointment after he led the Leafs to the 1940 Cup Final. The Canadiens were coming off 10-win season when a successful night yielded 3,000 fans inside the Forum. There was little discipline in the dressing room: players smoked and drank beer, shaved when the mood struck them and took little pride in wearing the *C*. It was no coincidence that during the season prior to Irvin's arrival, Montreal won just 3 of their final 35 league games, including a record 15-game winless run on Forum ice that spanned 3 months, setting the standard for over 50 years.

"It was every man for himself," Ray Getliffe, who was traded from the Stanley Cup champion Boston Bruins to the Canadiens before the 1939–40 season, remembered in Irvin Jr.'s *The Habs*. "Pit Lepine was our coach and he never seemed to worry. I remember one night, Boston beat us 6–2 at the Forum. Right after the game, Pit put on a big coonskin coat he always wore in the winter, gave us a big wave and hollered, 'So long, boys, see you tomorrow.'"

The situation had become so dire, rumors began circulating that the team could cease operations during the war as it continued to endure heavy financial losses amid its terrible on-ice performances. Senator Donat Raymond, the owner, had signed away all revenue streams: the concessions, advertising, the game program. The NHL called a meeting to address the woes before the city lost another club.

"They talked about the lack of discipline on the team, and everything was a mess," Irvin Jr. remembered. "And (Conn) Smythe said, 'I've got just the guy to send in there, we'll send in Irvin, at least as a start, to coach the team.' So that's what happened. My dad coached his last game for the Leafs on a Saturday night, came a day or two later on a train (to Montreal)."

Irvin and general manager Tommy Gorman, who had joined the Canadiens in the summer of 1940, agreed there were only a few NHL-worthy talents on the roster: recently acquired goaltender Bert Gardiner, Getliffe and Blake. Gorman left his entire roster, barring those three players, open to waivers.

Irvin went to work to address the discipline problems inside the locker room, instituting weekly weigh-in sessions and a strict diet of 3 p.m. steak lunches on game day—a habit that stuck with Blake when he took over as coach. Irvin showed no tolerance for ballyhoo, including with center Paul Haynes, who had been a steady scorer before injuries began to take a toll.

"My dad said, 'Where's Haynes?' And Toe Blake, who was the captain, said: 'Don't worry about him. He's here, but every time we come to New York on a Sunday he goes to the opera.' So, my dad said: 'Oh, the opera, eh?' . . . Haynes never played another game in the NHL. But that was the kind of stuff that was going on and somebody had to put an end to it and, obviously, he did."

When Walter Buswell demanded a $500 raise, Gorman sent the 32-year-old defenseman packing, and Irvin promoted Blake to take on his role as captain to start the 1940–41 season. Blake did not escape Irvin's wrath, either, as the 28-year-old forward seemed to be coasting off his Hart Trophy season.

Toe, when he showed up for Irvin's first training camp as Canadiens coach, was fat.

"Mr. Blake, you can play for this team this year, but if you show up at training camp next year looking like you do today, don't even bother to come," Irvin said. Toe laughed. He knew Irvin was right.

Blake may have been as tough on teammates as he was on opponents, but he was never unfair. This product of the mining country was kindhearted with younger players. His respect was hard-earned, but he believed in self-will and went out of his way to motivate even those who were struggling to make an impact.

"He was a very difficult guy to get to know," Lach said, "but once you broke through, you realized he was the cream of the earth. It just took him a long time to decide whether you were the right kind of person."

This might have seemed unexpected from a player who ran his mouth at referees and swung his stick at opponents. What Blake did not possess in finesse, he made up for with hard work.

In the *Montreal Herald*, Elmer Ferguson wrote:

> He isn't showy; he is no wheeling, handsome, straight-up Busher Jackson who took passes on his toes and hurled them forehand or backhand at bullet speed; he is no Sweeney Schriner, with expressionless face, lightning-shift, cool stickhandling skill and deadly shot; he is no hawk-faced, vivid Johnny Gottselig, who bewilders an opponent with his wheeling, pirouetting style; nor is he any hurdling, leaping Herbie Lewis; nor yet a Cowboy Anderson. But he's the best left wing in the National Hockey League.
>
> He's a hockey workman, a hockey worker, a plugger, a tireless, driving, game, rugged young fellow, whose main idea is to score goals himself or stop his check from getting any. Blake is on the short side of stature, but his shoulders are wide, his chest is thick and muscular, his hips and legs are thickly and powerfully constructed. He's

> a rugged piece of stuff, out of a rugged country. Blake isn't what you'd call a stylist. He's a good sound puck-carrier, but not sensational. When he came into big-time hockey with Maroons, he wasn't much of a skater. But he kept plugging and today he can match strides with the fastest. What makes Blake really great is that he digs in, battles in, shoulders hunched, shoving, bumping, elbowing, fighting . . . he's a fighting hockey player, one of the toughest and most effective in the game.

Blake signed his new contract—reportedly one of the highest in the league—promptly in October 1940 and joined the team camp in Saint-Hyacinthe as an untouchable. By the start of the season against the Stanley Cup champion Boston Bruins, he was named the 11th captain in club history. Blake's attitude fit into Irvin's plans nicely. The 48-year-old Irvin felt lucky to have a trusted voice in the locker room that could do some of the dirty work for him. Irvin spent his free time away from the rink, commuting between Montreal and Regina for his first 11 seasons in charge of the Canadiens.

The organizational shake-up left the roster with nine new players out of 17, including three promising rookies: center Elmer Lach, winger Joe Benoit and defenseman Kenny Reardon. Lach, for one, obeyed everything Blake and Irvin said, to avoid being handed a second-class bus ticket for the return journey to Saskatchewan.

"As you practice, so you play" Blake would yell to his teammates, words Lach would never forget as the pair played together on the Punch Line years later. Blake's affinity for motivating younger players searching for confidence was felt by the rookies. Toe, meanwhile, wanted his scoring title back—and the "nice, fat bonus" that accompanied being named a First Team All-Star.

He figured 10 goals by Christmas would put him in the running for the Hart again. "Last season I had five different centers and four left wingers. It's pretty hard to get going under those circumstances. This year the line seems to be settled. All Benoit has to do is pop in a few goals and it will be a big help to me. If he does that then the opposing line will have to pay less attention to me. Just give me those 10 goals," said Toe with a grin, "and I'll let the rest take care of itself."

But the season didn't start well for Montreal. The Canadiens went winless through their first six games, and Blake didn't get near 10 goals by the holidays. His frustration enhanced his already loud and foul-mouthed on-ice presence and his perpetual dislike of referees. Blake's long-running feud with referee Mickey Ion reached a boiling point that season. He insulted Ion's ancestry in a game at Toronto and was handed a match penalty. Ion was working the next game against Chicago, and when Blake was clipped by a high stick, he replied similarly and received another penalty. Blake charged at Ion, who warned the Canadiens captain: "One word—just one word—out of you, Toe, and you're out of this game!" Toe was torn—control his fury and stay in the game, or follow through on his anger? He couldn't stop himself and yelled, "I'm not going to say a word, Mickey, but you sure as hell know what I'm thinking!" He was ejected, and when his teammates found him in the locker room and heard the story from Blake, they all erupted in laughter. Toe admitted to enjoying the episode and later spoke of Ion to Bill Roche: "I hope he lives to be a hundred. He was not only a great referee; he was the best mind reader in the business."

Blake's penchant for booze fueled his already intense competitive nature. He was once barred from the poolroom that operated within the Forum building because of his foul language. With Blake struggling to score and appearing unsettled, the rumors again started swirling about a trade—this time to Chicago.

"This player is not for sale at any price," Irvin said. "We could have already traded him for a couple of famous names in the league."

And while Irvin felt affinity for Blake, he didn't treat him any differently. During one intermission in Boston when the team was struggling, Irvin went around the room giving it to each player, saving his last jab for his captain. "Toe Blake, the man with the one-track hockey mind. Back about 1926 or somewhere, he must have scored a goal by dumping the puck between the defensemen and racing around them to pick it up and go in on the goalkeeper. He's still doing it, but he hasn't scored a goal that way. There are other ways of getting in on a goalkeeper, but you can't make Blake believe that."

While Blake eventually turned his season around, going on to collect 12 goals and 20 assists, his 32 points tied him with Benoit (16–16, 32 points) for second best on the club, behind Calder Trophy winner Johnny Quilty (18–16, 34). The Canadiens still made the playoffs as promised, and the rookie contingent developed as expected.

But with Lach missing due to injury, the best-of-three series against the Blackhawks began with defeat in Chicago. Blake, criticized for his vanishing act in the opening 2–1 loss, set the tone in the return match on Forum ice by "slicing a gap in Mush March's forehead on the opening play of the game," according to the *Sherbrooke Daily Record*. Blake's move down the left side exposed goalie Sam LoPresti for Benoit to tie the game. Blake picked up a second assist as he split the defense with a pass that found a streaking Benoit for 2–1. The Canadiens tied the series with a 4–3 win in double overtime. But LoPresti was up to the task in Game 3, robbing Blake at point-blank with the score 2–2 before the Hawks triumphed 3–2 to advance. Blake's old nemesis Ion returned to haunt him on the winning goal. The Canadiens players felt Ion had performed well except for a blown call in the third period when they felt Earl Seibert tripped Blake at the Chicago blue line to set up a three-man rush that led to Chicago's series-winning goal.

Still, Chicago coach Paul Thompson was impressed by the Canadiens: "That club is on the right path now with all those kids," he told the press. "We've found them tough to stop and they have the makings of a good hockey team."

The outlook was bright as Irvin's pre-season shake-up and character change in the dressing room paid dividends. Veteran center Charlie Sands—one of the players Irvin had asked during the pre-season to set an example for the youngsters—was quoted after the defeat to Chicago in the *Gazette*: "Every one of those kids was swell. They're quiet; well-behaved and serious about their work. And not a popoff among the lot. If we had the old club which had just finished its season, Irvin and Patrick would have gone nearly wacky checking the players into the train and wondering what bar or tavern this guy and that guy was in. Maybe they'd had to hold the train to get everybody on board. All our gang made straight for the station, mainly because of the kids."

After carrying the seasoned pros' bags on board, the "kids" stood around the train's bar-car counter, sipping on fizzy drinks. The veterans spent the train ride tucking into booze while the youngsters reportedly went promptly to bed. "Some of the rookies had their tongues hanging out for a beer, but they didn't know whether the big bosses would approve even though we were through for the season," said Sands as he drank his first bottle of beer after volunteering to refrain from alcohol for the entire season to set an example to the rookies.

Irvin closed the door to his train compartment that night—the sign it was okay to bring out the beer. Irvin usually made sure his compartment stayed open when the team was traveling on the eve of a game, since the players, especially Blake, might fancy a cold one. Irvin never imposed a curfew on his players over the course of his 26 seasons coaching, except in his final campaign, in Chicago. The players understood the rules, and that worked. Even for Toe, who was normally gasping for a beer after a game.

Irvin loved the movies and would often go to a midnight showing after a road game. Getting out of the cinema at 2 a.m. offered an opportunity to check on the boys, and one night he came across some of the players, including a rookie, stumbling home to the hotel. One of those players was a young call-up from the Royals farm team, so Irvin told him a train ticket home to Montreal would be waiting for him when the team arrived in Toronto.

"It turns out my dad wasn't as hard as you thought, because the kid started to cry and so my dad kept him," Dick Irvin Jr. recalled. "He played the next night against Toronto and played a hell of a game, he played his heart out."

As the train rolled toward Montreal's Windsor Station, Toe sipped on his beer, enjoying the methodic chug of the wagon and a feeling of comfort. This was finally a team—his team—and the future looked bright.

Even if it meant another summer in those fucking mines.

• • •

Blake once described how his pregame stamina could affect his in-game performance, explaining he played best when feeling "a little bit tired" in the first period. "If I go into a game feeling like a million then I invariably finish it feeling rotten and I generally play a poor game. But if I'm a bit tired at the start then I always feel swell in the second and third periods."

Blake's endurance was one of the traits that defined his play. "Toe is one of the sturdiest hockey players in the league," teammate and Canadiens scout Paul Haynes told the *Montreal Herald*. "He has tremendous reserve of stamina, backed by unlimited power in his legs. He can skate just as fast, just as aggressively in the last few minutes of a hard game as he can in the first period. In fact, it takes Toe several minutes to warm up after he's been sent onto the ice. He's the type of player who responds to plenty of work."

Blake deliberately worked hard in the off-season to stay in shape. Year-round workouts were something he embraced as a player, especially going into the 1941–42 season. Irvin had already warned him about his playing weight. So, even if the Canadiens could ill afford to lose him, he did not take his coach's warning lightly. Blake spent the last two weeks before training camp skating every day in Hamilton as he, Betty and Joan spent some time with the Walters. The physical part of the game was important, but just as important was finesse. Skating, he believed, was a fundamental every player should master.

"He always told me to make it in hockey I have to skate and skate and skate. Become a good skater to become a good hockey player," Toe's grandson Kenny Stuart remembers.

Blake believed in this principle as a player and as a coach, when he would often open his practices with marathon skating sessions to get the players warmed up. "At practice, mostly we skated," defenseman Terry Harper remembers. "We didn't have all these drills to do, no drills at all. We skated, maybe worked on penalty killing and power play, and scrimmage."

It must have pained Blake to see his youngest sibling, George, failing to keep up with the pace in camp that pre-season. George, given an invitation to come to Saint-Hyacinthe, was ultimately cut and sent to the Canadiens farm club in Shawinigan Falls.

The Canadiens' outlook continued to improve going into the 1941–42 season. Blake scored in the club's season-opening game for a sixth straight season, but Montreal succumbed to Detroit 3–2 while also losing Lach to a broken elbow. Despite the early setback, the club was improving and won 18 games—two more than the previous year—to finish sixth, in the final playoff spot. But another best-of-three series loss, this time to Detroit, followed. One year later, with the league now down to the "Original Six," the Canadiens edged the Blackhawks by a single point to finish fourth and clinch the final playoff position.

Yet another first-round series defeat—the club's 10th straight early playoff exit—followed. But the rebuild had paid dividends. The Canadiens were a genuine force in the league thanks in part to the original Punch Line of Blake, Lach and Benoit. Blake set a personal best of 59 points in 48 games, one better than Lach. Benoit's 30 goals helped him to 57 points to cement the group as one of the league's best lines. Benoit's arrival had coincided with Irvin's—the Canadiens had acquired his rights from the Maple Leafs in July 1940. His totals had improved every season since his arrival, scoring 12 goals and then 20 before joining the Punch Line. But Benoit decided to join the war effort, leaving the Canadiens with a significant loss on what was set to be their most important line heading into the 1943–44 season.

Luckily, Gorman had signed a young kid named Maurice Richard to an $800 contract prior to the start of the campaign.

CHAPTER 5

PUNCH LINE

ON JANUARY 10, 1948, the sound of men's breath was all that interrupted the silence in the Montreal Canadiens dressing room. Shoulders hung low, heads bowed, players stared into the abyss of empty hockey bags.

The silence had begun outside these walls, with the 11,211 seated in the red, white and blue Forum seats. Toe Blake had been bearing into the New York Rangers end but had to quickly stop and return as the visitors started a fast clearance in the other direction. The score was 1–1 at 9:12 of the third period when New York Rangers defenseman Bill Juzda caught Blake with a hard check into the southeast boards. Blake hit the wall heavily. His skate was caught, twisting his right leg in a knot. Pain overcame him, and then his head met the ice. Knocked out, he was revived by a collective gasp from the Forum fans. He came to with a jolt of pain traveling up his right leg. The former miner was used to knocks, so he tried to climb to his feet. But the pain did not subside, and he fell back to the cold comfort of the ice.

Players surrounded Blake, whose eyes were closed as he imagined the worst. *Had I just scored on one of those two opportunities prior to this moment,* he must have thought, *I wouldn't be in this fucking bind.* At that moment, almost instinctively, Rangers goalie Sugar Jim Henry tenderly placed his glove under Toe's head.

The words of trainer Bill Head were audible as the arena maintained its quiet hush. Blake tried desperately to climb up and off the ice under his own power—he was the Canadiens captain after all—but his body wouldn't have it. He had kept his head down for an instant and, just like that, he was smack on his ass.

A stretcher appeared, and the Forum Red Caps gathered up their captain to remove him from the ice. But one lost his balance and they all lost Blake, who fell to the ice for a second time. Perhaps this second unexpected scene left the crowd too frozen to applaud and give Blake a fitting goodbye. Perhaps it was the subzero chill that had descended on Montreal that weekend. Or perhaps they thought, *This is old Blake, he'll be back in no time,* as he had done on so many occasions in 12 previous NHL seasons. Blake was beloved by both the English and French fans, yet they were all quiet as he exited. It was a scene none had witnessed before, nor would they again. That image—of Blake being carried off on a stretcher—was enshrined in the minds of *Montreal Herald* readers the next morning as the front page was filled with the image, the headline reading: "Trail's End for Toe."

"With characteristic courage, though grimacing with pain," read the cover story, "Blake pointed to his ankle as he passed through the knot of fans gathered at the gate, as if to explain in pantomime why he had not left the ice under his own steam."

To Toe, that moment felt just as it appeared: like he was the oldest player in the league. One who maybe should have listened to reason and taken the Buffalo Bisons job before the start of the season. Blake's exit caused tempers to flare in what was largely a dull 1–1 contest. The hosts responded to their captain's exit as Jacques Locas tangled with Juzda, the pair whaling away on each other. Rangers forward Phil Watson swung his stick at Hal Laycoe after he delivered an elbow. But none of this changed the score. Nor the outcome.

The ambulance was waiting to take Blake to the Montreal General Hospital for X-rays of what would be diagnosed as a complete break of the fibula and a tear fracture of the tibia. Despite the pain of a double fracture, Blake insisted on returning to the dressing room before leaving. After he'd recovered from the initial shock, the bulldog tenacity that had marked this player was not broken. Teammates Ken Mosdell and Murph Chamberlain helped Blake limp from the Forum medical clinic to the locker room. "Take it slow," Head, the Forum first-aid man, implored them.

Toe's arrival was met with silence. The players sat in shock, some speaking in low tones. Trainer Ernie Cook and his staff hurriedly packed cargo trunks and dried skates, providing a stark contrast to the atmosphere of sadness and respect. The team had a train to catch to New York that very night. Coach Dick Irvin sat in his usual spot in the corner, staring at the ground, pondering the loss of his captain and its significance to the season. Blake's legs had slowed, but his stamina and experience had carried him. Irvin could always point to Blake's example when his team was lagging. Toe could get the same results by skating five feet as some of the youngsters got by skating five miles.

"Guess that could be the end of a great hockey career, after 12 years of great play for this club. He's a great fellow," Irvin said quietly before jolting back to the present. "Hurry up, fellows, we got to make the train."

Frank Selke took Blake's exit the hardest that night, with both men reduced to tears. For many, including Selke, Blake's injury brought back flashes of Howie Morenz's fatal exit. Morenz had suffered his leg fracture at the same end of the ice, but along the opposite boards. "It makes me just feel sick," Selke said, "and at a time like this when he was just trying to round out a great career in the league, one of the greatest of them all."

According to *La Presse,* Elmer Lach and Maurice Richard—who sat on either side of a seat that belonged to Blake (there were no lockers or cubbies, just hooks for the players to hang their civilian clothes on)—looked to be "suffering enormously" and they exchanged few words. The dressing room felt like "a funeral parlor." Players slowly got dressed, sobering to the reality that there was little time to reflect with a bus waiting outside to take them to a train to New York. One by one they wished him good luck as they filed out. Chamberlain and Mosdell remained to help Hector Dubois get Toe dressed. Toe stood on one foot, pulling off his nether garments, his face grimacing from pain as weight was applied to the injured leg.

"Give me a Coke," Blake said hoarsely before receiving an uncapped bottle as he struggled into his street clothes. "Where's Bill? Hey, please get my keys. They're in Durnan's cupboard," he said. "Better go and get my car. Tell my wife. She'll probably be waiting in the car. I'll tell her to meet us over at the hospital."

Trainer Ernie Cook was now the last man in the locker room with Blake. He picked up Toe's bag, which was suddenly alone on the floor after having been surrounded by his teammates'. "Here's yours, Toe. You won't need it on this train," Cook said, smiling wistfully. Bill Head came back from the clinic, carrying a pair of shiny, varnished crutches for Blake, who continued to struggle with his attire.

"I can't put on my shoe. Guess I'd better stick it in my overcoat pocket," said Blake. At Head's insistence, he put his shoe rubber over the bandage. He gingerly moved from the room on the crutches, leaving just the clubhouse boy to sweep up the tape and other bits of rubbish strewn across the floor.

"The most famous hockey line of modern times," lamented the *Montreal Star*, "seems to have reached Trail's End."

• • •

"The Mad Dog Line" was a fitting name for the original Punch Line.

After Benoit left the Canadiens in 1943 to serve in the war, the injury-prone Maurice "Rocket" Richard would be elevated to play alongside Blake and Lach. The Rocket's potential was certain, but his ability remained somewhat of a mirage after two injury-plagued seasons. Blake, meanwhile, had already firmly established his status as a star in the league.

"Toe was obviously better than average. He did not need the Rocket to help him—he was a star before the Rocket. He was right up there. Not at the top with Howie Morenz, but he was very good," Fischler remembered. "I don't know how good the Rocket would have been without him as a winger at that time. (But) the most significant thing Toe did as a player was his ability to integrate himself with Lach and the Rocket and turn them into a tremendous team. As a player, he was superior."

Blake welcomed this combination, as he now found himself on the other side of thirty. Playing alongside Lach and Benoit had helped him rediscover his best qualities as a player. The resurgence of Blake as a superstar was the talk of the league. Some said his play at the end of the 1941–42 season was better than that of his Hart Trophy–winning season as scoring champion, or of his First Team All-Star season one year later.

After another exhausting off-season in Ontario, he decided that the summer of 1942 would be his last spent underground. Most players were working in the war industry—aircraft and munition plants. Blake would spend the summers of World War II working in a shipbuilding plant as a welder. He also worked as an electrician, a trade he had honed during his time in Hamilton at National Steel. The family moved into an apartment on Côte St. Catherine Road in the more upscale district of Outremont. By now, Bill Durnan and Murph Chamberlain had joined the club. Blake had some standout drinking buddies to hang with, and they played exhibition softball games weekly. Toe was able to cut loose just ever so slightly. But he remained vigilant about allowing complacency to creep into his daily habits.

"Right after I turned 30, Dick (Irvin) told me I would have to drive harder, just to break even. It sounded silly at the time but he was right," Blake told *The Hockey News* years later. "Every season after that, hockey was more like work and less like fun. A broken leg finally stopped me. I might not have gone that far if I hadn't been playing with a great club."

Being paired up with Lach and Benoit was the first step in maximizing Blake's output. When center Terry Reardon left to perform military service, Irvin slotted Lach into the line for a December 19, 1942, 1–1 draw with the New York Rangers. The line really came together in back-to-back weekend games against Boston and Toronto to start the new year, when it racked up 16 points. Because of injury, Maurice "Rocket" Richard didn't return to the fold until the following season, missing out on the Canadiens' 4–1 playoff series loss to the Bruins. With the downsizing of the league to the "Original Six," best-of-seven playoff series now became the norm, and the red line was introduced to rid the game of "pitch and toss" hockey. A faceoff rule was also introduced, forcing both centers to stand square to the puck before it was dropped.

The former initiative aided the Punch Line when Richard joined in. It was Blake "the coach" who appeared to promote the Rocket to the top line: Blake scored a pair of goals in a 3–1 win over the Bruins on December 19, 1943, after having missed out on five games to an injured shoulder; Irvin flew home after the victory to spend the holidays back in Regina, leaving trusted apprentice Blake to run practices until he returned from the holiday break. "Dick Irvin made a happy choice when he left Toe Blake in charge of the practices," the *Montreal Gazette* reported. "Toe has not been a soft touch, by any means. He has had the players going at top speed in the practices all week and they should be in fine condition when they face the Hawks."

Richard was improving as he returned from his shoulder injury, and Blake was running practices more than adequately: "That's one of the best practices we've had all year," Ray Getliffe told the *Gazette*. The pace continued one day later as Blake introduced Richard to his line with Lach. Irvin didn't return in time for the 5–1 Christmas Day victory over Chicago; Tommy Gorman filled in behind the bench, even if it was really Blake who had played coach that week. Irvin's trust in Blake was unwavering, so when he returned from Regina, there was never any doubt he would heed Blake's recommendation for a new Punch Line. Richard scored a hat trick as the Habs crushed the Red Wings, and together the trio managed 13 points in the lopsided 8–3 win.

While Irvin humored Blake's coaching hubris, he didn't stick with the new line. Irvin swapped Richard with the more defensively responsible Bob Fillion. But he went back to Richard in the 8–2 trouncing of the Rangers over a week later, and the team reeled off a nine-game winning streak. The Punch Line helped propel the Canadiens to their first Prince of Wales Trophy win since 1925, and the first of what would prove to be four straight. It was a relief after years of toiling in or near the league cellar. Richard led the team in goals (32) and racked up 54 points, Lach led the team in points (72), and Blake enjoyed another 59-point season, with 26 goals and just 10 penalty minutes. Durnan won the Vezina Trophy after backstopping the Canadiens to 38 wins in 50 games, with the team losing just five games and recording 83 points—25 better than the second-place Detroit Red Wings.

"Playoff Madness" seized the city amid expectations the club would end a 13-year Stanley Cup drought. On the eve of the semifinal series against the third-place Toronto Maple Leafs, thousands thronged the box office by 6:30 a.m., in anticipation of tickets going on sale at 10. Scalpers were demanding $25 for a pair that normally would cost $5 each in the regular season. The Canadiens hadn't lost at the Forum for over a season, a stretch of 25 games; perhaps that explained why Irvin was cautious on the eve of the match. The Maple Leafs surprised with a 3–1 win to open the series. Leafs goalie Paul Bibeault—on loan from the Canadiens, with Durnan the clear number one—made 61 saves, with only Blake getting on the scoresheet, when it was already 3–0. "We all lacked drive except Toe Blake," winger Murph Chamberlain said.

But the law of averages was on the Canadiens' side, especially with their balanced attack. The Punch Line led the way, and the Rocket broke out to score all five goals in a 5–1 win that evened the series, with Blake getting assists on all five tallies. The previous record for goals in a playoff game was three, an accomplishment achieved by Blake against the Blackhawks in 1938.

The Canadiens moved on to Maple Leaf Gardens and its pigmented ice, which was almost as dark as the puck. The color made no difference, as the Canadiens swept the remaining games, with Blake netting two goals in the series-clinching 11–0 Game 5 win in front of 13,215 on the milky-colored Forum ice. Not only was the scoreline a new record, but the five goals the Canadiens scored in 3:36 was also a playoff first. The Leafs were forced to open up and chase the game, and paid the price—the Canadiens were too fast, too rugged and too precise for their young opponents.

Chicago, meanwhile, had also needed five games to dispatch Detroit. When the Stanley Cup Final series began over the Easter weekend, the *Montreal Gazette* reported, "the ladies

LEFT: Portrait of Toe from his Sudbury Wolves playing days, circa 1932. Blake was a key player on the Northern Ontario Hockey Association champion's run to winning the Memorial Cup and the only player from the team to crack the NHL.

BELOW: Toe (far right) spent his offseasons at home in Coniston working hard labour jobs, including in the mines where he had first started in his teens.

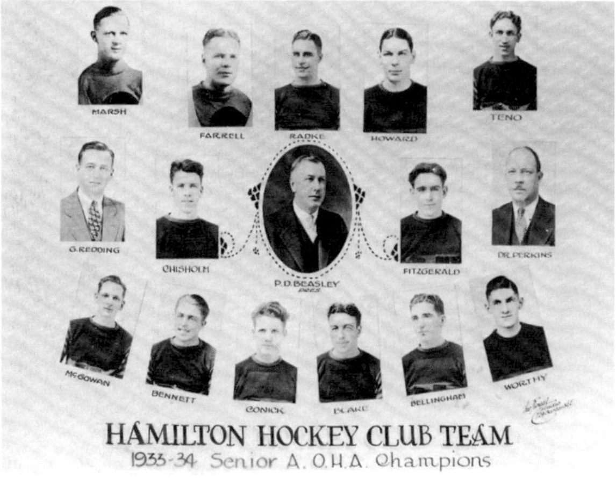

Toe spent two seasons playing junior hockey in Hamilton, winning the 1933-34 Ontario Hockey Association Championship with the Tigers.

November 24, 1934: Toe Blake and Betty Walters pose on what is presumed to be their wedding day, in Winona, Ontario.

Longtime friend and Hamilton teammate Maxie Bennett (on left) was likely Toe's best man at the ceremony.

Toe, who started his playing career with the crosstown Maroons, captained the Habs for eight seasons and won Stanley Cups in 1944 and '46. The Old Lamplighter is one of only seven players in NHL history to score a pair of Cup-clinching goals.

The 1936-37 season Montreal Canadiens: Toe (back row, fourth from left) scored 10 goals and finished with 22 points in his first full season with the Habs. The Canadiens lost the best-of-five semifinal series 3-2 to the Detroit Red Wings. Howie Morenz (bottom row, fourth from right) would tragically die from an injury later that season.

LEFT: Toe on the road in his playing days, where a bottle of beer and a game of cards — gin rummy, hearts or cribbage — helped pass the time during long train rides.

BELOW: The 1937-38 Montreal Canadiens team: Toe (bottom row, second from right) scored 17 goals to finish third on the team with 33 points. The Canadiens lost the best-of-three semifinal series 2-1 to the Chicago Blackhawks. Howie Morenz Jr. joins the team picture following the death of his father the previous season.

ABOVE: October 1939: Toe laces up his skates alongside teammate Charlie Sands at the start of a season when he won the Hart Trophy as the NHL's most valuable player.

LEFT: Toe won the Hart and Lady Byng Trophies, three Stanley Cups and was named a First-Team All-Star three times during his 13-year NHL playing career. When injury forced his retirement in 1948, he was only five points shy of Bill Cowley's NHL record of 591 combined regular season and playoff points.

The 1942-43 Montreal Canadiens team: Toe (front row, second from right next to rookie Maurice "Rocket" Richard) and the club endured a 10th straight playoff series defeat that season before finally coming good with a Stanley Cup win one season later.

Toe (middle row, third from right) with some Montreal Canadiens teammates and their families and friends enjoying a summer social event.

August 1944: Toe (back row, second from right) and his Montreal Canadiens teammates gathered to play softball often in the summer months.

Toe and Punch Line teammate The Rocket are interviewed by Granby radio station CHEF.

On the road, Toe (left) enjoys breakfast with teammate and friend Murph Chamberlain, including a tall glass of ginger ale.

Montreal Mayor Camilien Houde (left) fits Toe with a ring in front of Montreal Canadiens head coach Dick Irvin during a visit to city hall following the 1946 Stanley Cup triumph. Toe scored the second Stanley Cup clinching goal of his career in the 4-1 best-of-seven series win over Boston.

Toe signs the City of Montreal register while Montreal mayor Camilien Houde (foreground, right) and teammates from the 1946 Stanley Cup winning team watch on. Toe would also win the Lady Byng Trophy in '46.

Toe made a point of staying in good physical shape and enjoyed a long playing career by 1940's standards.

Toe and family at their home at 5259 Ponsard Street, around 1947. Toe holds Mary Jane while Betty looks at a book with Joan, who is seated at the piano.

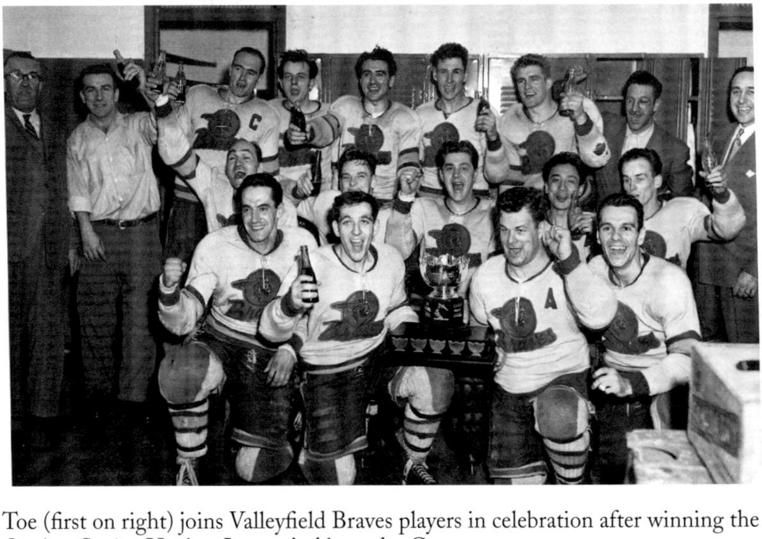

Toe (first on right) joins Valleyfield Braves players in celebration after winning the Quebec Senior Hockey League's Alexander Cup.

Toe and The Rocket pose with children on the ice at a benefit event.

Toe Blake won 11 Stanley Cups during his long hockey career, including eight in 13 seasons coaching his beloved Montreal Canadiens.

Toe has a word while leading a Canadiens practice.

Toe and Betty (second from left) dining at Ruby Foo's restaurant with Frank (second from right) and Lilin Eaves (left) during the 1955-56 season.

Toe shakes hands with Detroit Red Wings coach Jimmy Skinner prior to 1956 Stanley Cup Final.

Toe, fresh off the first of a record five straight Stanley Cup wins, performing first base coach duties in September, 1956. Ball games were Toe's sports passion after hockey.

The 1956 Stanley Cup champion Montreal Canadiens (Toe sits to the left of the Stanley Cup and Canadiens captain Emile "Butch" Bouchard).

Toe (right) celebrates Christmas with Jean Beliveau and his wife Élise and Canadiens owner Hartland Molson (center).

Coach Blake socializes with Canadiens players Don Marshall (to his right) and Dickie Moore (right, with cigar).

Toe's love of the game meant he rarely declined lacing up the skates for an old-timers or benefit game.

Toe having a word with Sergeant Jean Chouinard, chief of the defence staff of Canada.

During the record five straight Stanley Cups wins, Toe enjoyed some time off in the summer months at the family cabin in Venise, Quebec, on the shores of Missisquoi Bay.

Dickie Moore (left) and Bernard "Boom Boom" Geoffrion hoist Toe onto their shoulders as goaltender Jacques Plante celebrates another Stanley Cup triumph for the Canadiens during the record run in the late Fifties.

Toe's love of sports included an affinity for curling, pictured here at Caledonia Curling Club.

were all out in their holiday finery, and bright colors added to the spectacle. Despite the air of respectability, Chicago fans came prepared with missiles to the event, with police confiscating coat hangers, steel bolts, smoked fish, bags of rice and flour, fruit, boxes of soap flakes, rolls of toilet paper, megaphones, candies, bottles, large and small bells, pieces of steel, rolls of coins and several folding chairs." The Canadiens weren't intimidated; they won two tight, physical games in Chicago to take a 3–0 series lead back to the Forum. The team was loose and confident as judged by the demeanor of roommates Blake and Lach. But their conversation also revealed a stern, competitive streak.

"I get pushed around plenty at home but when we go on the road it's 10 times worse. I haven't got a say in anything, Elmer does all the thinking and all the talking," Blake said.

"If it weren't for me you wouldn't be here. I've kept you in the league for the last two years. You can't skate fast enough to keep up with me and Richard. You're always going in when we're coming out, or coming out when we're going in," Lach, who needed stitches over his eye in Chicago, retorted.

"I guess you don't read the papers. A Montreal sportswriter wrote the other day if they ran a popular player contest this season it would be won by Blake. I won once before. Know how I won it? One of my brothers was selling papers. Every time he sold a paper he pointed to the coupon and told the customer, 'just write Blake in there along the dotted line'."

Chicago's Smith-Bentley-Mosienko line may have been one of the NHL's finest, but in the final they were no match for the Punch Line. Blake, Lach and Richard not only carried the attack but were a coach's dream: they did not have a single goal scored against them in the playoffs.

The anticipation of Game 4 and a first Stanley Cup since 1931 was brewing before puck drop on April 13, 1943. The Canadian Arena Company—owners of the Forum—took the protective measure of compelling boys under 16 to sit in the north end unless accompanied by an adult, since so much damage had been done to the building by teenagers.

Going into the third period, though, it wasn't just the teenagers who needed to be surveyed. The near 13,000 spectators were so disillusioned by the 4–1 deficit after two periods that when the Habitants emerged into a smoke-filled arena to start the third, they were met by chants of "fake, fake" by the home fans, who were testing their championship mettle.

The stage was set for the Punch Line to star, and it was Blake who took the lead. The "grand old warrior" was the catalyst as he "broke up the game in typical Blake fashion." He racked up four assists, feeding Richard for the game-tying goal with 2:20 remaining. Blake clinched the club's fifth Stanley Cup by scoring the winner at 9:12 of overtime.

On the play, he took a pass from Butch Bouchard just inside the blue line and skated in alone, eluding the Blackhawks defense and cutting across goaltender Mike Karakas from the short side to leave him out of position before slotting the puck home into an empty goal. "Blake made no mistake when he got in on Mike Karakas," broadcaster Wes McKnight commented of the winning effort. Blake was mobbed by his teammates and carried to the center of ice as fans stormed the arena floor. The Conn Smythe Trophy for the playoffs' most valuable player had not yet come into existence, but if it had, Blake would have been a favorite to win it. The 31-year-old Blake's five-point night and seventh goal of the playoffs saw him set a new playoff record for points at 18—one better than Richard. The Punch Line set a playoff record by combining for 21 goals and 48 points.

"There have been better hockey games in the Forum this year but none was more exciting than this one" the *Montreal Gazette* pronounced, while *La Patrie* featured a picture of the team with the Cup on its front page beneath the headline "Dunkirk; Nazis in Crimea."

Broadcaster Andy O'Brien summed up the performance:

> They played for keeps tonight. It was a fitting finish to an aggressive 59-game schedule in which the Canucks gave the boys plenty to talk about and read about all the way. Tonight, was their greatest exhibition of all. They were offgear when they started, the machine was gummy, the usually smooth Canadien machine just couldn't get clicking. Hawks were aggressive, fighting boys from gangsterville plugged them in all corners. After 10 minutes of the third period, the old machine began to work again. Hawks were tired and out they came like the champions they are. Stirring drama all the way.

Blake's strength, smarts and experience led the turnaround, and even alternate referee King Clancy sounded off on the difference maker saying, "It couldn't have happened to a better guy."

The celebrations continued through the night into the following day, when a victory luncheon was organized for the team at the Queen's Hotel. Blake declared it was the best team he had ever suited up for. "I'm glad Rocket is on the line with me. He'll make me good for another five years."

• • •

But it was four years, to be precise.

In that time, the Canadiens won the Prince of Wales Trophy for the best regular-season record every season. The Rocket scored a record 50 goals in 50 games. Richard and Lach each won the Hart Trophy. Lach, Richard and Blake finished 1-2-3 in scoring in 1944–45.

"Elmer was the play-maker, the Rocket was the finisher and Toe was the insurance man on the line," Irvin later told *The Hockey News*. "They were exciting to watch and the rink was in an uproar most of the time they were on the ice."

Blake may have been the greatest benefactor of his linemates, but he was no slouch, either, and contributed significantly to making them better. Blake's former reputation for boisterous, truculent play had softened, though his edge always remained. He commanded respect around the league, and few were willing to challenge Lach or the Rocket, for fear of drawing his ire. Blake, who Lach and Richard affectionately called "Old Man," worked the corners and crease and provided a physical presence. He put his head down and let his actions do the talking.

The late 1940s enjoyed a "liberalizing process" that saw referees encouraged to call only the most flagrant violations of the rules. This left a growing body of poor or indifferent players to populate rosters and, in turn, cut down great players "by slamming them bodily into the sides of the rinks, massaging their ribs with fibre-padded elbows, inserting their sticks between rival players' legs or under their armpits and generally impeding what once had been considered their lawful progress," wrote Trent Frayne in *The Mad Men of Hockey*. Blake had done well to eliminate the violence from his game despite the obstacles set forth by opponents. He was even a front-runner for the Lady Byng nearly two-thirds of the way through the 1944–45 season, sitting atop the scoring table with only two penalty minutes accumulated. But his candidacy for most gentlemanly player was withdrawn on January 20, when he was suspended indefinitely for bringing his stick down over the head of New York Rangers player Walter Atanas. Montreal was top of the league and closing out a sixth straight win when "Ants" jostled Blake behind the Rangers goal with four minutes left in a 5–2 Canadiens triumph. Perhaps he was feeling sore after the commute by car from Chicago, which the players had been forced to endure in cold temperatures without food. Blake surprised even himself with the infraction, which saw him ejected from the Forum ice. He had picked up his first penalty of the year only a week earlier. Ultimately, Blake missed one game and avoided a fine since it was his first offense of the season, and because Atanas wasn't injured. It seemed almost a relief to *Montreal Herald* columnist Elmer Ferguson that Blake had snapped:

> He is something of a bad man, inclined to indulge in fisticuffs, to berate opposing players verbally, then attend to them physically. In later seasons, saddled with the responsibility of captaining the team, he has shown more restraint, trying to set a good example to the boys, and keep them on the ice. But at heart, he's a hard-hitting, truculent and aggressive player, and it's nice, in a way, to see Blake himself again, a rugged and pugnacious performer, not a candidate for a trophy that he just doesn't fit. Hitting opposing players over the head may not be nice, but it's more Blake, than was the Blake of no penalties.

It would have been hard to disagree with Ferguson to that point of Blake's career. Between Blake and Richard, the Punch Line's unpredictability unnerved opponents and unlocked defenses. Despite his small stature at 5-foot-10 and 170 pounds, Blake was as hard as the rocks he had mined.

"He had such a big, strong hand, he would talk and put his fist down and the table would shake," former Canadiens personnel man Howard Grundman would recall. "You could see how this guy with little said could intimidate his players."

Blake was never one to back down from confrontation, including against former boxing heavyweight champion Jack Sharkey. Sharkey owned a bar in Boston where Blake got into it with a bartender who he felt had shortchanged him. Sharkey backed his employee, and Blake offered to fight Sharkey on the spot, forcing patrons and staff to intercede. "That was Toe Blake," Ken Reardon, Blake's wingman on that evening at 156 Canal Street, told author Michael Ulmer. "He would be willing to fight the heavyweight champion of the world if he thought he was right."

While Rocket Richard benefited from this extra protection, he was prone to his own violent stick-swinging episodes, none more famous than his chop of Hal Laycoe of the Bruins to spark the infamous "Richard Riot" of 1955. Like Blake, the Rocket could brood over a bad call for days. Once, he tried to punch referee Hugh McLean in the Hotel Piccadilly lobby in New York over a call he felt had been mishandled the night before. The Rocket repeatedly escaped serious punishment because of his star stature, even after striking linesmen with empty gloves. He was often fined rather than suspended for his outbursts. Campbell said, "The suspension of a great hockey star is not justified if it reflects in gate receipts."

"Blake and I were just the opposite," the Rocket would say in his book *The Flying Frenchmen: Hockey's Greatest Dynasty*, coauthored with Stan Fischler. "Toe would hardly say anything. Even if you made a mistake he'd never say a word about it to you. In that sense he was somewhat like me. I never wanted to be mad at anybody. One characteristic the three of us had in common was a love of work. Even though Toe was 10 years older, he never stopped skating hard and, in that way, he was a tremendous inspiration to the line, especially to me."

Despite the line's success, it often stumbled against the Leafs. Toronto knocked the league-best Canadiens from the playoffs in both 1945 and 1947. Recording any type of triumph over them provided satisfaction, including on March 13, 1946, when Blake's late tying goal clinched the Prince of Wales Trophy—12 years to the day Conn Smythe blew his opportunity to ink him.

"You will never understand the regret I have felt for not buying that young player," Smythe told *La Presse*. "For over 10 years now he's been a star for the Canadiens and I have never seen him play a bad game."

Inside the Canadiens locker room, the business of winning was celebrated in measured terms as the team celebrated with a bottle of sweet liquor, quietly enjoying another Prince of Wales title. Smythe's remarks added to Blake's celebratory mood as the players celebrated Toe as much as the title. Irvin stopped at Blake's locker to deliver a passioned appreciation to his trusted captain: "My old Toe, thank you for providing the most emotional night of my career. Not only did you give me my third straight championship but you beat Toronto, the club that thanked me for my services a few years ago."

"This point meant more to me than the night I scored my 200th career goal," said Blake.

Rookie Gerry Plamondon was in the locker room that night, perhaps one of the happiest to have clinched his first piece of silverware. Plamondon, who passed away at age 95 in 2019, recalled that Blake "was a bon vivant. A real man's man, very honest, and when he said something, you listened because you knew it was true. He played to win and did whatever was necessary to win. And though he was aggressive, he was also soft—in a sense—and never got mad with us. He was an example for us, a real honest player."

The 1945–46 season was arguably the 33-year-old Blake's finest as a professional. He helped the club secure a third straight Prince of Wales Trophy, led the team in scoring with 29 goals and 50 points, and made up for his unexpected fury against Atanas one year earlier by winning the Lady Byng with just 10 penalty minutes in 50 games. Personally, it was a satisfying year, too, as the Blake family welcomed their second child, Mary Jane, into the family.

Irvin said no player he had ever known enjoyed hockey life more than Blake. The proof was in his constant evolution, from roughhousing thug to the sport's most gentlemanly player in 1946, when he became the first Canadien to win the Lady Byng. Only Mats Naslund has won it since. In true Toe Blake fashion, he even complained about the circumstances surrounding the penalty minutes he did amass. The Lady Byng was a shock to many who knew Blake as the hard-playing and hard-talking player who never relented in giving it to the referees, believing his complaints were always justified.

But Blake was no dummy, and he was able to use the guile of experience to curb the number of touchy spots he found himself in—even with feisty Detroit Red Wings great Gordie Howe. When Howe emerged, Blake knew he took liberties with rival players' ankles. Howe quickly learned not to test Blake after an initial attempt at the trick early in his career. "I didn't give it back to him," Blake said. "I just turned around and told him, 'Listen, youngster, my career is winding down and yours is just beginning. Keep that up and we'll both be leaving hockey around the same time.'"

Toe showed the trademark intelligence of a seasoned hockey man in these days. He had lost a step with speed but was playing more effectively than ever. He continued to insist he would not quit until he felt he was handicapping the club. "I'm not as tired as I was before," he told *La Patrie*; "my legs are still strong and as long as they are I still feel I can help the Tricolores' ambitions. When an athlete loses his legs, it's time to retire. But it's been the opposite for me until now, so I plan to continue."

Blake, a unanimous First Team All-Star, managed three points in the Canadiens' series-clinching victory over the Chicago Blackhawks as the Canadiens returned to the Stanley Cup Final. "Our Punch Line played its best hockey this season. It inspired the rest of the club," Blake said after the 7–2 win. "Our attack has never been more powerful. It would have had its way with any club in the league . . . It was simply irresistible."

The Stanley Cup Final against the Boston Bruins would provide the ultimate testament to Blake's personality as a player and leader of the Canadiens, one that is matched in few players today. The Canadiens opened Game 1 with a costly 4–3 overtime victory in which Blake injured his back—his spine, specifically. Blake crashed into the goalpost awkwardly, his back bearing the brunt of the first-period accident. He lay sprawled out on the ice for a long moment before eventually getting to his feet and gingerly skating off to the Canadiens bench. He played on with little impact as Richard potted the winning goal, and one look at Blake untying his skates in the dressing room afterward revealed a battered man. His face showed the wear of the playoffs, with cuts across the bridge of his nose, around his mouth and over his eyebrow. Sleepless nights followed due to the pain in his back, with the 33-year-old unable to even sit comfortably.

Blake's availability became a question mark. "I don't think I will be able to play (Game 2)," he told *La Presse*. "I'm heading to the hospital this morning to undergo some X-rays. I'll head over to the Forum to see the team practice after that, but I probably won't even put on the skates."

At the Forum, coach Dick Irvin tempered the worry by insisting Blake would be a game-time decision after being examined by team doctor A.A. MacKay. "Blake told me yesterday afternoon he didn't think he could play because he was having trouble walking," Irvin said. "We still have 36 hours. Anything can happen during this time, no?"

Blake suited up alongside Richard and Lach, but it was clear he was ineffective when Pat Egan and Bobby Bauer scored goals with Blake on the ice to take a 2–1 lead into the third period. Blake grimaced in discomfort as he shuffled into the dressing room before approaching Irvin ahead of the final period.

"Dick, keep me on the bench for the third period," Blake said to his boss. "I can't help the club in the condition I am in, I think I'm hurting more than helping."

Irvin agreed and left Blake on the bench for the remainder of the game, as the Canadiens were deep enough to sustain Blake's diminished role.

Defenseman Butch Bouchard tied the score before rookie Jimmy Peters netted the overtime winner to give Montreal a 2–0 series lead. Blake returned for a Game 3 victory in Boston, but the beds at the Hotel Manger did little to improve his sleep. Blake played sparingly in a Game 3 win and a Game 4 loss after picking up a shoulder injury, but he did pick up a fighting major after tangling with Bep Guidolin late in the defeat.

Blake's back was improved heading back to Montreal for Game 5. The Canadiens could clinch the Cup at the Forum, but two of their key cogs were nursing ailments: aside from Blake's back and shoulder worries, Bouchard was a serious doubt with a knee injury and a bout of the flu. "Blake told me he's doing better and that I can count on him," Irvin said. "We're going to do our best to win the Stanley Cup tonight."

The first of 4,000 fans began lining up at the Forum box office at 8 a.m. on the morning of April 9. By the time the puck dropped for the opening faceoff, 2,000 remained outside the arena without tickets. Police were forced to erect barricades to keep them from rushing the rink as they remained, wanting to be close to what felt like a historic moment. The Bruins did their best to demolish the Canadiens and add further misery to the already growing injury list, turning Game 5 physical. With the score tied 3–3 to start the third period, Blake was not riding the bench but back on the ice with the Punch Line. He had not played his normal number of minutes and had come off for longer stretches, but he was always going to be available and willing to grit through the pain with the Stanley Cup on the line.

Boston goalie Frankie Brimsek redirected a Blake pass up

ice, where one of his own defensemen blocked it, sending it right back into the goal crease, where it bounced over sticks and around a forming crowd. Blake swooped in from the corner and dug down to guide his shot along the ice inside the far post to make it 4–3 with just under nine minutes to play. Blake's momentum carried him across the goal line, where he raised both arms in celebration, his face a weary blend of exhaustion, combativeness and elation. There were no smiles—nothing had been won, yet. Richard would call this "the hardest game I've played in my career."

Blake's goal demoralized the Bruins and swung the momentum clear to the hosts, who were too fast, too strong and too opportunistic a rival. Chamberlain and Dutch Hiller added goals, but it was Blake's performance that had truly embodied the team's triumph. Blake was the unlikely hero. He was, as *La Presse* reported, "injured, a player who should have been watching from the spectator's seats, a veteran who preferred his role of helping his teammates triumph while displaying the quality the club captain should."

Blake was mobbed by his teammates after the final whistle, serenaded with hugs, handshakes and hands through his hair as he became the third player to score two Stanley Cup–clinching goals. He is one of only seven players of all time to accomplish the feat; the others are Jack Darragh (Ottawa Senators), Howie Morenz (Montreal Canadiens), Jean Beliveau (Montreal Canadiens), Henri Richard (Montreal Canadiens), Bobby Orr (Boston Bruins) and Mike Bossy (New York Islanders). No player has scored three.

"I'm glad to see Toe Blake get the winning goal . . . because he's played a lot of hockey and I think he deserves the credit of putting us in there tonight," Montreal defenseman Glen Harmon said.

After a dozen fans stormed the ice to join in the celebrations, the players made their way to the dressing room, leaving Blake on the ice for the Stanley Cup ceremony alongside NHL president Mervyn Dutton, Canadiens owner Senator Donat Raymond, Forum director M.D.C. Coleman and Tommy Gorman. Dutton presented the Cup to Senator Raymond before Blake was able to get his hands on it to bring it through to the Canadiens dressing room, where Irvin had already proclaimed his championship winning club "the greatest of all time." The scenes inside the locker room seemed to echo what had followed on the ice from the 11:06 mark of the third period, when Blake secured the win. With his career winding its way toward an end and his body aching, Toe became the focus of the celebrations. Senator Raymond spent extra time congratulating Blake inside the locker room. Bottles of champagne were brought in to celebrate the first Stanley Cup won after the end of World War II. Bruins coach Dit Clapper made his way into the Canadiens dressing room to offer congratulations to the team and, especially, Blake. "We were beaten by the best team in the NHL. Blake's goal was magnificent. I'm happy he scored the winner," said Clapper, echoing a sincere respect for Blake that reverberated around the NHL.

"Blake thoroughly deserved this honor; after a remarkable season, he was involved despite a painful backbone injury," one newspaper summed up. "He has always been the inspiration behind the club and the fans rowdily applauded his winning point."

Lach popped the cork of the champagne and took a swig, to the objections of his teammates, who yelled in good-natured scorn. Lach returned to pouring the contents of the bottle into the bowl of the Cup so Blake could take the first sip, to applause. Photographers got their final shots before racing to deliver the negatives to a waiting plane at Dorval Airport, from which the stills would be delivered to newspaper offices in Boston and across North America. Blake drank slowly from the Cup, seeming to savor each drop. Did Blake sense his playing career was nearing its end as he passed the Cup to Lach while Richard waited?

"I've never been so glad in my life to win the Stanley Cup," said Blake, who would go on to express that exact same sentiment with nearly every Cup victory as coach. "We have a real good bunch of fellas."

• • •

Blake's production did not slump the next season even though he turned 34 that August. He netted 21 goals and 50 points in 1946–47, and while he had been referred to as "the Beaver" in the past, this season he finally earned the nickname that would stick with him for the remainder of his hockey life.

The single "The Old Lamp-Lighter" by Sammy Kaye was released in late 1946, reaching number one on the Billboard charts for nine weeks between December 28 and February 8, 1947. It was the most-played song on jukeboxes across the continent, and its old-time feel lent perfectly to Blake's old-time hockey origins. Blake also tended to light the goal lamp throughout his career, making the nickname a good fit. The Punch Line was leading the team to another league title, with Richard leading the team with 45 goals and 71 points to win the Hart Trophy. Lach's career was threatened, however, after he was sidelined for the home stretch of the season by a skull fracture suffered against Toronto.

The Canadiens and Bruins met again in the playoffs, and Montreal again dispatched Boston in five games. But it was the Maple Leafs that once more proved the Canadiens' bogeyman, knocking them from the Stanley Cup playoffs for the second time in three seasons. Blake was gracious in defeat but also receptive to the criticism that followed, when some critics scored it a victory of youth "over invalids . . . just as two years ago," in the words of *La Presse*.

Speculation began over player movements. Frank Selke had settled into the GM job the previous August, when he named

Blake a "super scout" to keep track of amateur prospects. Selke was looking out for Blake's post-playing years—he had promised Toe an executive position with the Canadian Arena Company once his playing days were done—and had offered him an opportunity to coach in Buffalo. But Blake was determined to play one more season and surpass Boston Bruins center Bill Cowley as the league's all-time leading point getter. "Toe Blake had a fine season considering his age and soon we will discuss plans for next year," Selke said. "With Dick Irvin out west, Toe Blake is my sidekick regarding all hockey problems barring the Royals seniors."

Doug Harvey, Floyd Curry and Gerry McNeil were some of the Allan Cup–winning prospects populating the Royals, competing with Blake for a spot on the Canadiens. Selke publicly expected a handful of them to make the team in the next two seasons, and new prospects were being discovered as Selke began creating a Canada-wide farm system for the Canadiens. While Elmer Lach returned from his skull fracture to lead the league in scoring with 61 points in 1947–48, the Canadiens attack never found its feet due to injuries and several poor trades by Selke. Richard was hobbled by a knee injury but still contributed 28 goals and 53 points in 53 games. The offensive woes were so plentiful that Blake's 24 points (nine goals) from just 32 games in his last season were enough to place him third on the club, behind Lach and Richard. Any momentum toward a playoff run seemed to lose steam on the night of January 11, 1948, when Juzda finished that crushing bodycheck against the Old Lamplighter. NHL rules prohibited board-checking, but officials rarely enforced it. Lying flat on the ice, staring up at the Forum rafters, weighed down by the silence and the weight of time, Blake made up his mind to retire from hockey.

Two days later, Blake was forced to have the cast removed and reapplied due to the searing pain of his injury. From his hospital bed in the western division of the Montreal General Hospital, he was finally smiling after receiving hundreds of messages from fans wishing for his recovery. The brave face masked his disappointment at watching his pursuit of "Bristol Bill" Cowley close. Blake was 21 points behind Cowley's all-time regular-season points record of 527, but only five back of Cowley's 594 points in the regular season and playoffs combined.

Blake wasn't the only sports great hospitalized that night. Babe Ruth was a patient in New York, where he became one of the first patients to receive chemotherapy combined with radiation to battle cancer.

Blake retired the leading scorer in NHL playoff history with 62 points—nine better than Toronto's Syl Apps. Richard (52) and Lach (48) were not far off and would eventually surpass their teammate. Toe did not let go of the thought of catching Cowley, however, insisting during his recovery that he could return at the close of the season and be ready for a playoff run. He continued traveling with the team despite the injury, gripping on tight to the feeling of being one of the boys after it had been prematurely snatched away. Without Blake, the club struggled down the stretch and finished out of the playoffs for the first time since 1939. Blake's dream of returning might have been the last selfish act by a selfless player longing to hold on to his sense of self. But Selke snapped Blake back to reality by sending him to Houston to plant the first seeds of the greatest coaching career of all. Hours after his injury, speculation about Blake taking over for Irvin behind the Canadiens bench had already begun.

"One thing for sure is the team's fans would like to see him return as manager of the Canadiens, where he has earned an excellent reputation," *Montréal-Matin*'s Jacques Beauchamp wrote. "If Blake replaces Irvin, he won't have trouble improving on the ex-Maple Leafs coach. The players would be more interested in 'giving everything' for him since his character is more impressive than Irvin's, who seems to have become a nuisance to the local club."

Beauchamp went on to become a long-time friend of Blake's before ultimately being ostracized from his life during his coaching days. But he had always backed Blake, and it was no different following this night, when he criticized the Forum faithful's reaction to Blake's loss: "Murph Chamberlain received more applause than Blake did tonight after he fractured his ankle in Detroit."

There would be no official goodbye, no opportunity to provide the Old Lamplighter with the rightful send-off he deserved. That summer Blake would be on the move to Buffalo, which would reshape his relationship with the Canadiens until he was hired as coach in 1955. But it was clear from his time with the Punch Line that Blake had the capacity to translate his knowledge into a role behind the bench.

"When I was there Toe was considered the old man of the team. He and Bill Durnan would take the young guys under their wing," Elmer Lach told author Michael Ulmer. "The year Rocket scored 50, Toe should have scored 60. They'd put two men on Rocket and that always left Blake open. But Toe was one hell of a player. He played hard, he was never fooled. He had a lot of imagination, which you would have to have and which I think is missing today."

CHAPTER 6

VALLEYFIELD

THE CROWD HUDDLED IN the foyer leading to the arena, TV crews filming the speeches by men in suits and panning across the room to capture the ex-players in front of a suddenly swelling crowd. Everyone beamed with pride. The guests of honor—including the mayor of Valleyfield himself—watched from specially reserved seats. The surname Blake was placed on several of them.

Behind the podium, draped high up the wall, hung the centerpiece of the Toe Blake memorial space. After the speeches were completed and the lengthy video montage of Blake's career gathered from Google Images faded out, the guests of honor were called up to the stage to do the honors: to unveil a special monument to one of the great coaches in hockey history.

Former Montreal Canadiens player Rejean Houle looked on with a smile as the drape came down, revealing a pristine Montreal Canadiens jersey encased in glass. It hovered above pictures of Blake with his Punch Line teammates, Maurice Richard and Elmer Lach, and another picture of Blake gesturing with Jean Beliveau during his time as coach. Houle embraced Stephanie Blake—who had traveled from Toronto and was the lone Blake family member attending the special ceremony—and smiled warmly alongside former Valleyfield Braves players Bruce Cline and Gordie Haworth, and former equipment manager Paul "Bill" Guerin. Cline and Haworth had played for Blake; Guerin worked for him. A vintage Valleyfield Braves jersey hung alongside the Canadiens jersey, above a few photos from Blake's five seasons spent as coach of the Braves.

Gaston Legault, a resident of Valleyfield and Blake's greatest admirer, watched with a mix of pride and indifference. The Braves' decision to honor one of the greatest coaches in NHL history was largely thanks to his own tireless work. Legault had published his own 82-page account of Blake's time in Valleyfield, from 1950 to 1954. The Braves won the Alexander Cup during Blake's final coaching stint before returning to the fold of the Montreal Canadiens organization. Blake's exit from his beloved Canadiens in 1949 led him to Valleyfield, to this minor league hockey team just beyond the western tip of the island, about an hour's drive from Montreal.

Legault has been a tireless promoter of Blake's legacy and has pushed the Canadiens to retire Blake's No. 6 jersey. He has written open letters to newspaper editors and directly to Canadiens president Geoff Molson. Legault is incredulous that a storied organization like the Canadiens has allowed Blake's number to remain in rotation, worn by 17 players since his retirement. Tonight, in Valleyfield, Legault—who had printed commemorative tickets to mark the special occasion—watched on as his two-year effort to have a minor-league club pay Blake a major honor was achieved. Yet he remained unsatisfied.

"It's disappointing," Legault exhaled. "Two jerseys hanging there like that, it's not what I would have liked to have seen done. I would have put a great big picture of Toe as the centerpiece. That's how you honor the man."

Few expected Blake to make his first major coaching mark at a club like Valleyfield. Blake's coaching journey wasn't supposed to lead him here.

• • •

"Toe Blake was my man," swoons Bert Bourassa, repeatedly, over the course of a conversation about his former Valleyfield Braves coach. "I was so happy to play for him, I adored him as a player. He could have asked me to do anything and I would have done it. I will never forget him. He was a sensation."

Blake's signing by the Quebec Senior League club in 1949 was, in fact, a sensation. Bourassa couldn't believe his luck when he joined Blake's Braves in 1950.

A sturdy if slightly diminutive defenseman, Bourassa was on Valleyfield's roster for Blake's two brightest seasons at the club. Bourassa, who left the Trois-Rivières Reds to join Valleyfield, found his future perspectives changing as he suited up for Blake.

"The fact he had confidence in me, a skinny player weighing 155 pounds who played on defense—are you serious?" Bourassa says. "He trusted me, and he helped me. He saw a future for me. I gave everything for him."

Bourassa had few vices in 1950, which might have made it easier for Blake to picture a future for the kid. He didn't drink or fraternize with his teammates after hours. His lone vice was the pipe, which he enjoyed twice a day. That, and the women. "Back then a lot of players and coaches went out drinking and having fun, but I was more focused on playing shape. I didn't like the bottle, but I liked the girls and, let me tell you, Valleyfield was full of them," the 88-year-old remembers with a laugh. "The town cherished us; we were treated like kings."

Blake spotted potential in Bourassa and helped him break into the American Hockey League after the Braves won the title in 1951. The defenseman went to Providence to play for the Reds, just as

Blake had during his own professional career. After two seasons in Rhode Island, Blake helped engineer Bourassa's move to Detroit Red Wings affiliate the Springfield Indians in 1955. But that's when the first of two serious concussions took their toll on Bourassa.

"Gordie Howe gave me my first concussion. I lined him up in the corner and he saw me coming and got me with an elbow as I came down on him. He left me on the ice on my ass," says Bourassa, who featured in 56 games with Springfield during the 1955–56 season. It was hard going following that concussion; Bourassa bounced between the QHL's Trois-Rivières Lions and Cleveland Barons before stepping away from hockey for two seasons. He returned in 1959 to play for the Sherbrooke Castors of the Eastern Townships Intermediate Hockey league (ETIHL) for several years, but his career was never the same.

"No one was like Toe Blake. He was my idol," Bourassa says. "I never saw a coach like him, and maybe that's why I had trouble breaking in after that. I couldn't get along with anyone else. Not like with him."

Valleyfield, like its former players, still figurately pinches itself over the early 1950s, when an out-of-work former Canadiens captain decided to accept the job of Valleyfield Braves manager. It remains a great source of pride for the town of approximately 40,000 residents.

"Was I surprised he coached here? For sure," former Braves center Gordie Haworth said. "Valleyfield was very lucky to have such a hockey figure like that. I don't know how they got him."

Timing, courage and a little luck, it seems. While Blake envisioned returning to the ice with the Canadiens once his injury healed, Selke had other plans for him. A Canadiens farm team in Houston suddenly found itself without a manager when player-coach Mike McMahon was recalled. Buffalo Bisons scout Rudy Pilous had stepped in to take charge of the club until Blake arrived as the fourth coach of the season (George Boothman had begun the campaign). Though Blake was only three weeks on from suffering his career-ending injury and still hobbling on crutches, Selke decided to ship him to Texas to cut his teeth with the struggling Canadiens farm club. Blake had a new cast put on his injured right foot on Monday, February 2, and was on a plane to Houston within three days.

The Houston Huskies—formerly known as the Skippers—were hoping to challenge for the United States Hockey League's Southern Division title. Blake's arrival was engineered by Art Chapman, the owner and general manager of the Canadiens farm team in Buffalo, who would play a pivotal part in Blake's initial coaching career. Blake remained on the Canadiens payroll.

Blake joined the Huskies during an eight-game road trip that left it in solid position to qualify for the playoffs. Houston had 12 of its last 16 matches at home, and there was incentive to finish top of the division to earn an extra playoff series bye.

Blake imposed himself on the club immediately, instilling an 11 p.m. curfew. "You play hockey, or you go home," he told them.

It did not begin well for Blake. Houston, with only 13 bodies on the squad, lost a road game 3–0 to the Northern Division–leading Minneapolis Millers in subzero temperatures after netminder Harry McQuestion foiled the new coach's debut. But Blake quickly rejuvenated the Huskies with a 5–0 win over the Southern Division leaders, the Fort Worth Rangers, that moved Houston within one and a half games of the division lead.

"The gang made me think for a minute I was back in the National League," Blake said. "I think we've got the best team in the league, and unless we get a bad break through injuries, I feel sure the Huskies can beat (Minnesota) in a long series."

Blake's arrival provided the Huskies with a jolt of enthusiasm, but his lack of experience was also highlighted. Blake uncharacteristically called off a practice scrimmage after just 20 minutes, with the team at the top of the division and the playoff chase in full swing, fearing his players were getting too rough for their own good. He was then forced to ride a backup goaltender when his starter was injured. Still, he was showing a steady hand despite the pressures of the title chase against Fort Worth, as his offensively talented team continued to pour in the goals and move closer to the Southern title. Blake was learning to manage the fear of injury, a worry the manager on crutches alluded to continuously over his stint in Houston. But it was a notable concern, since his players' own enthusiasm was proving costly. Winger Leo Gravelle, one reporter noted, "skates with blinding speed, and often, after a making a shot crashes on into the boards before he can pull up." Blake's patience was tested.

Even so, Toe was enjoying the transition to coaching, if the picture of him donning a cowboy hat over the headline "Rootin' Tootin' Huskies Boss" was anything to go by. With Pilous—now manager—at his side and leading on-ice practices, Blake guided Houston into the playoffs, taking the division title by 10 points one season after the team finished last. The players bought into his philosophy from the start and saw his treatment as fair. Blake dropped the curfew once the team clinched a playoff spot.

"A jump from the cellar to the lead is a real step," Blake said. "But with the talent that was sent to Houston, there was no excuse for this team to fail."

Blake showed his aplomb at managing egos straight away, channeling his own experience and emotions. "Some of the older players were a bit upset over being sent to Houston this year. And I understand how they must have felt. But in spots, the play in this league can be just as fast as anything I've seen in the American, and sometimes the National (leagues). Of course, we don't have the consistency found in the big leagues, but when you get some of this fine Texas rivalry to work, anything can happen."

Blake was treated to the nerve-racking experience of a dramatic playoff series from a different perspective as he watched his Huskies go up 2–1 in the best-of-seven opening series with the Kansas City Pla-Mors. The Huskies dropped two straight before back-to-back blowout wins advanced the team directly to the best-of-five final.

The series with Kansas City showed Blake was an adept scout—just as Selke had hoped prior to Toe hanging up his skates. Selke was in constant talks with Blake, prodding him for information on potential talent for the organization. "There's a fellow with the Kansas City team named (Bert) Olmstead who's a pretty good hockey player," Blake relayed to Selke.

Despite injuries to his defense, Blake quickly exhibited some of the qualities that made him a standout coach, working with what he had and looking to make the most out of the talent on his team by putting his players in an optimal position to succeed. "We have a high-scoring club, so there is no use trying at the last minute to perfect a defense to match our power. We are simply going to go out there, keep possession of the puck as much as possible and keep firing at goal," said Blake. "Some of them have to go in."

Blake's philosophy helped lead the Huskies to the Paul Loudon Trophy with a title-clinching 4–3 victory over Minneapolis in their final playoff series. Blake was voted alternate coach of USHL All-Star Team for leading Houston to the Southern Division title and the USHL Trophy.

Despite his coaching success, Blake still harbored hope of returning to the Canadiens starting lineup for the 1948–49 season and surpassing Cowley's record. He planned to spend the summer of 1948 getting his right ankle into playing shape on the softball diamond. "If it doesn't go well," he told the *Globe and Mail*, "Houston is a pretty good job to go back to."

But a meeting with Selke changed Blake's perspective. Selke saw an opportunity with the Canadiens farm club in Buffalo, which Blake had already turned down the summer previous. But this time Blake was outside the game looking in, unlike one season ago, a predicament Selke stressed to him. Selke saw a future for Blake within the organization and appeared to be grooming him to take over the reins from Dick Irvin, whenever that might be. Some newspapermen were already writing about the possibility. Selke had already named Blake "manager of Forum hockey affiliations" in the summer of 1946—the "super scout" position for keeping tabs on young players and tracking the progress of the organization's amateur hockey teams. The role meant Blake was assured a Forum executive position once his playing career ended.

Montreal's farm team in Buffalo was coming off a strong campaign capped by a bittersweet final series in which it was swept in four games by the Cleveland Barons. The head coaching position opened up after owner and general manager Art Chapman decided to make Leroy Goldsworthy his executive assistant (Goldsworthy ultimately swapped positions with Blake and took over his old post in Houston). Selke recommended the Old Lamplighter seriously consider Buffalo's offer "as it meant a lot to his future."

Chapman, spurned by Blake one year prior, traveled to Sudbury in August to meet with Blake, who was in Coniston to celebrate his parents' golden wedding anniversary. Chapman must have been convincing—either that or Toe finally realized his ankle would not hold up under the rigors of a 60-game NHL schedule—because, on August 8, Buffalo named Blake its head coach for the 1948–49 season.

The new endeavor started in familiar quarters for Blake—the Montreal Forum. The minor-league team was set to play the parent club three times to start the pre-season, beginning in Montreal. This allowed Selke and Irvin not only to evaluate the team's minor-league talent but to get a glimpse of Blake. Training opened on September 20, and so, too, did the dial-up of expectations.

Blake was "the Babe Ruth of modern hockey," according to the *Buffalo Evening News*. Reporter Tony Wurzer, who covered the Bisons throughout the season, provided a snapshot of Blake, the coach on his first day of work: "He is expressive, like most French-Canadians. He talks with his hands. Directs the team with his shoulders. He moves about in rapid, little sliding steps. Like he still has on skates. But he knows what he wants."

Blake skated onto the ice to look over his players. It was evident to the young coach this wasn't the team he had gotten used to sharing the Forum ice with. There were no Rockets, no Lachs, no Doug Harvey. "I see we have lots of men. And everybody has skates," Blake said. "That is a start."

Blake's squad possessed some players with NHL experience, including right winger Floyd Curry—who would turn into his closest friend. There was a promising 20-year-old defenseman named Ray Gariepy who marked his arrival as a physical specimen by dumping all players in his path onto the ice in his first practice. But Gariepy would ultimately linger along for a few seasons without a glimpse of the NHL. Starting goaltender Conrad Dion, from Asbestos, Quebec, was a 5-foot-3, 140-pound sportswriter who played goal in his spare time. "For a little guy, he's the biggest goaler I've ever seen," Indianapolis Caps coach Ott Heller said of the 30-year-old netminder who would duel with the likes of the Indianapolis Caps' Terry Sawchuk and the Cleveland Barons' Johnny Bower. Dion's tenacity was unwavering as he played out a victory in which he required 12 stitches to his cheek.

Veterans like center Ab DeMarco complemented youngsters like defenseman Tom Johnson, who would go on to be a key cog in the Canadiens' Stanley Cup–winning teams coached by Blake. The mix of youth and veterans was there, but Blake was going to have to work hard to make them gel. That was apparent from the opening exhibition 7–3 loss to the Canadiens at the Forum. This defeat was far removed from present-day norms of pre-season play whereby star players are kept from the ice to avoid injury. This violent exhibition opener featured 13 penalties and closed with players from the same organization swinging their sticks at each other.

The bad blood carried over to Buffalo's Memorial Auditorium a few days later, on September 28, as 5,615 fans watched Maurice Richard and Les Canadiens romp to an 8–0 win. The Rocket scored two goals, opened up a two-stitch cut over defenseman Lloyd Finkbeiner's right eye, and was subsequently tossed from the game for bodychecking the referee after being penalized for cutting Finkbeiner. Several of Richard's teammates had to guide him off the ice to keep him from checking the official again. The Canadiens' dominance left Blake dazed, especially after a 5–0 loss the next night in Barrie, Ontario. Blake's hurried character was learning about the importance of patience, quickly.

"I never thought I'd be so happy to see my old teammates go away," Blake said while wiping away the sweat from his brow.

As a coach, Blake was prone to panic, his anxiety allowing him to believe the situation was escalating beyond his control—in this case, with no time to practice, evaluate tactics and restore confidence with another exhibition game the very next night. Blake was also saddled with operating the Bisons' entire training camp since Chapman was hospitalized with a lengthy illness. The Bisons lost again in Barrie, 5–1—this time to the Springfield Indians. It was still pre-season, but frustration set into the camp and left Blake with a challenge he had never before faced. Toe had been on poor teams as a player, but he had never had the responsibility of turning around morale and developing game plans as he did now. The Bisons dragged themselves back to Montreal to cap a 400-mile road trip that featured four defeats in five nights.

"From now on it's four-hour skating sessions until I am convinced the boys are serious about this business. We are going to start looking like a hockey team if I have to shake them down to the last man," Blake was quoted as saying in the *Buffalo Evening News*, dissatisfied with the team's back-checking. "Actually, this is a pretty strong squad. Just what is the matter is a puzzle at this moment."

Blake was prone to using tough love throughout his career, and in this instance he hoped it would shake his players out of their disappointing start. "Our boys have been more or less resting on their reputations. You might say they have been rusting, actually . . . I think I've got that idea out of their heads. That is, if they want to play for me this season."

The extra days to recover from a grueling road trip paid off as the Bisons picked up their first pre-season win in Quebec City with a 3–2 triumph over the Aces. But the punishing pre-season schedule would not relent: the team pushed off for another game the very next night, in Shawinigan Falls. As the start of the regular season approached, Blake focused on the positives, including a 5–3 victory at Valleyfield. Newspapers had now begun openly suggesting Blake was set to be Irvin's successor. The Bisons broke camp on October 10 to open the 68-game season with three straight games on the road, starting in St. Louis against the Flyers. Blake marked the start of his full-time coaching career with a 4–0 defeat.

"Maybe the boys need someone to go out there and show them what a goal looks like," Blake said, donning full equipment in the very next practice. Toe also knew about the Indianapolis goaltender from his time in Houston—Terry Sawchuk was not going to be a pushover. The Bisons lost 5–1 to the Caps before a 9–3 loss in Pittsburgh completed the 0–3 start.

Uncertainty overcame the team, and Blake was already under pressure. He tinkered with the lines and cracked the whip in practice, and the Bisons won their home opener at the Memorial Auditorium, 3–1 over the Hershey Bears, in front of 8,328. While the victory was welcome, it also brought out the first signal of Chapman's discontent with the squad and tactics and demonstrated his heavy-handed involvement in the running of day-to-day affairs. This would ultimately sour the relationship with Blake.

A 5–0 win over the Providence Reds dispelled worry until a winless two-game road run sprung Chapman back into action, to Blake's chagrin. The 36-year-old coach started practicing with the team with an eye to playing, and the *Buffalo Evening News* was buoyed by the thought that "a Toe Blake patrolling left wing would just about insure another playoff post for the Bisons this year." Blake admitted that he would need about a week or two to get into playing shape and that the thought of lacing up again was exciting for him and the players. After a 2–2 home draw with St. Louis, Blake and the team seemed ready to the turn the tide, with a full week of practice providing an opportunity to work on tactics. Chapman looked on.

"They look like they have finally hit their stride. We should see an entirely different team in action against Washington Sunday. I believe we'll start to move on from now," said Blake, who felt early-season jitters explained the shaky start that had Buffalo last in the five-team Western Division.

Blake's instincts were spot on: the Bisons thumped Washington 10–0 on home ice. The record-tying victory against the league's worst club was more like shooting practice for Buffalo, as Washington coach Frank Beisler's team possessed, as the *Buffalo Evening News* put it, "as much fight as a broiled porkchop." Beisler couldn't stand it and even left the bench at one point to order "double cokes . . . one could hardly blame him."

The victory had made "new men" of Blake's squad. "The team seems to have taken a new lease on life. Their passing is sharper. They have drive and above all, they're disgusted with their weak showing. I'm confident they will look like a new bunch from now on," Toe said with Chapman hovering, nodding in approval.

Despite four games in nine days, the Bisons went 3–1 on the road and looked to have turned the corner. They won 9 of 11—including a 16–4 win over Philadelphia on November 14—as the team gelled under Blake's tutelage.

"This Buffalo team begins to look like the class of the league," Detroit Red Wings coach Jack Adams said as he watched the

Bisons rout Sawchuk—who had to exit for a period to receive four stitches after a puck struck near his left eye—and the Indianapolis Caps 8–3 on November 17 to climb into second place.

Blake did in fact need to lace up for game duty when injuries began to mount. He went on to feature in 18 games that season: while he was "obviously not the Toe who starred with the Montreal Canadiens through 13 years," as the *Buffalo Evening News* proclaimed, he "still is some shakes as a player." Blake made a sizable impact in his first appearance—a 4–1 victory over Springfield before 9,504 home fans on November 22. Blake turned in a "hard-rocking game" and displayed "the fierce competitive spirit that made you understand why he had been an outstanding star for Les Canadiens."

But it was in the dressing room after that victory that Blake's affinity for players revealed a softer side that would obviously stick with his charges throughout his career. Blake slumped into his locker like one of the gang, asking about injuries, commending his teammates' play, making their sacrifice feel critical for the success of the team. Blake showed a natural ability to tap into and understand the camaraderie of a dressing room, having been there himself. "That's what makes hockey a great game, that kind of spirit a million dollars can't buy," Blake said afterward. "If we can only hang together a little while longer, we'll be all right."

Blake's star power was drawing record numbers at the Memorial Auditorium, with nearly 10,000 spectators in attendance for a 5–3 win over the Pittsburgh Hornets on November 28. The team was also markedly improved and looking like title contenders early on. They were set to begin practicing at the newly rebuilt Peace Bridge Arena, which would eliminate the need to travel back and forth to St. Catharines, as they had for more than eight years. (The new arena would also welcome the arrival of flamboyant wrestler Gorgeous George and his exploits as they were broadcast on TV.)

Blake's relationship with Chapman continued to be strained, however, despite the turnaround. Chapman disagreed with Blake's methods and was not above expressing this to reporters as he chomped down on his cigar. Behind the scenes, Chapman was also orchestrating trades that Blake didn't entirely agree with.

Blake wasn't fazed, however, and continued to coach how he saw fit. In one game, trailing by a goal, he sent on six forwards in the waning moments, unafraid to commit himself with much-needed points on the line. Blake notched the lone goal of his time in Buffalo, an empty-netter, in the waning moments of a 4–2 triumph over the Philadelphia Rockets on January 3, but the Bisons languished in last place in the Western Conference despite just seven losses in their first 28 games.

Some games were probably best played without Blake and his temper, which rubbed off on his players. In a violent 5–3 win at the Memorial Auditorium on January 10, Washington player Dave Maguire was driven so hard into the boards he went through them and into the seats.

"Wednesday night the Bisons played the kind of hockey that could easily make it an odds-on threat to win another AHL crown," the *Buffalo Evening News* wrote. "They were a hard-checking, two-way team outskating one of the circuit's fastest teams. Outpassing one of the circuit's finest passing teams."

"We've been behind the eight ball since the opening of the season," Blake said after a 3–2 win over Providence. "We dropped five of our first eight games. The division is much stronger all around this year and we're just having fits trying to catch up. Judging off Wednesday's game, the Herd (a popular alternative nickname for the Bisons) definitely is on its way. Things are looking up."

That optimism came crashing down on January 17 with a 2–0 loss to the Springfield Indians in front of 9,046 spectators. The sluggish defeat undid all of Blake's work and sent Chapman on a rampage. Chapman placed all but six players on probation for indifferent play and announced the team would return to playing the Eddie Shore powerhouse style that had been so successful in previous seasons.

"The rest either start to play hockey or out they go," said Chapman before launching a full-out assault at his coach. "The club hasn't even looked good in winning. The players are out of position. They're scrambling. I don't like it. Neither do the fans. We've never been in this poor spot at this time of the season since the club came to Buffalo. We'll take steps to remedy it right away."

Blake, already steaming, was infuriated when *Buffalo Evening News* sports editor Bob Stedler touched on the team's tactics in a timely editorial, which was unusual in he rarely contributed his opinions to the paper. "Local fans have noted the lack of co-ordination on the part of their players," Stedler wrote. "The club seems to have the material but somehow it has not clicked."

A day later, Chapman announced Blake's contract had been terminated by "mutual agreement." The conflict between Chapman's desire—to return to powerhouse hockey that focused on a quick breakout counter—and Blake's preference for the National League style, with all five players accountable and the wingers driving into the corners to retrieve pucks, was not going to work. Goldsworthy stepped in to relieve Blake for the next game, against the New England Ramblers.

Blake told Chapman that under current pretenses "he did not think he would be of any further value to the organization." At a press conference that started at 10 p.m., he said he had "taught a definite system of play, but some of the players simply wouldn't follow instructions." He felt he could have produced a stronger team if not for Chapman's meddling. "I'm not quitting. I won't quit. But I can't carry on under the present set-up. After we lost the first three games of the season, my system of play was criticized in front of the players. I gave warning then that I would not tolerate such action." Chapman's decision to publicly call for a new system was the last straw. Blake said he would only reconsider if Chapman would publicly provide him with full on-ice authority. "Maybe Art Chapman didn't figure that that was interference. I did. It was never my intention to quit the team in the middle of the season but I felt I couldn't give the best of my ability because this shadow was being cast over my authority."

The decision was unpopular with Bisons fans, who heckled and whistled Goldsworthy in the following contest, a 3–3 tie with the New England Ramblers at the Memorial Auditorium. The Bisons won just eight of their last 24 games and finished last in the division, out of the playoffs.

Selke, meanwhile, also seemed to side with Blake, who traveled to Toronto to meet the Canadiens general manager and his former coach, Dick Irvin. "It's an old story," Selke said. "A coach is always the goat when a team loses."

Blake visited Irvin in his room at the Royal York Hotel, where the Canadiens coach tried to straighten out his former player. The Old Lamplighter was at his wit's end, depressed, yet his relationship with Irvin remained steady. Irvin tried to settle Blake down after the upsetting chain of events in Buffalo.

"If there had been assistant coaches, I'm sure Blake would have become an assistant to my dad," Irvin Jr. said. "But if these guys wanted to coach, they had to go to the minor leagues or somewhere because there just wasn't enough places in the NHL, nor any support staff."

Despite the setback, Blake joined Selke as they watched his beloved Canadiens win 4–1 at Maple Leaf Gardens, with Blake attempting to decide on his next move. Toe was suddenly a 38-year-old unemployed former player with no prospects and a third child on the way. His son, Bruce, would be born in March.

"I told Art it was essential for a manager and coach to get along if the team was to succeed and if we were to keep harmony among the players. I didn't have to leave but it was no good staying around just to open the gate," Blake said before announcing his plans. "I want to remain working as a coach and will listen to the highest bidder."

• • •

"Hey, stick-boy! Get your skates on, we need you on the ice!" That might sound derogatory today, but in 1949 it was like a royal horn to Robert "Bill" Guerin.

"Mr. Blake practically adopted me as one of his kids. He gave me my own uniform and dressed me, so I felt like I was one of the players. I took great pride in having everything ready for him as he liked it." Guerin's voice swells with pride when he remembers Blake, who used his junior equipment manager like an assistant upon his arrival at Valleyfield. Guerin was told to make Blake feel welcome, to help him settle in. The 18-year-old Guerin made himself available to Blake at all hours—he was the former captain of the Montreal Canadiens, after all. Guerin made sure to get to the rink early to mop the dressing room, set up the chalkboard and the coach's office just as Blake wanted. He even went so far as to shovel out the coach's parking spot in the winter months; Blake was making the 56-kilometer daily commute from Montreal West.

For Guerin, getting an invite from the boss himself for any social function outside the rink was an honor. Joining Blake at La Lumière restaurant in St. Henri, when the team was in Montreal for a date with the Royals, was worth more than the small salary he earned. Guerin knew he was lucky to be part of something special, and he could tell very early on that Blake's arrival was going to transform this Quebec Hockey League club.

"Everyone was on the moon," Guerin says, "people celebrated his arrival."

Blake's sudden move to Valleyfield after those tumultuous months in Buffalo was a shock. The idea of signing Blake had first dawned on owner Arthur Vinet in October as he watched Blake's Bisons beat up on the Braves in pre-season. When news broke that Blake had left Buffalo, Vinet reportedly reached out to Selke to learn what plans the Canadiens had in store for their apparent heir to Irvin. Instead of batting away Vinet's suggestion, Selke saw an opportunity for Blake. "Toe asked me if I had any objections to his taking the job," Selke told the *Globe and Mail*. "I told him none what-so-ever."

There may not have been a better apprenticeship for Blake than the Valleyfield job. He would be responsible for handling the team's finances, travel bookings and player personnel—tasks NHL coaches of the day typically tended to. Now that he was no longer playing hockey, Blake had few options left and little money saved. He also realized he'd be finally throwing in the towel on Cowley's record.

Weeks of speculation followed, with Blake denying reports in late January that he had signed with Valleyfield. Blake said he had received offers from several amateur clubs but was waiting to hear from Selke before deciding his future. Finally, Vinet announced Blake had accepted his carte blanche proposal to take over the Braves on February 10, 1949. Vinet called Blake "a true benediction for hockey fans in the area. He is a true idol . . . Everyone has the utmost confidence in Toe and his directives are followed religiously."

"Toe Blake's hiring has created some panic in sporting circles, most notably with the Braves adversaries," the *Gazette de Salaberry* wrote on February 17. "We can assure Blake will be better protected in Valleyfield than he was in Buffalo." Valleyfield was so honored that a local artist presented Blake with an oil painting, a portrait that would go on to be hung in his tavern.

"Toe wanted to get the most out of every player, so once our contracts were signed we were expected to be happy. He would take us one by one and tell us you have received what you wanted to be happy, so I expect the most out of you," former Valleyfield forward Andre Corriveau says.

Blake lost his third straight coaching debut in Ottawa, with the game report suggesting the "players trying too hard to impress their new coach" in the 8–5 loss to the Senators. His players regained their legs to score a 4–2 win over Sherbrooke in his first game at the Valleyfield Arena, on February 13, 1949. The club finished Blake's first half season in fifth to miss out on the playoffs. But Blake was unconcerned, as he was constructing a side he could be comfortable coaching. Blake reshaped the roster through trades and signings, with as many as eight new players joining the club by the start of the next season. Blake occasionally relied on his own reputation to persuade players like defenseman Jacques Deslauriers to leave Cincinnati of the AHL to play for him in the Quebec Senior League. Blake's communication skills were unique for a time when gruff, disconnected coaches seemed to be the norm.

"He communicated like no one else. If an error occurred (in practice), he didn't blame anyone but looked to correct it," Guerin remembers. "He'd take out his chalkboard and go over the play with the player before working it out on the ice until he got it right. He would whistle the play dead and start over until the player got it right."

Blake wanted this squad to match his own playing philosophy: puck possession, precise passing and physical play. "In that time, the coaches never got on the ice and rarely showed you how things should be done, they just whistled and pointed. Toe did," Gordie Haworth says. "He got on the ice and taught you how to play offensively, defensively, tactically, on the power play, shorthanded, how to take the faceoff, how to forecheck, all these little things that other coaches didn't do. Toe put the accent on hockey, skating, handling the puck, shooting the puck, and that's why he enjoyed so much success in hockey. He prided himself on the philosophy of the Canadiens. He emphasized skating. If you couldn't skate, you couldn't do much."

Working with a professional of Blake's stature immediately rubbed off on the players, who felt their confidence growing each time they stepped onto the ice. Blake ensured the Braves would be the finest-conditioned team in the league. The team had no superstars, and Blake recognized that. "He helped us gain a strong comprehension of the game. He knew the players' strengths and capacity beforehand," says Corriveau, who played for Valleyfield for nearly five years and shared ice time with Blake as a linemate for 20 games.

Players respected Blake's experience with the daily rigors of hockey life. The average salary was $90 per week, and all players worked jobs outside of hockey season to support their careers. Blake recognized this, and while he had a little saved from his playing days, he never boasted about his glories or rested on the laurels of his reputation. Blake kept the spotlight solely on his players. He listened and engaged just enough to straddle that line between coach and player. Sometimes Blake would put off his commute home to Montreal to join the players at forward Larry Kwong's restaurant or offer cigars to his players on the bus ride home after a victory. Perched in the front seat of the bus, Blake would smile as he heard the occasional coughs between the good-natured talk that accompanies a winning team on a road trip.

"I came out of the bus green!" Haworth said. "Later on, when he had his tavern, after the games against the Royals at the Forum on the weekends, he would invite us all to the tavern and say, 'OK, one draft and then everyone goes home.'"

Ever the quintessential teammate, Blake always jumped at the chance to have a laugh, including the night Corriveau celebrated the birth of his son. "I also welcomed a newborn into the world today," Blake joked. "Yes, the cat at my tavern finally gave birth this morning, but only to four kittens!"

Still, being away from his beloved Canadiens gnawed at Toe. He had expected Selke to protect him in Buffalo. And when the general manager had not offered him a position back within the organization following his dismissal, Blake took Selke's stance as a slight. So Blake took delight in making life difficult for Selke, which occurred every time the Braves played the Montreal Royals. Blake thumbed his nose at Selke and Canadiens management with hard-nosed negotiations over series dates whenever the teams were involved in a playoff series at the Forum. The QHL was effectively owned by the Canadiens, yet Blake still felt aggrieved.

"He gave Selke a lot of trouble during the Valleyfield stint," Kenny Reardon told author Michael Ulmer. "The Forum ran the Royals team and the league, too. The Royals would always want the best home dates and Blake would say 'tell the Forum to go fuck themselves.' He would go to senior league meetings and give Selke all kinds of trouble."

The Braves only lost five games between the end of October and the end of January to move five points ahead of the Quebec City Aces in first place. As early as December, Blake had signaled that his team could win the championship. The Braves would ultimately finish nine points better than the Aces to clinch their first regular-season championship in six years.

"He had no voice by the end of the season. The first month he screamed after everyone and then couldn't quite keep up after that," remembers Corriveau, who was battling his own health issues with an ulcer that same season.

In the playoffs, the Braves cruised past the Royals and goaltender Jacques Plante to go up against Blake's future Maple Leafs nemesis Punch Imlach and the Aces in a best-of-nine Quebec semifinals series. The series went the distance, with each of the final four games decided by a single goal.

Tied at 3–3, the series shifted back to Valleyfield. The Braves led 3–0 after one period before inexplicably unraveling. Referee

Ken Mullins, who "on top of lacking judgement is also presbyte," according to the *Gazette Valleyfield*, left Blake bewildered as he ejected a player after adding 10 minutes to a penalty. After the ice was cleared of peanut shells, the Aces immediately rallied, and the Braves saw a 5–4 third-period lead slip away in a 6–5 loss.

Valleyfield would have to sweep the remaining two games, starting with Game 8 in front of 14,000 fans at the Colisée. "I'm more confident than ever that we'll win in Quebec tonight," Blake said before the life-or-death game. He entered the dressing room as on any other night, not seeming overly excited or emotional despite staring down elimination. With an unwavering voice, Blake laid out the game plan then sent his players out, asking only for their full effort.

"I never heard him give hell to nobody. Even if the guy made a mistake, even if it cost a goal from a mistake. Never, never," Haworth said. "His character was good. That's why he was so great—in the dressing room, on the ice, all around, he was always calm and always a good word to say. That's why he was so great."

Valleyfield beat the Aces 3–2 to force the Game 9 decider back home, where a propensity for dramatics would test Blake's blood pressure. Dick Gamble put the Aces ahead 2–1 with just under 10 minutes to play. Blake pulled goalie Paul LeClerc for a sixth attacker with three minutes left, only to watch Roger Roberge's empty net goal make it 3–1 with 2:28 to play.

Four thousand home supporters slowly streamed from their seats toward the exits. But they were stopped in their tracks, turning around to return quickly as they heard the roar that accompanied 39-year-old "Kitoute" Joannette's goal with 62 seconds to go. The ice was pelted with debris, and the ensuing pause offered Blake a chance to gather his team and draw up one last rally. With 31 seconds left, Joannette netted his own rebound to force overtime as celebrations broke out throughout the arena. The Aces never recovered: Georges Bougie scored the winner at 2:48 to send 500 fans onto the ice in celebration. The

Braves had secured the QSHL's Thomas O'Connell Memorial Trophy for the first time.

The celebration was short-lived, as a trip east to play the Sydney Millionaires awaited in the best-of-seven Eastern Canadian Final. The first three games would be played in Nova Scotia and the return four at the Montreal Forum to meet demand. Despite the long-distance travel, Valleyfield emerged on top of the opener before their exhaustion caught up with them. Blake was sent to the dressing room for protesting a little too vocally in a 3–2 Game 2 loss, with one local fan graciously offering Blake his seat right behind the bench so he could continue belching out instructions. After the final whistle, Blake tore off down the players' tunnel to corner the referees to speak his mind before the next game in the series.

The Braves dropped Game 3, and though they now trailed 2–1, they never looked in danger as the series moved to the Forum. Blake had finally come home, regardless of what color jersey his players wore. Selke, Maurice "Rocket" Richard, Canadiens president Senator Donat Raymond, Eddie Shore and Gerry McNeil were among the 9,000 in attendance for a 9–6 Game 4 victory. Blake's fine-tuning of the power play proved particularly useful, as the Braves netted four goals in 65 seconds of five-on-three play in the second period. A 3–2 victory pulled Valleyfield ahead 3–2 in the series, and after the 7–1 Game 6 thrashing was over, the only sore spot before the trip to the first Alexander Cup Final was losing defenseman Jacques Deslauriers to a broken ankle.

Blake had won major trophies nearly everywhere he had played: this best-of-seven Canadian championship series against the St. Michael's Monarchs offered up another opportunity to add to his expanding trophy cabinet. For the Braves, it would be a first major honor, and a caravan of 25 cars escorted the team bus to the Forum for the opener. Six thousand fans filled the arena stands. Inside the locker room, Blake did his best to keep his charges loose before the start of the biggest series of their lives.

"Where are your skates, Jacques?" Blake launched in the direction of injured defenseman Deslauriers. "Don't let a little thing like a broken ankle keep you from playing tonight. Don't you remember? Eddie Shore played a whole game with a pair of broken ankles!"

Blake's pep talk worked: the Braves opened with a 4–1 victory. They were set to play the next two games, maybe three, at Toronto—the schedule was still not set. But the series started to deflate once it reached the Queen City. Only 1,902 fans were at Maple Leaf Gardens for the 4–1 Monarchs win. Double that showed up three nights later for Game 3, which was halted at midnight with the score tied 4–4 due to an Ontario law banning games on Sunday. Blake decided to take his players to Niagara Falls to unwind on Sunday's rest day.

The series was tied but there was little buzz, so when the Canadian Amateur Hockey Association announced Game 4 would be played in Toronto, Blake was "sizzling mad"; the Braves had been expecting to return to the Forum for Game 4. "If Toronto fans aren't interested enough to come out, then why should we play any more games here?" Blake said.

Finances played a big part in boiling Blake's blood. Teams received between $140 and $180 per day on the road, an amount expected to cover 10 hotel rooms at Hotel Barclay and three team meals for 20 people. And Valleyfield's players hadn't received their salaries for a couple of weeks due to the club's poor financial situation. Still, Blake felt confident about his team, believing the Sunday outing and off-day had reenergized his charges. Instead, the team ran out of gas in a 6–1 defeat in front of 1,542 spectators—the smallest crowd the Braves had played in front of all season.

That pitiful number led the CAHA to announce the series would be transformed into a first-to-nine-points series. Game 5 would be worth four points instead of two to help speed the series along, leaving St. Michael's in position to clinch the Dominion Championship on home ice with a win. Sensing the end could be near, the Braves responded with a 7–3 triumph in a rough, penalty-filled affair. There were 27 penalties, including six majors for fighting and a match misconduct for St. Michael's Jackie Meldrum for scuffling with fans behind the penalty box. Spurred on by a pair of bench-clearing brawls, the unruly Forum crowd forced police into action to break up three separate melees between the Monarch bench and fans behind it, tossing fans at the same time. Monarchs coach Johnny "Peanuts" O'Flaherty called for the officials to be bounced from the series following their "terrible," "incompetent" display that was "a disgrace."

While Valleyfield needed just a tie to claim the Alexander Trophy at Maple Leaf Gardens, the Braves scored a commanding 4–1 victory to lift the cup. Jack Schmidt's goal at 4:55 of the second energized Valleyfield, and the contest was never in doubt after Paul Larivee scored early in the third. When Don Menzies netted the fourth goal in the last minute of play, Blake was mobbed by Valleyfield players, technical staff, executives and the 250 Braves fans in attendance.

"I've never been hugged or embraced like that, not even after winning those championships with the Canadiens. I've never been so emotional, either, so if you see some tears under my eyes it's because I am happy for myself and the entire population of Valleyfield," said Blake, who watched on as a bonfire was lit at center ice of the Gardens to symbolize the close of another hockey season.

In victory, Blake showed the traits that would make him one of the sport's great champions: humility and leadership. "It was a tough series, anybody might have won, my boys played hard and well," he said, declining to pay tribute to any individual player. "They were all great. No one man was responsible for the victory. It was a team effort."

Thousands were on hand at Bellerive Station to welcome the team home the following day. Blake would never match such success with Valleyfield again, guiding the club no higher than third over the course of three more seasons with the Braves. He had molded a group of players into a unit, squeezing the most out of them for a full season before finding the sponge drying up. It wasn't a ragtag crew but a working bunch, without superstars: a well-coached club that played a tough game and capitalized on their strengths and took advantage of their opponents' weaknesses. "That's why we were champions—everyone respected him, and no one questioned him," Guerin says. "It was a sad time when he ultimately left. But we knew it was only a matter of time before he moved up to coach the Canadiens." Today, Valleyfield continues to play in the spirit of Blake's philosophy, its junior team not afraid to apply some grease on the forecheck and use its speed to produce offence.

Blake left the club on August 24, 1954, to focus on his tavern, which he had opened two years prior, and to also work as an umpire for summer baseball leagues across the province. It wasn't glamorous but Toe enjoyed it. The Braves were sold off to Trois-Rivières a year later. And then Toe would satisfy what to many seemed his true destiny as he was named coach of the Montreal Canadiens.

For many, the signs had been obvious for some time, especially after the Braves' improbable Alexander Cup win. "Blake endured a number of difficulties since the start of the playoffs, but his teams held such admiration for him that they never stopped believing. Toe Blake once again proved he is a worthy coach," Jacques Beauchamp wrote in *Montreal Matin*. "Don't be surprised if he earns a coaching job in the NHL within the next few years. If Art Chapman had been fairer with him, he'd probably already be in the NHL."

CHAPTER 7

COACH OF THE CANADIENS

"The most pressure of all during my coaching career was the first year. I knew I had to win because it was dangerous to my job. I had the feeling we had to win every game. I was very fortunate, I give a lot of credit to the players."

UNDER THE GLARE OF camera lights and the swarm of a buzzing press corps, Toe Blake gingerly picked at his collar and wiped away the beads of sweat forming on his brow. He shifted from one foot to the other. His toothy smile showed nerves even if this was, perhaps, one of the proudest moments of his 42 years of life. Betty and the children were with him inside vice-president William Northey's office, alongside president Donat Raymond and assistant manager Kenny Reardon. And then Frank Selke officially informed the media that Toe had been chosen as the next head coach of the Montreal Canadiens. Within five minutes of signing his contract, Blake, the former Canadiens captain who had strained and sweated and devoted himself to hockey without recourse, was thrust before some 30 newspaper, radio and TV men. "Whew," Blake gasped from inside the Forum on June 8, 1955, "I'm sure coaching the club won't be as hard as this."

Rumors had swirled about Blake's appointment since Dick Irvin's resignation on May 2. Toe was one of the heavyweights on a long shortlist of candidates. It included future general manager and current Junior Canadiens coach Sam Pollock; former Toronto Maple Leafs star Joe Primeau; the coach of the Western Hockey League's Calgary Stampeders, Frank Currie, who had been in the organization for years; former Montreal Royals coach Frank Carlin; Billy Reay, coach of WHL's Victoria Cougars; former Canadiens defenseman Roger Leger, the Edinburgh Cup–winning head of the Shawinigan Cataractes; former Punch Line center and Junior Canadiens coach Elmer Lach; and current Canadiens captain Emile "Butch" Bouchard.

Despite the French media angling for Bouchard, the 35-year-old defenseman ruled himself out by confirming he would return to play his 15th—and final—season. Senator Raymond preferred Reay, while Selke gave the edge to Leger. Reardon appeared to be the only executive siding with Blake.

Montréal-Matin was one of the few francophone newspapers pushing for Blake, with sports editor Jacques Beauchamp lauding "one of the most courageous, most combative players in Canadiens history" as an ideal new man in charge. The French-language newspaper would label Blake's hiring as "The Year's Best News." Beauchamp felt Blake had all the qualities to succeed, especially his profound understanding of the player psyche. Plus, Blake will "provide great copy for journalists, which is very important."

Inside the Forum, Reardon's support of Blake was crucial in swinging the decision. A tough defenseman whose career had been interrupted by military service in World War II, the Winnipeg native had played alongside Blake for nearly five of his seven professional seasons. After retiring, Reardon worked as a scout for the Canadiens organization and often mingled with Blake while he was coaching at Valleyfield. Reardon had watched how Blake led the Braves to the Quebec Senior Hockey League title. He was already won over by Blake's character, tenacity and determination as his former teammate, and Blake's record in Valleyfield only cemented his feelings.

Being firmly entrenched in the front office as Selke's right-hand man, and son-in-law to Senator Raymond, helped Reardon plead Blake's case. Reardon had seen the trouble Blake had caused Selke and the Canadiens with their league fixtures during his stint at Valleyfield, and felt it was better to be working with him than against him. He also recognized Blake's value as a former captain and teammate of the Rocket. At 34, Richard remained an unpredictable, prickly force thanks to Irvin's antagonistic treatment. Canadiens management had had enough after Richard was banned for the playoffs, with the Canadiens losing the Stanley Cup Final to Detroit in seven games. It was obvious Richard would have likely been the difference-maker. In Blake, Reardon and Selke recognized a personality that Richard knew and trusted. Blake knew his former Punch Line teammate better than almost anyone else. The Rocket had nothing but respect for Blake, especially after watching him pay his dues in Valleyfield.

Reardon called Blake four days prior to the announcement of his hiring to verify his interest. Blake had, after all, been out of the game, professionally speaking, for over a year since leaving Valleyfield to focus on his tavern. There was concern about Blake's ability to juggle the tavern alongside his Canadiens duties. There were never any doubts on Blake's part. Reardon told Blake he would have to bite his lip and work with the players Selke gave him—if he couldn't do that, he wouldn't have a chance of lasting.

Blake knew what team he was inheriting and was no dummy: he could work under these conditions.

Toe was confident he could step in and replace Irvin successfully, and he was fully aware of the expectations accompanying his appointment. Few were as committed to winning or as dedicated to the Canadiens cause as their former player. From his perch in the blue seats, where he had season tickets, Blake was aware of the strengths and weaknesses of this club. Montreal had been Stanley Cup finalists just two months earlier and were expected to immediately challenge again. "When a club hires a coach, the priority is to maintain harmony between the players and in their play," Blake said at his unveiling. "You have to work hard on the collective because the majority of players who make the jump into the NHL don't have much more to learn in terms of fundamentals. But they can all contribute to improving team play and that's where the coach comes in."

The Richard Riot of March 1955 was a pivotal moment inside the organization, setting off a chain of events that would lead to Blake's hiring. The Canadiens were two points atop the league and the Rocket was leading the scoring race when an altercation with Boston Bruins defenseman Hal Laycoe ended in a brawl. NHL President Clarence Campbell suspended the Rocket for the remainder of the season, including the playoffs. "No sports decision ever hit the Montreal public with such impact," Sidney Katz wrote in *Maclean's*. "It seemed to strike at the very heart and soul of the city."

After announcing the decision, Campbell attended the very next Canadiens game at the Forum despite warnings not to. The majority of the francophone fans viewed the ruling as unjust, another example of the English Canada looking to control and keep the Frenchman down. Campbell was pummeled with rotten fruit and eggs and punched by fans, and when tear gas went off inside the Forum, fans flooded the street, where hundreds were already protesting the decision, and a full-scale riot proceeded. The St. Patrick's Day Richard Riots led to 137 arrests, and considering Richard's status in Quebec—he transcended religion—many see the event as the spark that lit the fuse of Quebec's Quiet Revolution.

The riot had also led Selke to do some organizational soul-searching, and it was agreed it was time to move on from Dick Irvin. Irvin had guided the Canadiens to three Stanley Cups, including two with Blake as captain, in 15 seasons at the helm. Irvin's departure seemed a foregone conclusion as early as February, when Selke granted Chicago permission to speak with his coach. The Richard Riot one month later confirmed and accelerated this process. Selke felt there was no choice but to part ways with his dear friend at the end of the season. Club prestige had been affected, and Irvin's acid tongue and gloomy demeanor—perhaps attributed to his failing health—were irking many. Selke wanted a coach who would back his players in public—not call them out—especially the temperamental Rocket. Selke and Reardon were already working behind the scenes to tame the Rocket, and the popular belief was that Toe could be the extra positive force. Any of Selke's lingering doubts were refuted when Richard and Bouchard dampened claims that the players would be upset with the appointment of Toe. "Don't you worry about that, Mr. Selke," the Rocket said. "We all love the Old Lamplighter. We'll give him every ounce we have!"

When Selke called Blake into his Forum office for a visit two days prior to the official signing, he had been assured that Blake would be unanimously supported in the dressing room. He just needed to be certain for himself. Selke had spent time with Blake off the ice, starting in 1947, when he named him a "sidekick regarding on all hockey problems" with the Canadiens. Selke had strategically moved Blake along his coaching path until his exit from the organization, and their relationship had soured during Blake's time in Valleyfield. But this wasn't personal, and Selke felt Toe, as the senior man from the organization, deserved the opportunity.

And so, it was Selke who walked out to the gathered scrum of media men at 10:05 a.m. on Wednesday, June 8, to reveal that Blake had signed a one-year contract "that could last a lifetime."

"This is a momentous occasion in the long history of the club," Selke said. "When Dick decided to go to Chicago, we started to look for someone who had learned hockey in our system. Our headlong type of game, which was always endorsed by Irvin, has made the Canadiens the most popular club in hockey, and we intend to keep it that way with 'Toe' at the head of the club."

Blake, who was named the ninth coach since the club's founding, "walked jauntily into the midst of the swarm of buzzing reporters," wrote the *Montreal Star*; "it was the job for Blake, no one else."

With wife Betty and children Joan, Mary-Jane and Bruce nearby, there was no doubt Blake was exactly where he had always wanted to be. "It has always been my great ambition to coach the Canadiens, and today I realized my dream. I realize that I have a big pair of shoes to fill in my new post, because I always regarded Dick Irvin as the best coach in the National Hockey League," said Blake, who followed Newsy Lalonde, Sylvio Mantha and Pit Lepine as the fourth ex-player to coach the club. "With the help of Mr. Selke and Ken Reardon and the players we will continue to keep the Canadiens hockey name on top. The team won't let the fans down. I am not going to promise a Stanley Cup but we will continue as a great fighting club."

As reporters lobbed questions at Blake, who answered in English and French, "Selke stood by grinning broadly as Blake parried newsman's questions with the aplomb of a diplomat," according to the *Montreal Star*.

• • •

> *"You have to understand that each player has their own style even if it seems as if they are evolving similarly. If you asked an entire team to play the way I did as I came up the Canadiens, it would be pure folly. You have to blend the styles and hope it creates something as close to perfection as possible."*

Toe spent the summer of 1955 as he normally would—playing softball and the occasional round of golf when away from the tavern. He had the added responsibility of plotting his first season in charge of the Canadiens. Irvin did his best to put the pressure on his former charge. The new Blackhawks coach predicted the Canadiens would win the league by 20 points over Detroit and go on to lift the Stanley Cup.

"It's a good choice (of coach) even though I thought Emile Bouchard would have been chosen," Irvin told *Montréal-Matin* from his home in Mount Royal, where he carried a cane, looking fatigued and 20 pounds lighter than he had when he left the Canadiens. "No team in the league can match their talent. I really believe the Red Wings have hurt themselves with recent transactions. Glenn Hall is not Sawchuk."

Irvin's words surprised Blake, even if his former coach was now his rival. Prior to joining the Canadiens, Blake had telephoned Irvin several times for advice on negotiating his first contract. In 1955, Irvin was the highest-paid figure in the NHL, on a contract worth $20,000 per season. His final deal with the Canadiens was a two-year contract worth $15,000 per season, an amount Blake did not seem likely to dent as a rookie coach. "What they're offering you is a joke," Irvin told Blake over the receiver.

Toe would ultimately spend nearly 50 years inside the Canadiens organization, wearing different hats: from vice-president of hockey operations to special ambassador to scout. It was partly to help supplement him with an income after having been underpaid throughout his career. When Dickie Moore quit the Canadiens during the summer of 1963, he came out of Selke's office, and the first person he bumped into was Blake.

"You're crazy to quit now," Blake said.

"That's easy for you to say," was Moore's retort, "with all the money you're making."

Moore would quickly regret lashing out at his coach when Blake admitted to making less than what Irvin had earned during his final season in Montreal.

Meanwhile, the defending Stanley Cup champions, the Detroit Red Wings, were making off-season personnel moves of their own. Detroit general manager Jack Adams was worried about the future of his ageing squad despite having won four Stanley Cups since 1950. He had shocked the league by trading away Sawchuk to Boston for a package of young players to promote highly rated rookie goalie Glenn Hall. Still, despite being led by a rookie goalie and rookie coach in Jimmy Skinner, the Red Wings remained favorites to meet Montreal in the final thanks to a lineup that included Gordie Howe, Sid Abel, Alex Delvecchio, Ted Lindsay and Red Kelly.

Blake still felt the Canadiens were the better squad. In the previous playoffs, Detroit's Glen Skov–Tony Leswick–Marty Pavelich line had held Jean Beliveau–Bernie Geoffrion–Ralph Olmstead in check, but Blake was confident his men would bounce back from that experience. Leswick was now gone. Blake knew immediately that anything less than the Cup would likely be failure: "I feel if we finish anywhere but first I'll feel I've done a very bad job. If things go right we should win by 10 games. But any hockey man will tell you that things don't always go right."

Being back with the team in September for pre-season training at the Verdun Auditorium bolstered Blake. He loved the hockey lifestyle and the camaraderie that came from being around the boys. Being back among Les Tricolores rejuvenated him and the team. Blake didn't differ much from Irvin in his approach, but he did differ in how he related to the players.

There was no period of transition—Blake immediately stuck in with the team as if he was just another player, completely at ease with everyone. Toe recognized there was team harmony and with the Rocket, Bouchard, Floyd Curry and Doug Harvey still in the fold, he also enjoyed a link to the players through his former teammates. There was no need to whip the team through fear—Blake could sense the disappointment of previous years and the desire to prevent it from occurring again. "I couldn't help be amazed once we started holding our first workouts. I was glad I was as young as I was. Otherwise I would have been killed. All those great shots. The puck was flying around with such speed I thought I was in the shooting gallery."

The Rocket was a pivotal ally for Blake from the start; and Richard, Bouchard, Floyd Curry and Kenny Mosdell made extra effort to help him settle in. For the Rocket, it was clear that Toe was the perfect choice. Blake wanted Richard—and the rest of the team—to use their skating to keep possession, rush the play and shoot as much as possible. Blake pushed them to play to their strengths but did not point the finger when mistakes were made.

As Rocket Richard put it in *The Flying Frenchmen*:

> As far as I was concerned, no other man was qualified for the job but Toe, for lots of reasons. Most of the team had played with Toe. They knew the kind of competitor he was, a fellow who hated to lose, who knew his hockey, and was liked by everyone who ever met him. The French players knew he was half French Canadian so that solved one problem . . . So he wasn't coming into the job cold. I had idolized Toe as a kid and played with him on the Punch Line for many years. As far as we were concerned, there couldn't have been a more perfect choice. It didn't take long

> to realize we would work well under Blake, perhaps even better than Irvin. Toe had one quality that marked him from Dick. It was Irvin's policy to roast a player publicly for his mistakes. Blake would never give anybody hell in front of other players. When he had something to say he would take them out to a private room, or his compartment on the train, or into his office to discuss it. Make no mistake, Blake was a tough man. You never heard a good word from him on the bench. If you made a good play he wouldn't walk over and pat you on the back. But that doesn't really matter. In the dressing room you knew he was behind you and as long as I played for him Toe was well-liked by the players.

Toe also set out immediately to work on the Rocket's emotions. No one knew Richard's psychological triggers—what turned him on or tuned him down—like the new coach. Following the troubles of last season, this was an important job. "Blake was also a soothing influence," said Richard. "When he took over as coach he said 'If I ever say anything that hurts you, don't come back and say anything to the press. Wait, and come and see me and we'll talk about it.' Toe was always afraid that I was going to talk in front of the other guys and to the newspapermen and hurt the team morale, but that never happened."

Blake had the aid of Selke and Reardon on the Rocket front, with the trio doing all they could to ensure Richard's emotions never boiled over. In January, Reardon even took it upon himself to sprint into the dressing room between periods at Madison Square Gardens to play peacemaker after defenseman Lou Fontinato caught the Rocket with a looping right cross that opened a four-stitch cut over his eye. "You've got two strikes on you now in the league head office. One more and you may be out," Reardon told Richard, as reported in the *Montreal Gazette*. "Nobody questions your courage. You've been in the league a long time and you've proven yourself over and over again. You've got everything to lose and nothing to gain by going back at him. Let the thing ride."

Inside the locker room, Doug Harvey's ability to crack a joke at the right moment also proved a soothing influence. Blake worked diligently on the Rocket—he would make him captain one season later after Bouchard retired. "I often had to cool him out—right on the bench," Blake said. "He glared at me, but he took it maybe because I was an old linemate. He knew we had been through a lot together and most likely because he didn't want to make my first season as an NHL coach tougher."

With the Rocket appeased, the Old Lamplighter now had a clear task: dislodge Detroit and win the Stanley Cup. "It was not said aloud but implied by Frank (Selke) that you win the Cup, or you're gone," Toe's son, Bruce, remembers. "So, he won the next five."

• • •

Blake walked into the Canadiens dressing room to find a familiar sight. Irvin had put a poster up on the wall with a quotation from Abraham Lincoln. "I do the very best I know how, the very best I can, and I mean to keep on doing so until the end," the former United States president is quoted as saying. Blake was just fine with that, and the quote would remain through his tenure as coach.

Irvin had already applied the pressure with his pre-season predictions, and Blake was already applying pressure upon himself. The league title was not up for debate—the Canadiens had to seize it back from the Red Wings, who had won all the team trophies the past two seasons. Luckily, that feeling was mutual among the players when camp opened in Verdun. Some speculated the team was frayed and shaken from the Richard Riots. "Nothing Remains but Shame," was how the *Montreal Star* newspaper described the long-term damage of that fateful night. Blake knew success or defeat rested on his shoulders and his decisions, starting with training camp. Plante had been erratic last season. A fractured cheekbone in December seemed to unnerve him, and now he was fighting for his spot with a new coach and another goalie—Bob Perreault—aiming to take his spot. Kenny Mosdell was working hard to stay with the parent team, while the Rocket's kid brother Henri Richard also looked as if he might challenge Andre Corriveau for a spot at center. Corriveau had played for Blake at Valleyfield and was brought in to fill the loss of Calum MacKay, who was sidelined following knee surgery.

"If there is one man who will be on the spot it is Blake. Blake takes over an intact team," one report suggested. "Blake has shown no worry over being in the position of having to keep his club battling at the top or having the wolves on his neck. He has been decisive and an indefatigable worker at training camp." Undoubtedly, Blake relished jumping back on the ice with the boys when they moved their workouts to the Forum.

"He knew when it was time to get tough and when it was time to have fun. That was in comparison to Irvin, who never smiled and was hard to read," Geoffrion remembered in his memoir. "It was obvious the change in coach would change the mood from training camp."

Blake was critical in settling things down. There was no language divide with this bilingual coach at the helm—one who could still get on the ice and prove himself when tested. The Canadiens farm system had produced most of these players, and Toe certainly felt this core had matured enough to be champions. While there was pressure to make sure the team won, there was no other way but greatness in Blake's mind, anyway.

"What he instilled in players was the ability to be hard

workers, the engrained work ethic. He was a hard player himself, worked his way up, nothing was handed to him. This made him a very strong practice coach. His practices were well constructed, he had good players, but he needed a good system," recalls Scotty Bowman. "He recognized hockey was a team game and you had to rely on all of your players. He had a good rapport with all his players but what I really learned from him is that your top players have to feel comfortable in the style you are coaching. Do everything in your power to support the stars and back them in any situation. You can't have any controversy with those kinds of players."

Blake didn't put his players through fancy drills but tried his best to recreate in-game situations for his charges. Irvin believed in rugged, exhausting practices, and many believed this played a part in the Canadiens' drop-off down the stretch. With Blake, there were no long, grinding practices but efficient 60-minute sessions where skating was the focus. Blake liked to have his players do an extended amount of skating to get warmed up. In camp, Blake surprised himself by gravitating toward Henri Richard over Corriveau. The "Pocket Rocket" was a wild card, while Corriveau offered security, a much-desired quality for any newcomer to a high-stakes job. In Detroit, Jack Adams had been the busiest general manager in the league, bringing back only nine players from the Stanley Cup–winning Red Wings, who possessed the biggest team in the league, with the 18 players averaging approximately 184 pounds each. Boston had its roughest and toughest team in years, with Sawchuk backing them up, while Toronto's squad had also undergone a shake-up; GM Hap Day predicted the Leafs could win it all or finish fourth.

How would the Pocket Rocket hold up in the face of all these bruisers, Blake kept himself up wondering. "This kid needed more time in the minors to bulk up," he recalled, as quoted in Boom Boom Geoffrion's autobiography. "I don't want the Rocket feeling like he has to go out of his way to protect his little brother."

But Blake relented and, on the eve of the opener against the Maple Leafs, he okayed a three-game trial for Richard. Blake lost his first official NHL game as he took charge of the NHL All-Stars in a 3–1 loss to Detroit. Blake's career with the Canadiens started with a 2–0 triumph over Toronto that came with the cost of Geoffrion being sidelined by injury. Blake slid the Pocket Rocket into Geoffrion's spot on the right side beside Beliveau and Olmstead, and the Canadiens started the season with four straight wins. Meanwhile, the Red Wings lost their home opener for the first time in 17 years.

"They can all handle the puck. They know what they're doing every second they're out there," Bruins coach Milt Schmidt said. "They never make a move without a purpose. If you make one false move, you're sunk. They make the other teams' power plays look feeble."

Even Irvin was impressed with his successor's start, sending Blake a telegram: "I wish you luck, and hope you can do what I failed to do."

"Maybe, he means getting the puck out of our end," a puzzled Blake told the *Montreal Herald*. "I should wire him collect that whatever it is he meant, we've done it all right so far."

Irvin played spoiler in his first return trip to the Forum, where the Blackhawks emerged with a 6–0 victory. Three games later, against the Red Wings, Blake brought up Claude Provost from Shawinigan Falls to play right wing on Beliveau's line, and had the Pocket Rocket center the Rocket and Dickie Moore. The Rocket could now keep a close eye on his brother, even if ultimately it would be unnecessary.

The Canadiens beat Detroit 2–1 in their first meeting and didn't lose again for almost a month—a run of 11 games. With Detroit's reshaped roster struggling to find its rhythm, the Canadiens were the clear class of the league and building a cushion atop the standings. Just like the Canadiens, the city of Montreal was full of ambition that winter. Leo Dandurand was talking about bringing Major League Baseball to the city, with plans to erect a 40,000-seat stadium at the current site of the Olympic Stadium with the capacity to expand to 75,000. The 21-storey Queen Elizabeth Hotel was one of 15 buildings worth more than $20 million reshaping Montreal's downtown skyline. It promised to be the largest hotel in the British Commonwealth.

Blake, who could be found puffing on five-cent Peg Top cigars in the executive offices of the Forum alongside the pipe-wielding Reardon, was the toast of the town even if, as the *Montreal Herald* described it, he "dispenses conversation with the frugality of a Scotsman compelled to forfeit a coin with each word. A pleasant contrast to his predecessor who placed no value on words at all."

"I'm pleased with the work of Toe Blake as coach. Blake has done well," Selke told *The Hockey News*. "I'm more convinced than ever that we made a good choice in signing him to guide the team."

"He had Butch Bouchard, Maurice Richard—a lot of players who already knew him, so he didn't need to speak up much," remembered Jean-Guy Talbot, who Blake called up as a rookie that season. "The players helped him in that sense. He was a player's coach and they certainly helped him. He explained the kind of game he wanted us to play but not much more than that. He didn't need to say much. The dressing room respect helped him. To see Maurice and the other guys who played with him hold such respect for him and his authority also helped us respect him. Sometimes I didn't agree with him, but I always respected him and followed it."

Blake worked tirelessly on improving the Canadiens power play, which he saw as the ultimate weapon for all his offensive talent. Penalties were served for a full two minutes, allowing the Canadiens to run up goals with the man advantage such as in the 4–2 win over Boston on December 11.

In Boston that night, Schmidt was still recoiling from the onslaught of Beliveau, Richard, Geoffrion and Harvey that Canadiens forward Ray Getliffe termed "Murder, Incorporated." Back in Montreal, the possibility of murder had been brewing two nights earlier: 110 were arrested when students shut down the city overnight in protest over a tram fare hike. Service was totally cut off when, according to the *Montreal Herald*, "a hooligan fringe mob" slashed power lines, flattened bus tires and burned tram cars to the ground. The monetary damage was pegged at $102,000, but the city's image was devalued even more on the heels of the Richard Riots. These were delicate times, and the two incidents "gave Montreal an extremely bad name all over the continent, creating in distant minds the idea that this ordinarily peaceful city is a cross between a lawless frontier town . . . (with) an underworld center composed mostly of thugs and hoodlums." On that evening, Blake was more concerned for his tavern.

Through 29 games, the Canadiens were one win better than the season prior, had lost four fewer games and surrendered 20 fewer goals. Blake's obsession with discipline had resonated with Harvey and the defensive corps, who were clearly instructed on how to play.

Terry Harper, one of the key figures on the Canadiens blue line under Blake during the 1960s run of championships, said Blake's principles were clear, well understood and, if followed, would mean playing time:

> The first thing was to head-man the puck, always pass it ahead of you. If someone ahead of you was open, you pass it to them. Rule number two was always to have one defenseman in front of the net—never leave the front of the net. Thirdly, the other defenseman was tasked with working it out of the zone, mostly through the centerman, but also with the wingers. And fourth, the blue line: never get trapped by the blue line. Always get

> the puck over it. From your own zone, get over it and out. In their zone, get over it and in. And you never stop short of the blue line.
>
> These were cardinal rules with him. Those were the kind of things that would get you benched if you didn't follow. But as long as you were doing the things he wanted and trying hard, he didn't use that as a motivator. He stuck by you. He'd emphasize these things all the time. If you broke these rules you could end up sitting out several shifts, maybe even a game or two. Like carrying the puck back over your own blue line—never. Never.
>
> To have a goal scored on when a defenseman was in front of the net—no, that doesn't happen. Head-man the pass, head-man the puck all the time was the hockey brand he wanted to play. Forward, aggressive hockey—you don't score goals skating backwards. And going deep, he always went deep. Never stop just over the blue line. He went deep all the time and then try to play the puck back out to the front of the net or the defenseman. Let defenseman shoot it and converge on the net. And taking a shot on goal on the way in was good, too.

Blake would practically eat his hat when any of his players passed the puck in front of the Canadiens goal, screaming "Away, get it away!" It was all part of his stressing the fundamentals of playing a simple, tactical game to beat your opponent. A center should maneuver the puck to create scoring opportunities for his wingers and himself and play a sound checking game. The wingers stayed out wide and skated their lanes without crossing over the ice or penetrating too deeply, for the risk of getting caught out in the event of a turnover. On defense, Blake paired a good bodychecker with a sound, steady player. And the goaltender was the heart of the team. Blake would not tolerate laziness or indifference, preaching to his players to always keep their sticks on the ice if they wanted to catch a pass. Some suggest he was the originator of the European/Russian style of the 1970s and '80s with his emphasis on puck control in all three zones. Blake was one of the first coaches to push his defensemen to jump up and join the rush, to play at the blue line rather than behind it. "Hockey is very easy it is played with two Vs—one moving away from our net and the other moving towards theirs," Blake would explain, holding his arms up in a V.

The Canadiens had a stranglehold on the league. The Red Wings' poor start had left them with too much ground to cover, although they had started to turn things around in December and were slowly climbing back up the standings. While Blake had warned about Boston's potential at the start of the season, he knew the Red Wings remained formidable as defending champions. Blake's strategy involved both mental and in-game tactics.

"The most important chore we can do for ourselves is win a game in Detroit," said Blake, whose team had surpassed his 50-point demand for Christmas with 51. "Wings are going to be the team to beat and it would hoist our morale and lower theirs if we won there. They have a lot of class and I rate them the team that sooner or later will force us to slow down. We divide our season into three sections. Christmas ends the first season, the end of the regular schedule closes another and the playoffs are the third. The spirit of the club is wonderful."

Now, a new objective was made: score 51 points in the second half of the season to set a record 102-point total for a full 70-game season, which would be one better than the 1950–51 Red Wings total.

Blake figured such a demand would motivate his players and keep them focused on hockey—and beating Detroit. Still, Toe had some concern with the spirit inside the team, particularly in relation to his captain, Butch Bouchard. Bouchard had returned to play one more season at Blake's beckoning, but a combination of injuries and age had slowed him enough for Talbot to claim his place in the lineup. There was no better team man than Bouchard, who had played alongside Blake and replaced him as captain. Talbot was anxious about unseating him, but Bouchard quickly eased the rookie's tensions and encouraged his replacement. "I tell my club that four or five stars don't make a team," Blake reaffirmed in a *Sports Illustrated* interview. "Everyone in uniform is important."

While the Richard Riots were voted the top Canadian sports story of 1955, Maurice was quickly putting the episode behind him. The Rocket marked the close of the year with his 500th goal (including playoffs) in a 5–2 victory over Toronto. His season had been relatively free of controversy, as he simply ignored the goading that would normally tempt him to drop his gloves. His lone weakness was a penchant for sticking up for his brother, but that was slowly dissipating as the Pocket Rocket showed he could defend himself.

Blake's next set of season objectives got off to a rocky start when Harvey broke his hand in a loss to the Rangers on Christmas Day. Conn Smythe had already begun talking up the need to reign in the Canadiens power play, and Harvey's injury did that. Dollard St. Laurent soon shattered his jaw, and the Pocket Rocket was sidelined by an ankle injury, while Plante was showing jitters following his return from a broken nose. With five rookies in the team—Talbot, Provost, Bob Turner, Jacques Deslauriers and Connie Broden—the absence of the veterans was being felt, particularly on the power play.

The team started January with four defeats in five games, including a particularly upsetting 2–0 loss to Boston on January 14. Sawchuk was out to injury, and backup Long John Henderson's size-13 skates did not arrive with the team. Blake refused to release backup goalie Gerry McNeil to the Bruins, so Canadiens practice goalie Claude Pronovost filled in and earned a shutout in his first NHL start. Blake was livid. To Blake, the causes of this losing streak were clear: he blamed Beliveau's popularity for putting off the centerman, with the press phoning his hotel room as soon as the team checked in on the road, photographers rushing to snap pictures of him at all hours, "even while he eats!" Opponents were taking liberties with the team since his defenseman weren't using the body enough, with Talbot easing off, too, and Tom Johnson not laying a finger on anyone.

"One thing about these defeats," Blake told the *Montreal Herald*, "they're taking the curse of that phrase 'greatest team of all time' off of our shoulders. Some of the players had got not only to reading these overdone puffs, but got to believing them. So, right now, we're just another hockey team, taking our bumps like any other team, and with a chance we might finish third. Red Wings are the club I've always feared and they're coming like Gang Busters."

The Boston loss was followed by a third straight defeat that allowed the Rangers to move within six points of the NHL leaders with a game in hand. It was becoming clear that the first real strain of adversity was beginning to test Blake's short patience.

"I've everything to lose and very little to gain. The Canadiens team is expected to win and if they don't, it's my fault. I've got to win this year. Can't say wait until next year," Blake told the *Herald* after a 2–0 loss in Detroit.

> My team isn't getting any younger. The Rocket is 34. He's getting goals now but will he in another year? Butch Bouchard is all through after this year. So is Mosdell. Doug Harvey and Floyd Curry are in their thirties. Another year may be too late.
>
> (Irvin's) putting a finger on me. If the team is good enough to win by 10 games this year, it should

> have been even better a year ago when all those stars were a year younger. Why didn't Irvin win the NHL title by 10 games? He didn't even win it.

Toe even started receiving phone calls and letters criticizing his decisions and his management style.

> It's the guys who call in and tell me how to run my business. Just a little while ago, some guy called up and, with no introduction, nothing, he snapped at me: "What kind of a coach do you think you are?" I thought he might be kidding, so I said I didn't know yet, I had been coaching only a few years. So this guy wasn't fooling. He snapped right at me: "You don't know a thing about coaching. Why don't you get some young fellows and junk a lot of that worn-out deadwood you're carrying. Why, you haven't developed a single youngster yet. You're stringing along with old has-beens like yourself."
>
> That really burned me. Here I've brought up five kids this season. All these were playing that night, and this guy talks about no new blood on the team. He should have blood on his nose, already.

Money had always been an important motivator for Blake as a player, and he snatched onto using the ploy as a motivating tool as coach, too. "This was the worst game they played this season," he told the *Herald* after a 5–1 loss at Boston. "They looked to me like guys who don't care about money. These two losses to Bruins, one here and one there, could be very expensive. They could mean we finish second, and that means $500 per player. But the indifferent way they played made me think they don't care about $500. Either that, or they've become too sure of themselves and of their leadership. We'll have to play a lot better hockey tonight. The boys can't get by any longer on their clippings."

Despite Blake's public prods and unnerved temper, the players' faith in their coach grew. Blake was forward-thinking, never reminding his players of past mistakes as Irvin tended to do. Blake praised more than he criticized, and his makeover of the defense and fine-tuning of the power play were getting noticed. Blake wanted to show up Irvin, above all—the public spat, the gap in pay and his former boss's skeptic welcome all motivated the Old Lamplighter.

And that feeling seemed to translate back to the players by February, as the Canadiens found their rhythm during an unbeaten run of 12 games. The dressing room was loose as Beliveau looked to hold off Gordie Howe in the scoring race. "Le Gros Bill" was transforming into a more physical player under Blake as he ran up 143 penalty minutes that season. He set a record for goals by a centerman with 47, winning the Hart and Art Ross Trophies. Left winger Bert Olmstead set a record with 56 assists on the season as the Beliveau-Geoffrion-Olmstead trio notched 220 points (88, 62 and 70, respectively) to equal the record set by Blake and his Punch Line during the 1944–45 50-game season.

The Rocket racked up 38 goals on the season but provided Blake with a fright during a 5–2 win over the Blackhawks. Rocket fell headfirst into the post, leaving him unconscious and crumpled on the ice. He was rushed to the hospital in uniform for scans and to close the five-stitch gash on his forehead, but he returned to the Canadiens bench to start the second period. Blake's fears over his former teammate were soon put to rest, and when the Canadiens finished the season 24 points ahead of second-place Detroit, Blake could exhale, if only briefly.

"We ran into a bad streak in January," he told the *Sherbrooke Daily Record*. "I told the boys not to get panicky or start blaming anyone for losing a game. I told them that was my job. I don't call down a player in front of everyone in the dressing room if he did something that cost us a game. I try to sleep on it first because I might say something I'd be sorry about the next day. I went along with most of Irvin's disciplinary rules, but I wasn't quite so strict. Perhaps when your club is on top you're inclined to be less strict."

The Canadiens went into the playoffs on the back of two straight victories over the Rangers, which left the blueshirts behind Detroit in third place and a first-round matchup with Montreal. To Blake, the playoffs were akin to a game of poker. The regular season had been a killing, and now they were throwing the winnings into the pot for a single cut of the deck.

Across the ice was another driven rookie coach in Phil Watson. Watson was as stern and unrelenting as Blake, but he was petulant and tended to undermine his own players. Watson, who played one season alongside Blake with the Canadiens, forbade his players from drinking any type of liquid refreshment during games and reprimanded anyone caught sneaking small drafts of water in the penalty box. During intermissions, Rangers players were served tea in tiny Dixie Cups. Watson loved the limelight, hogging the glory while passing along the blame in defeat. Watson had once said his squad was full of "horseshit players" and needled his team at every opportunity. Goaltender Gump Worsley was one of Watson's favorite whipping boys; once, after a morale-building win, he told his goalie: "Worsley, you think you're a hot shit now. You stink." Watson criticized Gump all season long, keeping the threat of demotion in his mind with Johnny Bower ready to come up from Providence.

For Game 1 at the Forum, Watson changed his routine: his players were served small cups of very strong tea liberally sugared, without cream or milk. Blake, meanwhile, had his boys sucking on oranges in the Canadiens locker room. The Rocket notched a hat trick in the opening 7–1 triumph. Watson lambasted Gump, who played through a knee ligament injury, and picked Gordie Bell to start Game 2, which turned out to be a 4–2 Rangers victory. The physical contest bothered Blake, who yanked on his collar as he sidestepped reporters afterward. Fourteen minor penalties were called in a game where the timekeeper's clock malfunctioned, leaving MC Jacques Belanger to update the crowds about the time in intervals. Inside the Canadiens dressing room, Blake stewed to himself, and the silence spread. Blake sat there, hunched over with his fedora perched up and his head down. He rubbed his chin as he replayed all the faults of the evening. His defense had kept backing up on Plante all night, and the guys in front of them looked like figure skaters—they hadn't hit a body all night! How could they allow a breakaway in a playoff game—sacrilege!

Watson had taken a number of gambles—he benched Lou Fontinato following a poor display in Game 1. But he also ensured the Rocket and Beliveau were tightly checked throughout the contest. And now he was basking in the result. "We'll take two in New York and meet Detroit in the finals. We've got the Canadiens' number," he proudly cried.

The Canadiens boarded the train to New York, where the Hotel Piccadilly awaited. Playing at the old Garden was as far from the bright lights of Broadway as could be. The dressing rooms were small and smelly. The players were forced to hang both their street clothes and uniforms from the dry pipes since there were no lockers or clothes racks. The fans gathered outside on 49th Street to yell insults through the open windows, which couldn't be shut without turning the cellar into a steam bath. Just getting in and out of the room meant climbing over bags, bodies and tables where a trainer might be working on a player. But the cramped confines suited Blake and the Canadiens fine. It helped their focus, and the Canadiens always helped the Garden draw at least 15,000 fans, who provided extra energy as they serenaded their team with vaudeville classics like "That Old Gang of Mine" and "Marching Along Together." A late 9 p.m. start for Game 3 didn't bother the visitors, who held the Rangers to nine shots in a 3–1 victory. Rangers fans showered the ice with eggs, oranges, rubber balls, coins, a bottle, overshoes and toe rubbers over the course of the game.

Over 1,000 Canadiens fans bought one-dollar tickets and made the trip south for Game 4, which Montreal won 5–3 for a 3–1 series lead. Despite the victory, an outraged Blake called it the worst refereeing he had ever seen. In lieu of celebrations, the small sauna of the dressing room the Canadiens were parked in was cloaked in silence. Blake rambled on while his players watched in awkward silence like children waiting for a petulant parent to finish a rant. While Blake's discontent for the men in stripes was a big part of it, the changing dynamics of the players' relationship with the game was also a factor. Blake couldn't understand how a player could struggle one day and perform well on another. Executives could get away with a bad day at the office—hockey players couldn't. For Toe, the pride of playing in front of your fans and succeeding was a heavy burden, never to be taken lightly. He noticed that even the Rocket would ease up, whereas before, on the Punch Line, he would have steamrolled through. The Rocket responded in Game 5 with five assists to match Blake's 1944 record in one game as the Canadiens closed out the series 7–0.

"We played a heck of a good game because the Rangers played a heck of a bad game," said the Rocket from the dressing room, where Blake went around shaking each individual player's hand after earning his first playoff series triumph. Blake used the moment to remind his players—as he would remind Ryan Walters during the Canadiens' Stanley Cup run 30 years later—that they hadn't won anything yet. Much hockey remained to be played.

Detroit had beaten the Leafs in five games to set up the rematch hockey fans had wanted. It would be the fourth playoff meeting in five years for the two teams, with Montreal starting out as slight favorites this time around, now that the Rocket was available. Montreal had never beaten Detroit in a final before. Blake expected a "long, tough and tight" series. On the eve of Game 1, Toe welcomed a photographer into the family home. Six-year-old Bruce is seated on his father's lap, his mother, Betty, at their side, looking much older than her 44 years. Mary Jane smiles politely while Joan—also appearing older than her 19 years would suggest—stands behind her parents with a grin. Blake and his family look calm and confident beside the matador lamp that looks on from the side of the picture.

Any calm Blake may have felt had evaporated by the end of the second period of Game 1 at the Forum. Tensions had been high coming into the opener, reverberating among the 13,694 fans prior to the first faceoff. The Red Wings had succeeded in establishing a physical game from the start, going on to score a pair of power-play goals as a result. The physical play came despite defenseman Red Kelly's ineffectiveness, as the powering blueliner wore a face mask to protect his mouth: he had lost three teeth and received 12 stitches after a puck found his face against Toronto. Detroit had led twice before the Canadiens had twice rallied to tie it at 2–2. But the visitors replied with two more goals to go into the final intermission with a small cushion.

Blake hustled his players into the locker room, these grown men on skates prancing on their tiptoes as they rushed to stay ahead of an unhappy man. Blake closed the door behind him and, after a glance around to make sure everyone was in, unleashed on his players. The only result he wanted was a response on the ice. He yelled, pleaded, teased, joked—nothing was off-limits. A man's feelings were inconsequential to the glory of winning. He'd seen little honor through those two periods, no trace of the champion's pride he understood so well. Did they realize that a $500 bonus was awaiting alongside victory? That was a substantial sum, unimagined in his playing days, Blake thought as he curled his lip in anger at the pompous, spoiled display his players had showcased. Alibis and excuses were no good inside these walls he said, pointing the finger at all players, whether English or French, rookie or veteran. Blake berated his team for the entire intermission until it was time to return to the ice.

Blake's talk shook his players, and his subsequent tactical changes led to one of the greatest third-period rallies in playoff history. Blake shifted right-handed shot Claude Provost to the left wing for the first time on a line with his reliable workhorse Floyd Curry and rookie winger Jack Leclair. Leclair, Geoffrion, Beliveau and Provost each tallied in a thrilling comeback, and the Canadiens emerged "from the ashes of tragedy with a ferocious third period assault," in the words of the *Montreal Herald*, to take the series opener 6–4.

"I always wondered, if we had lost that game, whether we would have gone on to win the series," Blake told the *Toronto Star* decades later. "I always think if we'd lost that game, everything might have turned out differently."

The Canadiens took a 2–0 series lead back to Detroit, where Red Wings general manager Jack Adams called out his players' pride and focus, unconcerned about wounding their feelings. "They weren't tired, they just quit hustling," Adams said. "Hockey isn't their main source of income anymore. Some of our guys have lost their desire. I wonder if they will have any pride left. Maybe we will find out tonight."

Far from displaying brittle egos, the Red Wings players responded with a 3–1 victory at the Olympia to get back into the series. The closing scenes of Detroit's 12th straight home playoff win saw Canadiens defenseman Doug Harvey tangle with a Red Wings spectator named Steve Kemeny, who was positioned behind the visitors' bench. Harvey was taken to a police station for allegedly hitting the 37-year-old laboratory technician in the face with his stick, leading to three stitches.

"This guy was abusing me all night, using the type of language that is sometimes scrawled on the walls of men's washrooms. So I told him to sit down and shut up. Then he and his gang wanted to fight," Harvey recounted. "They probably would have had trouble licking a postage stamp, but they might have started a riot."

Inspectors were embarrassed about the warrant, since Harvey was one of several Canadiens players who lent their time to the local March of Dimes campaign conducted by the Detroit police. The bench-side brawl returned some extra tension to a series the Canadiens had been in control of until the unwanted distractions. Blake was keen to reassert control over proceedings. The violent scenes weren't limited to Harvey; a Detroit fan slashed Beliveau across the face with his match program as the players left the ice after Game 3. Beliveau put it behind him quickly: the Canadiens center was "smooth as syrup and just as slippery" with a pair of goals in 3–0 Game 4 victory. Blake's astute line changes provided Beliveau with the right matchup to dominate a game in which he drew applause from the same Detroit fans who just two nights earlier had assaulted him. But the game again descended into chaos after the final buzzer as a melee developed when both teams left their benches, forcing Blake onto the ice to herd his players into the dressing room. The Old Lamplighter was desperate not to rattle the momentum. The rookie coach was looking to lift the Cup on Forum ice and finally cleanse the Canadiens' home of the Richard Riots.

Fittingly, it was the Rocket who ended up with the Stanley Cup clincher in the 3–1 Game 5 victory that kicked off the first of a record five straight Stanley Cup triumphs for the Canadiens. Fans, who had paid $1.75 for tickets, began flooding the ice after the players had shaken hands, while Blake was lifted onto the shoulders of Butch Bouchard and Jack Leclair for a lap of honor. Blake waived his fedora and saluted the crowd, and his grin grew even larger when Bouchard brought him in for a sip of champagne from the Cup. Bouchard had played Game 5 only because Blake sensed the club would close out the series and he wanted his captain—a man who had postponed retirement for one season at Blake's request—to accept the trophy on behalf of the team.

Inside the dressing room, Toe quietly made the rounds, shaking hands and thanking each of his players as champagne corks popped all around him. Mayor Jean Drapeau, accompanied by two policemen, arrived in the dressing room, handing out cigars and announcing the team would be welcomed at the Hélène de Champlain restaurant on St. Helen's Island for a special banquet following the victory parade in a few days. That forced a number of players looking to leave for Florida to stretch their plans. Selke lauded Blake's work in keeping the club focused all season, and Blake admitted afterward that few changes to the roster would be needed the following season.

"Those newspapermen really put a lot of great pressure on the club when they called us to finish in first place—after all, I thought Detroit had won the league last year. They not only picked us to finish first place but to win the Cup," Blake said on the CBC radio airwaves postgame in his distinct voice, which was high in accentuation but not in pitch, akin to a man with a fresh lozenge lodged in his throat. "I thought it put a lot of pressure on the boys, but they came through whenever they had to win an important game. They played well under pressure."

Toe marveled as 250,000 fans lined a 30-mile route through the city for what turned out to be a 6-½-hour parade celebration. It was a season Toe would never forget. The Canadiens felt Blake's mastery had shaped the beginning of what was certain to be a prolonged period of success.

CHAPTER 8

RECORD RUN

SCOTTY BOWMAN STROLLED UP to his usual seat in the reds behind the Montreal Canadiens bench, settling his paper bag lunch containing an egg salad sandwich at his side. Practice was already under way. The future Hall of Famer was coaching a local Junior B team part-time and was eager to watch a professional like Toe Blake in his element. Toe held practice from 10 or 11 a.m. to noon, so Bowman would excuse himself from his daily duties at the Sherwin-Williams paint company on Centre Street at 11 and take the 15-minute bus journey up Atwater Avenue to the Forum for lunch. He enjoyed his meal in the company of Bernard Geoffrion, Jean Beliveau, Dickie Moore, Jacques Plante and Doug Harvey before packing up to catch a bus out to the depot in LaSalle, where his paint inventory work continued.

Blake's practices suited Bowman well—not a long, grinding training sessions but a swift, impactful hour of useful drills meant to replicate game-time situations. The players did a lot of skating, starting right from the warm-up, and followed a regimen that fine-tuned all aspects of the game. Bowman watched as Blake fretted over the little things: where a player positioned himself without the puck; entering the zone smartly so the linesman couldn't whistle offside; working the lanes on the power play. The Old Lamplighter was quick to whistle when he noticed careless or sloppy takes. The fundamentals were crucial, and Blake expected his players to learn them and play their role. But there was also flexibility in his manners. He wanted to tap into a player's skill and help it flourish rather than bend him away from his natural ability for the sake of a system.

"He was an innovator," Bowman says. "He let the players attack. He didn't try to take their individuality away. He was also very firm with how they would play without the puck. He knew the importance of that part of the game. He was firm but very fair with his players. He knew both sides, and there aren't too many players that are like Toe; those kinds of players don't often make coaches. He knew how to get the best of his players. He'd tell me, 'You have to be patient with some of these young players, they are going to make mistakes and you're going to have to get over them.'"

Blake understood the importance of every player. The idea of "fire-wagon hockey"—offensive, attacking hockey in a two-way game—was Blake's mantra. Let those creative players use their individual ability without neglecting defensive commitments while channeling a miner's work ethic. Simple enough, Blake surmised. Find the right role for every player for the benefit of the team, regardless of their star power. Blake's frustrations with Plante's shopping list of medical excuses didn't keep him from using the star goaltender. There was never an inopportune moment to discuss strategy: Blake once, as they made their way through a city in a taxicab, asked defenseman Bob Turner to start killing penalties.

"He knew the value of every player on the team. That was his strong suit," Bowman says. "He stressed little things to me: every player was important, especially if you get in the playoffs, with injuries . . . changes. He was a star player himself. That's why players that weren't stars performed above their ability—he was able to glean that from them."

Bowman watched as Blake implored defensemen Doug Harvey and Tom Johnson to move the attack forward themselves rather than set things in motion from their own zone. Blake pushed Harvey harder than the rest, and the Montreal native ultimately won seven Norris Trophies playing under him. While Harvey confidently set up much of the Canadiens' attacking play, Blake still couldn't help but grind the few real teeth he had left anxiously watching on. To Blake, Harvey's casual demeanor left him feeling like his star defenseman "played the game in a rocking chair." Blake pushed Harvey in practice to keep him fit. Blake was labeled a tyrant by some, but there was no doubting the joy he felt and displayed being on the ice with the players—the boys—and transmitting his knowledge. His respect for the game was instilled in his players, while his love for it provided success and joy. If Bowman was lucky, he might see Blake playing take-away/keep-away with the players once practice had subsided. "We used to tell him 'Hey Toe, you're over the hill,'" said Boom Boom Geoffrion in his autobiography. "'You're finished. What are you trying to do taking the puck away from us?' Then we'd all laugh."

Bowman also observed another particularity of Blake's. "He often kept two players together a lot. You'll see Beliveau and Geoffrion played most of their career on the same line together. He would often add a player here and there. The Richards virtually always played together after Henri broke in. He was pretty big on lines and even more on tandems. If it worked for him, he was going to do it. That's basically the way he coached."

Bowman wished he could listen in as Blake and the Rocket chatted away like old teammates do, both resting on the butt end of their sticks. Blake's arrival had been transformative for Richard and a coup for the Canadiens, who not only got a coach but a psychologist. Following Bouchard's retirement, Blake's first order of business was to put the *C* on the Rocket's No. 9 sweater.

"He was respected by the Rocket," said Stan Fischler. "When Toe goes behind the bench that was good for the Rocket, good for the team. The team gelled behind him. The philosophy was fire-wagon hockey. He let them do their thing. You didn't need any analytics for these guys, they were loaded. He didn't have to do anything special but play the game. He tamed the Rocket."

Blake went into each of his first six seasons in the NHL trying to temper the same overwhelming expectation—that the club would walk away with the NHL championship yet again. He went mad trying to keep his team from believing the hype and to keep them motivated.

"Everyone is conceding us the Cup without a fight. They think we're crazy to play games. We should just go away on holiday and come back for the finals. That's ridiculous. We're bound to lose games. All clubs will be out to give us a battle to enhance their own prestige. It's going to be a long, rugged season. And remember, the Canadiens aren't supermen. They're just good hockey players," Blake told reporters while puffing away on a cigar before the start of his first Cup defense. "I guess it looks that way to everybody but me. But believe me, we can have our troubles, too. There'll be no complacency on this club. Our work is cut out for us."

A rule change related to power plays saw the penalized player return to the ice if the team with the man advantage scored. Designed to slow the Canadiens' potent attack, it hardly succeeded. Geoffrion missed nearly half of the season to injury but returned to enjoy a spectacular playoff as the Canadiens breezed past the Rangers and Bruins in five games each for a second straight Stanley Cup. The team continued to brand itself the class of the league. By the mid-1950s, Montreal—just like the game of hockey—had changed, with the city so clean that it put the Montreal police department's vice squad out of business. The club raised ticket prices by 50 cents, and the Canadian Arena Company issued warnings to season ticket holders that use of foul or indecent language, throwing of objects on the ice or fighting would see their tickets withdrawn.

Every pre-season featured nearly 100 players trying to make the team in camp. To assess the talent, Blake was joined by up to six other individuals, including Selke, Junior Canadiens coach Sam Pollock, Frank Carlin and Montreal Royals coach Elmer Lach. Blake split the teams into four groups—A, B, C and D—to play each other over three weeks for the pre-season title. The results and standings were often printed in the dailies.

The players received $25 per week, free lodging and food at the Queens Hotel. Players could also head out to St. Catherine Street and spend $1.90 for breakfast or $3.90 on a steak, and partake in other distractions. Toe knew the majority of the players stood little chance of making the team. He made it clear that those who were using the tryout as a vacation would be quickly spotted. "I don't want to see any deadwood in training and all of you who don't do your best in practice will quickly be relieved of your services."

There were very few open roster spots because Blake had enormous trust in the players which had succeeded for him thus far. They were his veterans, his guys, and to dislodge them was a difficult task.

"Once you made the team with him, he stuck by you," says defenseman Terry Harper, who played for the Canadiens from 1962 to '72. "He was good to the veterans. If you made errors or something, he'd put you right back out there. He'd say 'These are my guys, they can do it, let's not panic, let's not change things, these guys will do it—they've done it before, and they'll do it again for me.' Once you were on his team you played for him. You would have to die before he would finally change you for someone else. That was a real incentive, it made you want to work harder for him."

Phil Goyette, who made his breakthrough as a rookie with the club during that 1956–57 campaign, said the deep farm system kept players on their toes. "Every game you had to give 120 percent if you wanted to keep your job. You couldn't even trade yourself to anyone after your contract was up—you belonged to them," said Goyette, a smooth-skating center who spent his summers working in a customs broking office which eventually turned into a 43-year full-time job after hockey. "You had to keep yourself motivated if you wanted to stay with Montreal as your team. If you didn't, bye-bye—someone in the farm system would take your place."

If a roster spot opened up, it normally came down to necessity, whether it be because of injury or because a player was losing his legs. Plus, Molson had recently purchased the Canadiens for a reported $5 million and didn't want to lose any of the product's shine. The beer brewer was eyeing TV broadcasts for the first time, and the Rocket's popularity was a driving force behind this decision. The Richards-Moore line was generating so much attention that one paper asked readers to vote on a line name for the trio in the tradition of Richard's famed Punch Line. "Les Rimochards" won the contest, but it never quite caught on. Such was the clamor to see the Rocket that even Prince Philip, Duke of Edinburgh, reportedly enquired about Richard during a visit to Canada with Queen Elizabeth.

But even losing the Rocket to an Achilles injury early on in the 1957–58 season did not slow the Canadiens. The 36-year-old Richard, who had recently scored regular-season goal number 500, would recover in three months from the same injury that had forced Joe DiMaggio from baseball at age 33. Geoffrion, Olmstead and Talbot also suffered major injuries, and Beliveau, Harvey, Richard, Johnson, Plante, Curry, St. Laurent and Turner all missed time. The farm system replenished the lineup when necessary, and Blake still managed to lead the Canadiens to a third straight Prince of Wales Trophy by 19 points. The press threw around words like *dynasty* and *records*, which ate away at Blake.

"No one other than Toe Blake is responsible for the great success of the Canadiens this season. He has a knack for getting the best out of his players always, so I give him all the credit. The Canadiens wouldn't have been as dominant without Blake," said Rangers coach Phil Watson, who earlier in the season had said that without the Rocket, Geoffrion, Olmstead and Talbot, "these jokers are lucky to win."

Blake's working-class approach gave him the ability to understand the psyche of the player and was critical to maintaining stability and success amid injuries, dips in form or off-ice clamoring. During the record five-year run, he never allowed any situation to escalate. At the start of the 1957–58 season, Dickie Moore felt he was hurting Henri Richard's game as he played through a fractured wrist. Moore took the matter to Blake, who called a team meeting during a train ride and left the decision to the players. Moore remained and went on to win his first scoring title that season.

"He's the greatest guy you'd want ever want to meet. He gives you confidence so that you go out there and try things you'd never think of before," Moore told *The Hockey News*. "With him there aren't any stars on the club. In the dressing room, the rookie and the vets get the same treatment. He wants to give everyone a chance to play. Like I've said before, if he had a dog on his team he'd give it a chance."

Blake's experience of molding regular prospects in Houston, Buffalo and Valleyfield into championship teams nurtured the former captain's sense of the collective triumphing over everything. "They didn't come into their real own . . . their peak came after Toe took over," Bowman argues. "He recognized hockey was a team game and you had to rely on all of your players. Good rapport with all his players . . . But what I really learned from him is that your top players have to feel comfortable with the style you are coaching. Do everything in your power to support the stars and back them in any situation. You can't have any controversy with those kinds of players."

Blake earned his players' trust and respect with poignant acts like ordering the trainers to leave an injured player's equipment in their stall with the expectation they would return before season's end. While no player wanted to lose his roster spot to injury, such acts inspired them to return even quicker for their leader, who, stated the newspaper *Samedi-Dimanche*, "was as true as Napoleon."

"He knew how to instill the desire to succeed in the players even when stars were falling to injury every night," wrote Plante in his regular newspaper column. "The club followed the instructions of the coach, who knew what to say at the right moment. I raise my hat to him because I have never seen such a competitive man as Toe Blake." Even with half of the roster left, he never stopped fighting and his desire to win translated to the players. The coach remained confident even when the trainers told him this player or that player was lost for the balance of the season. He never got discouraged."

Apart from the fedora on his head, Toe practically blended in with the players on the bench, sometimes nestling into a spot at the far end. He appeared ready to jump on the ice, his face full of fervor, nervousness and anguish until the red goal light went off and elation won the moment. In those moments, any coach/player boundary was eased, with Blake giving up his coach's crown for that old thrill he longed for as a former player. But it was always only for a moment, as he quickly tightened his tie, returning to his rightful place in the pecking order.

When Blake got upset, he'd chirp "Get mad!" to his players as he paced behind them. His players' ears would perk up as he lapped the area behind them, his head swiveling furiously. "Toe was a man of discipline," said Geoffrion. "He knew how to handle the guys, what to tell the guys, but he never, never pushed anybody to the wall. He would grab a guy and talk to him. I remember him giving hell to Doug Harvey. He didn't give a damn who you were."

"Toe was the boss," said Claude Prevost.

Montreal—already considered one of the global capitals of boxing and wrestling—was padding its reputation as a hockey center as the Canadiens saw off all challengers despite key injury setbacks. With the club sporting its red jerseys on the Forum home ice, Blake matched Toronto Maple Leafs coach Hap Day's record of three straight Stanley Cups, amassed from 1947 to '49, when the Canadiens beat the Boston Bruins in six games in the 1958 final.

But a third straight Stanley Cup as coach seemed to take a toll on Blake. "In my first (season) I felt like a kid with a new toy," he later told *The Hockey News*. "I really enjoyed coaching. It was a wonderful experience. Second year was almost the same. Then it started to get harder. It's pretty hard for me to get myself up for every game. Sometimes this feeling gets me down."

Beliveau's five-year, $100,000 deal had expired in the summer of 1958, leaving the future captain to negotiate a new contract. Blake saw this as an opportunity to remind his charges about staying focused over the summer months after he saw a group of his players at a golf tournament enjoying the fruits of life a little too liberally. He didn't single anyone out but reminded them all that while they were slinging back beers on the softball diamond, training camp was only around the corner. If there was a problem, players remember Blake calling them into his office to get to the root of why they weren't performing, what needed to be fixed and how he could help fix it. So while Blake would slam doors, kick sticks and throw equipment around the locker room, he also understood the pressures of the game and the life of a professional player and could relate.

"One thing I know for sure is that some of my young players are currently letting themselves fall out of shape or taking things too lightly," he told *Parlons Sports*. "If several veterans arrive in camp in poor physical shape they will have problems keeping their spot on the team. It's unfortunate but they have no one to blame but themselves. Of course, I do not want to see this happen but it has in the past and history has a way of repeating itself. If they don't arrive at my training camp in shape, they won't be part of my team next season. The pressure will be even greater on my players. We must win a fourth Stanley Cup—no matter the cost—and I won't be able to accomplish the feat with athletes who come in heavy."

Blake's stress was magnified after Frank Selke called this Stanley Cup–winning group "the best hockey team in the world, the strongest I have had in 12 years at Montreal." Maple Leafs executive King Clancy felt the Canadiens enjoyed "a lock" on a fourth straight Stanley Cup. Blake paid these opinions no credence, remaining focused on his team and what had to be improved. There was no celebrating the Rocket's 600th goal (regular season and playoffs combined) after the Rangers scored three unanswered goals to rally for a 5–3 win in New York.

"In the dressing room afterward, steam was coming out of Blake's ears," Geoffrion recounted. "There was a knock on the big, steel door. Blake opened it and saw two New York reporters standing there waiting to interview Rocket. Toe slammed the door so hard you could hear the reverberations in Montreal. That kind of behavior told me that Blake had become a lot edgier. It was clear the pressure had gotten to him."

Blake's face would turn beet red whenever he was questioned about his tactics; he'd turn to a reporter and stammer, "It's come to this? I have to explain to you the decisions I make?" Add the Rocket's tetchy personality, and strolling into the Canadiens locker room after a defeat was never an easy task for a writer assigned to the team.

Blake even took to holding closed-door "secret" practices to try out new plays and lines in response to defeats. As frustrated as he was, the players were often as disappointed as their coach. Donnie Marshall explained how the Canadiens players felt after losing: "Disgusted with yourself. You don't want to see anyone or talk. You analyze things that caused you to lose. Things you could have done better."

• • •

In mid-January 1959, the city of Montreal was buried in snow after a 42-hour storm. Blake was buried in self-made doubt. His nerves could suddenly come unhinged, win or lose. Toe just couldn't comprehend how a team of such great talent could have an off night. Fresh off a 5–2 win over Toronto, Blake lauded the team's skating and speed but seemed puzzled why such a performance couldn't be repeated. Toronto came out of that defeat in poor standing for the playoff push—seven points behind the fourth-place Rangers, with just five games to play. But Punch Imlach's men still snuck into the postseason. Toronto went on to upset the Bruins in the semifinals to set up a final showdown with the Canadiens, where Imlach predicted the Leafs would win the Stanley Cup in six games. "I won't make any predictions," Blake replied. "We'll play the best we can. Anyway, predictions are for gypsies."

Henri Richard scored 36 seconds into Game 1, and the Canadiens never looked back as they won a fourth straight Cup in five games. "Boston put up a better fight last year," said left winger Dickie Moore, who was celebrating his second straight Art Ross Trophy. Toe was named the series' second star (his team was the first) after clinching the cup in Game 5. The PA announcer said the Toronto Maple Leafs had been picked as third star.

The players paraded Blake around the Forum ice in the annual rite of celebration, snatching his fedora off his head and passing it around. Blake was the first coach in NHL history to win four straight Stanley Cups. He once again uttered his

"I've never been so happy in all of my life" catchphrase after the triumph. Blake's passion for the Cup was clear to all as he bear-hugged the "Stovepipe Cup" with all his might, the hardest embrace he could give anything or anyone.

Suddenly, in 1959, talk of retirement began to surface for the first time. Toe Blake's Tavern—the city's unofficial hockey headquarters—was a success and could use more of his undivided attention. But Blake was no fool. As champagne bottles were uncorked and beer sprayed in the locker room, he was well aware his team had the capacity to win a fifth straight title. He could think back to the 1944 Cup-winning team led by himself, Richard and Lach, the Punch Line: *We had one line that could score. This team has Beliveau, Rocket, Pocket, Moore, Harvey, Boom Boom . . . three lines capable of winning a game.* He knew he'd be a fool to walk away. Toe's biggest problem in his fifth season would be cramming all that talent onto the bench. The legacy he could leave, winning five straight championships, would put his team in another category . . . it would transcend the sport. Everyone knew the New York Yankees team that won five straight World Series titles between 1949 and '53. Bill Russell had just led the Boston Celtics to the first of eight straight NBA titles that same spring. Australia would become synonymous with the Davis Cup after their teams won 15 titles between 1950 and 1967 (but never five straight). Soccer's Real Madrid was on the cusp of a significant five-peat, dispatching the continent's top clubs in the European Cup competition five straight times between 1956 and 1960. Holding this rare opportunity energized the Habs and the entire city, and the Canadiens started the 1959–60 pre-season with a 6–1 All-Star Game victory. "If everyone picks us to win . . . what are we going to do, make liars of them?" Blake said.

Blake's only real headache of his fifth season turned out to be a significant moment in NHL history: Jacques Plante coming out onto the ice wearing a face mask.

Blake hadn't been impressed with Plante's performance in the 1959 final against Toronto. When Plante started showing off his face mask in practice the following season, it rubbed him raw. Plante had received approval from the league office and subsequently did his best to instill the image of a goalie wearing a mask in the public eye by posing for pictures and showing it off to the press at every opportunity. Behind the scenes, Blake was fuming, saying Plante would never wear the mask in an official game. To his coach, Plante already displayed weakness with his litany of medical ailments, and now this would damage the team. It was an unthinkable act to an old-time player.

And yet Blake says he and Ken Reardon were the ones who first gave Plante the idea to don a mask as he recovered from a broken cheekbone. "I had been an umpire in the old Provincial baseball league, you know," he would tell the *Toronto Star* in 1981. "So I brought down my old mask. Kenny and I asked Jacques to wear it in practice."

The real turning point came on November 1 at Madison Square Garden, when Andy Bathgate's backhand struck Plante's upper lip, leaving a trail of blood on the ice as the netminder skated off to receive seven stitches to repair his face. With no backup goalie available in those days and only the house goalie available on loan, Plante knew Blake expected him to return. Although the injury was far from the worst he had played through, he'd swallowed a fair amount of blood. But it mattered little. Toe, who thought his goalie's vision would be compromised with the face shield, was forced to relent when Plante refused to return.

According to sportswriter Red Fisher, Blake asked: "How bad is it?"

"It's sore," said Plante, who was also sporting a five-stitch cut under his chin from a game against Chicago one week earlier.

"Why don't you wear the mask for the rest of the game?" Blake suggested, and Plante returned with the flesh-colored protective shield.

"I don't think I can go back in without it," Plante said.

Plante's performance with a mask in a 3–1 victory left Blake with a sour feeling. Plante didn't wear the mask in the following game but returned with it after that despite Blake's stance against it. The goalie had already won four straight Vezina Trophies without the protection; why did he need it now? By the turn of the new year, Blake was making overtures designed to get Plante to scrap the new equipment, deriding his "loose" goaltending and blaming the mask. Club management even signaled Plante would undergo vision tests so science could confirm his vision was not interfered with.

But Plante's playoff performances swung Blake's opinion enough to accept that the mask was here to stay.

"Blake also has to deal with some of hockey's most accomplished tragedians and most sensitive artists," *The Hockey News* wrote. "He handles them beautifully."

Montreal swept past Chicago and Toronto without a single defeat in eight straight playoff games to clinch a fifth straight Stanley Cup and solidify what remains the NHL's most successful dynasty. Blake took no chances in the series-clinching victory over Chicago, telling reporters he wore the same suit in which he had clinched the Stanley Cup one year prior.

The Canadiens' success led to criticism regarding the champions' stranglehold on hockey's top prize, but league president Clarence Campbell was hearing none of it. "It is the very nature of hockey to run in cycles. I disagree that it is harmful to the league. I believe that it is always a good idea to have a good standard to shoot for. If the Canadiens are that good and everyone is trying to equal them, it is good for the league and the standard of play," Campbell said. "I don't visualize any legislation aimed at curbing Montreal's current supremacy. I think the draft will do the job."

The Canadiens won a fourth straight Prince of Wales Trophy in the 1960–61 season but failed to make it six straight Stanley

Cups. Blake's first losing playoff campaign was, naturally, his most frustrating to date. During the season, Blake admitted the strain of aiming for number six filled him with enough tension that "on days of some games I'm not even human." To relieve the pressure, Toe would send Bruce and Mary Jane to church on Sundays so he and Betty could spend time alone.

"He'd give us money and tell us to stop for cherry Coke and fries, and to take as much time as we wanted," says Bruce. "We'd ask him, 'Why don't you go to church?' 'Well I go when I'm on the road.' 'But you're at home and it's Sunday.' 'Just go,'" Toe would finish, closing the door behind his children to join Betty.

That instant relief from pressure didn't last long. After an early-season 8–4 defeat in Chicago, Blake railed against his players, the referees, his rivals—just about anyone who could have played a part in the humiliation. The players were lackadaisical and complacent, lazy, without fighting spirit. Plante was struggling, and Harvey—who now replaced Maurice Richard as captain after The Rocket retired—was battling injury. The Canadiens were battling with Detroit for first place but seemed to have lost their defensive composure, allowing 3.5 goals per game through the first 16.

"We're just not biting . . . we're not hitting. For that matter, we're not doing a lot of things right defensively," Blake said following a 9–7 win over the Rangers. The defensive woes continued all season long, and at a certain point Blake sounded embarrassed. "My wife has been trying all week to get our set connected to the network," he told *The Hockey News*. "I'm glad she didn't have it done in time to see the game."

"When things weren't going well he'd have us all in the dressing room and start on one corner and go all the way around and tell each of us what we were doing wrong and what we needed to do differently," remembered Donnie Marshall, who watched as Blake no longer had to skip over the Rocket as he had the previous five years with this routine. "When he chewed you out you knew it."

That frustration boiled over into Blake's infamous swing at referee Dalton McArthur in the 2–1 triple overtime loss of Game 3 in Chicago that turned the series. An enthralling game of end-to-end hockey saw goalies Jacques Plante and Glenn Hall combine for 96 saves. McArthur waved away a Donnie Marshall overtime goal because of a borderline high stick. When Chicago scored the power-play winner after a questionable penalty call against Moore, Blake had seen enough. He swatted away restraining hands, swung the gate open from his bench and marched across the littered ice toward McArthur. Up in the stands of the Chicago Stadium, Toe's wife, Betty, wasn't shocked. She knew what was coming as Toe, his fedora cocked at an angle and his face red as ketchup, eyeing McArthur, who was already surrounded by belligerent Canadiens players but still spotted Blake coming his way. Meanwhile, over 800 miles away back in Montreal, Toe's 11-year-old son, Bruce, was puzzled to see his father striding across the ice in the direction of McArthur on the TV. Toe delivered a right-handed swing at McArthur that grazed his shoulder before his players restrained the Old Lamplighter and led him back toward the dressing room.

At 5 p.m. the following day, NHL President Clarence Campbell issued a statement titled "Toe Blake Assault" to journalists who had crowded into his 15-square-foot hotel room. The 25-line communiqué said that with the absence of a bodily injury and considering Blake's exemplary tenure over the previous 20 years as an NHL player and coach, the league president saw no need for a suspension but would fine Blake $2,000—one-ninth of his yearly salary and the largest in league history—with the condition it could not be paid off by the club.

The $2,000 fine was the equivalent of the Ford Monarch that a 35-year-old man named Jean Serge Renaud had stolen from the Blakes on Valentine's Day earlier in the year. Renaud was sentenced to two years in prison, while Blake was told his fine could not be paid with outside assistance. But Toe's standing in the NHL saw him escape any suspension. Surprised by the amount, Blake had little argument: "It's stiff but I won't kick it. A suspension would have hurt me more."

Betty, meanwhile, jumped to her husband's defense. "Toe didn't do it for himself, he did it for the players, who were robbed," Betty said after the game. "Besides, if he hadn't done it, I would have done it myself."

Toe felt Betty might have been more concerned about the fine cutting into a proposed vacation to Mexico, which she had brought up to the attending press on the train ride to Chicago. Mexico "was never really on," said Toe, who at the time had hoped the fine wouldn't be more than $5,000. "She bought a lot of presents here (in Chicago). Now she'll have to take them all back."

"How could you do something like that?" Betty Blake asked her husband, according to Red Fisher. "That was stupid."

"He doesn't allow a goal in the second overtime, and Moore's in the penalty box for what—hooking—when they get their second goal," Blake snapped back. "That's what's stupid."

When Toe walked in the door at the family duplex in Snowdon, near Ponsard Park, the first question Bruce asked was, "What happened, Dad?"

"I accidentally fell into the referee," Toe replied.

"I thought it was a nice way to schlep it off," Bruce says now with a smile. "Most of the time he didn't like to talk about hockey. He liked to keep things separate at home."

Ultimately, it made no difference. While the Canadiens rallied to win Game 4 to even the series at 2–2, the Blackhawks clinched with back-to-back 3–0 shutouts before going on to beat Detroit for their first Stanley Cup since 1938. Blake had clung to the belief his players—such tremendous playoff performers—would come through under pressure as they normally did. Blake continued to believe, even up to the third period of Game 6, with the team trailing by three goals. But it was not to be. Toe pointed no fingers nor played the "prophet of doom," as he had been accused of doing during much of the record run. Even the fans were resigned to this run of success eventually coming to a close, with Blake receiving letters from well-wishers rather than the barrage of criticism he was used to opening.

That would not last.

CHAPTER 9

QUIT, YOU BUM!

"What he loved was to win. Losing was what he hated."

IRONICALLY, HOCKEY WAS ALWAYS taboo inside the Blake home.

Toe and Betty had agreed early in their relationship it was best that hockey talk remain out of family conversations because of Blake's temperament and obsessive competitive streak. Betty never deviated from this agreement, maintaining "religious silence" on the matter. It had been this way since their marriage in 1934, and Toe had no desire to tinker with a winning formula. "A long time ago, Toe made the following recommendation: you take care of the house and kids, Betty; I'll take care of the hockey. I'm happy just to be at the games," Betty Blake said.

When the Canadiens were winning, the Forum was a release for both Toe and his wife. Toe rubbed his temples in apparent pain behind the bench, while Betty anxiously squeezed the purse on her lap or her daughter Joan's arm. From the stands, she acted as a veritable extension of Toe's suffering.

Betty raised the children with the help of a Scottish nanny, Mrs. Salter, who was married to the head bartender at the Tavern. Bruce remembers her as a "phenomenal, wonderful woman" who helped restore some calm and clarity in a home often shaded by the latest result. Mrs. Salter regaled Bruce and Mary Jane with Scottish songs and piano tunes, encouraging the children to join in and sing. Bruce went on to take up the guitar, introducing his father to the sounds of the Beatles and the Rolling Stones in a home that had been dominated by the sounds of Lawrence Welk and Glenn Miller. Toe wasn't a fan of the guitar. The Old Lamplighter associated it with hippies and drugs and used to let Bruce hear it whenever he noticed his son's hair reaching his ears. "Look at him, he's a Beatle," Toe would comment. Toe used to get a kick out of wearing pillows over his ears whenever he walked into a room where Bruce and his gang were strumming away. Toe wasn't musically inclined, and his library was a throwback to his Great Depression youth. But it wasn't all just noise to him—he could still recognize a good song when he heard one. "That sounds pretty good, you guys," Toe said of a particular Bob Dylan tune. And if one of those songs kickstarted a winning streak, you bet Toe asked Bruce to keep on practicing it.

Superstition took up a surprising amount of shelf space in Toe's books. If a player had touched Toe's fedora before the game and they won, he would demand that the player keep up the ritual. While Betty enjoyed wearing a mink coat to the games at the Forum, underneath it could be the same dress night after night, for as long as a winning streak stretched. Betty was found frantically searching grocery stores for specific mushrooms to accompany Toe's steak if her own grocer had run out. When the Canadiens played at home, Betty and Joan would often go to the games at the Forum, while Bruce and Mary Jane were normally able to join for the Saturday night game if a family member wasn't in town and using Toe's personally paid season tickets.

"We'd go to games in the '60s, and I'll always remember watching Toe: the fedora, the chewing gum, the pacing behind the bench. Intense and involved. It was an education," niece Margaret McKie remembers. "But he was much more relaxed outside of that sphere. Much more relaxed with the family."

Stephanie Blake remembers moving to Montreal at 16, working downtown in Karen's Flower Shop in the CIBA building on McGill College Avenue. The shop closed once construction of Place Ville Marie got under way, but she was able to get a job at McKenna's on Côte-des-Neiges Road because she was Toe's niece.

"The whole city was enamored with Toe—he was a celebrity," Stephanie recalls about a man who always picked up the cheque—except on Christmas day. "Toe took the whole family to Desjardins Seafood House. We were treated like royalty. No hesitation with him—if he wanted to do it, he did it. Toe would leave tickets at the Forum box office for when mom and dad came to town. I wanted a mink coat so badly—everyone got all dressed up to go to the Forum! Men wore suits, women in coats and gloves and hats, it was like going out to the theater. Every time I had a new boyfriend, I would phone Toe and ask him if he could get me tickets to the game. And he would!"

Toe's generosity extended to road trips—especially in Toronto, where both sides of the family would make the journey to catch the Canadiens' visit. Toe would make the time before the game to meet family underneath the Gardens clock to dispense tickets and, in return, rid his mind of a million questions for a time. If his schedule permitted, he'd stay for a longer visit, especially if it meant seeing one of his siblings, who loved to tease Toe at every opportunity. Blake hated waiting around with family and friends in front of the dressing room door; he was shy and did not relish wading through the waiting crowds. The narrow corridor outside the team locker room was filled with well-wishers and autograph seekers mingled with hockey wives waiting for their husbands. There, the latest rumors and gossip were bantered about. While Toe normally rushed from these scenes, one particular night in Toronto one of Toe's brothers was at the game—unbeknownst to Toe—and he presented his program for an autograph. Toe did not look up, so the brother presented a little hockey stick, and still Toe did not look up. When his brother took off his hat and asked Toe to sign the inside band, Blake finally looked up and they shared a good laugh. While the team was on the road, Betty found time to organize clippings related to Toe's successes she was collecting from the newspapers. "At first Toe found it a silly idea, but I know he enjoys leafing through them now," Betty said of the various collections she had started cobbling together around the time of Toe's second Stanley Cup win.

"Betty was amazing," remembers her niece Margaret McKie. "She had a great sense of humor; she was very nurturing. She sang in the choir at church and she was quite a singer." Toe's wife provided moral support, but it was often in private, away from the children. And most notably after defeat.

"Betty was very loving, sweet and kind. My mom and her were extremely close," says granddaughter Judy McDonald. "She was probably the rock that calmed him down."

"She treated him like gold," Bruce says.

"She's the only one who would ever put up with my shit—I'll never find another one like that," Toe would say.

When Toe would grumble about things, she was the only one able to reason with him, saying, "Knock it off, Duck" (the affectionate nickname only Betty used with him). If anyone else attempted to ask Toe to cool down, he'd normally reply, "Don't tell me what to do."

Bruce admitted living with Toe was a little suffocating. Toe earned his grouchy nickname "the Bear" rather easily. "He didn't talk very much about his upbringing or parents. We heard early,

'Don't even ask,' because he didn't want to talk about them. When I asked, he would ignore me or give me some trivial statement like 'You wanna work hard; he was a hard worker,' and just blow it off. You weren't going to get any information from him, so you didn't bother because you also didn't want to change his mood or cross him. His discipline was strict, that was his style, the old style."

Bruce had the luxury of a lookout in Mrs. Salter, who would warn the youngster about the Bear's movements. "She would look out the window around 4 p.m., when Dad was getting home, and say, 'Mind yourself, you little shit—the big shit's home.'"

Toe's purposely insular personality inside the family home was strikingly different from his predecessor Dick Irvin's, despite the two coaches' outwardly similar approaches to the game. Both brooded over defeats for days, to the detriments of their families—Dick Jr. remembered one Christmas ruined for the family because of a defeat. But Irvin was always keen to speak with his brood about the sport that consumed his life. "The last night of his life we talked about hockey. He was laid out in one of those hospital beds—we had it in the house—and he couldn't move, but we talked hockey. I had questions for him which he loved for me to ask," Dick Irvin Jr. recalled. "Hockey in the house right to the end—it was what he loved to do.

"I was a bloody nuisance when I was studying at McGill University—I wanted to hang out with my dad. Any chance I got I went to the dressing room, go to the practices, go to the games, I'd go down to pick up my dad to take him home after the game. I'm sure I drove my father crazy with the questions—but he wanted to answer them. I don't think half the players knew if Toe had a family. He never said very much to anybody."

The end of the record run provided Toe with a new reality check—one he was struggling to balance off-ice. After 1961, the Canadiens were no longer viewed with the same awe that had accompanied the run of five Cups. The Rocket was gone, and Chicago had exposed Montreal's physical limitations. As the new decade began, the rest of the league found belief: the Canadiens were beatable.

This ate at Blake. He had but one objective: to win back the *other* love of his life—after Betty, of course—the Stanley Cup. Toe beamed with pride when the club won the Prince of Wales Trophy for a sixth time in seven years in 1962, showing a commitment to returning to their winning ways. But the strain remained. Behind the bench, he could regularly be seen stewing, cursing to no one or grabbing his hat and trying to pull his head right through it. That behavior seemed to translate into his daily battles with the press, who he felt he needed to beat back at every opportunity, especially with reports of retirement continually resurfacing.

Toe was bewildered when asked if he would rest any players before the start of the 1961–62 playoffs and the first-round rematch with the Blackhawks. It sounded like a great excuse, perfectly engineered to breed failure. Toe was tired of these questions, and suddenly felt he was the one who deserved a break. "If you work 10 or 12 hours a day down in a mine, you might need a rest to keep you healthy. But well-conditioned hockey players who play only 20 minutes a game don't need time off unless they're injured," he said. "That's a load of baloney. I'm convinced after listening to all the newspapermen, the only one who needs a rest is the coach."

Excuses were like spoiled milk to Blake. The thought of a team of "happy losers" milling around the dressing room, trading barbs after a defeat, was the stuff of his nightmares.

"That was a steady expression from Blake and other coaches of the time. It made it very difficult to interview guys after a loss," said former *Hockey News* reporter Gil Smith, who covered the Canadiens for much of Blake's coaching career. "That attitude was prevalent and anyone who was a happy loser would not be around long."

Blake would not be plagued by playoff anxieties for long that spring, as the Blackhawks again bounced the Canadiens—despite having finished 23 points behind them in the standings. Seven Montreal players had scored 20 or more goals during the regular season, but only Dickie Moore had managed to notch more than two goals in the series. Blake was exasperated by the collapse. "I'm terribly disappointed. Despite all of our injuries, I never thought for a minute that we would lose in the playoffs. We suffered a letdown at the wrong time. This time, even if it hurts, I have to admit that Chicago was the better team . . . We just fell apart in the playoffs.

"It has been my hardest year as coach, my most disappointing year. But I'm not giving up," said Blake, who spurned a three-year extension to remain as coach on a one-year contract. "The way I look at it is that if I can't win with this team, then I don't deserve to earn more than I'm being paid by the Canadiens."

The entire Blake household could finally exhale. While it wasn't gratifying to close on a losing note, the end of the season would relieve the tension that permeated their home throughout the spring. Yet the tension was a little more significant that season—the family learned 16-year-old Mary Jane was pregnant. Toe and Betty seemed to take the news in stride, however, pledging to support their daughter as she prepared to marry the father-to-be, Roddy Stuart. Despite her mischievous personality, Mary Jane was Toe's favorite, and now that his teenage daughter was about to become a mother, he became even more protective of her. "Mom always told me that if anyone ever asked, tell them that she was 17," Bruce remembers.

Despite the household drama, summer provided relief. It was the only time of year when Toe could truly unwind. There was summer baseball, and softball leagues with his old pals Murph Chamberlain and Bill Durnan on a team managed by future Habs general manager Sam Pollock. He seemed to disregard all his worries at the family's cabin in Venise, Quebec,

Toe, surrounded by Canadiens players, signing the register at Quebec's National Assembly in the early Sixties.

In the locker room, Toe goes over tactics with forwards Dickie Moore (left) and Jean Beliveau.

Toe has a word with goaltender Cesare Maniago during the 1962-63 season.

Toe was at home behind the bench of the Montreal Forum, where he also guided the Canadiens to nine Prince of Wales Trophies as the NHL's top team.

Toe (front row, fifth from right) and one of the Habs teams from the mid-Sixties.

Toe and his son Bruce at a social function late in his coaching career.

Toe receives a birthday cake from Montreal Canadiens General Manager Sam Pollock as owner David Molson (third from left) joins in the celebration.

Toe with Montreal Canadiens owner David Molson.

Toe and Betty pose for a photograph at the Blake residence on Sheraton Drive before heading out for the evening.

The stress of maintaining the Canadiens yearly Stanley Cup expectations coupled with his wife Betty's battle with cancer took a toll on Toe in his later coaching years.

Montreal Canadiens coach Toe Blake laces on the skates for a Quebec old-timers game.

Toe Blake's final NHL game came as coach of the 1969 Eastern Division All-Stars.

Toe enjoyed golf in the summer months after retiring as coach of the Canadiens.

Toe mingles at a Hockey Hall of Fame Induction Dinner in 1972, with Albert Allmark on right.

Toe is joined by his son Bruce, daughters Mary Jane (with two of her children), and Joan (right) on the Forum ice for Toe Blake Night in December, 1972.

Bruce Blake and Henri Richard look on as Toe addresses the Montreal Forum crowd on Toe Blake Night.

Toe receives a small Stanley Cup replica from Jean Beliveau on Toe Blake Night as Elmer Lach (left of Toe) and Butch Bouchard (left of Lach) look on.

Canadian Prime Minister Pierre Elliott Trudeau and his wife Margaret (far right) congratulate Toe upon being appointed to the Order of Canada in 1982.

Toe Blake poses for a portrait after being appointed to the Order of Canada in 1982.

Toe Blake and Al Arbour are honoured with an 'Appreciation Night' held on July 21, 1983, at the President Motor Hotel in Sudbury.

Toe loved nights like these, slotting in with former Canadiens players like himself to pay tribute to the club's proud history.

Toe at his desk inside his office at the Toe Blake Tavern prior to its closing in November, 1983.

Toe enjoys a beer with daughter Joan at the tavern — which enjoyed a male-only policy — prior to its closing.

Toe soaking up one final drink at the tavern prior to its closing after 31 years of business.

Toe Blake is escorted to center ice at the Montreal Forum as Bob Gainey looks on from Canadiens bench.

Toe, in his later years, enjoying a sunny, summer afternoon at his son Bruce's home in the Laurentians.

As coach, Toe Blake won eight Stanley Cups in 13 seasons with the Canadiens, including an NHL record five-straight from 1956-61.

on the shores of Missisquoi Bay. It was a place where Toe could find solitude in a space with those he trusted. There was no telephone at the cabin, and no one could bug him, as he put it. Blake would make the 56-mile drive to the summer home on Wednesday evening and stay the night, before returning to Montreal to do it all over again come the weekend. He never took more than two weeks off because of the tavern. And even in brief-vacation mode, one look at Blake and there was no doubt he was a product of his upbringing.

"Ninety-nine percent of the time he'd be dressed in a button-up shirt, dress pants, with a coat at hand if needed. He'd wear his suit for the drive to and from the cottage and wear a less formal button-up shirt at the cottage," Mary Jane's son Kenny Stuart recalls, immediately debunking the myth of the city slicker loosening his tie and unbuttoning his top button with work done. In fact, Blake always maintained appearances, whether he was attending a banquet, visiting a friend or dropping in on family.

"He was always in a suit and tie. He'd come up to our house in the country for the weekend and he was in a suit, shirt and tie," Bruce says. "They didn't have much money growing up, and they might not have had nice clothes, so he dressed well.

"He survived growing up in a family of 11 . . . perhaps why he was so hard. We had hardwood floors on Ponsard, and he always had these big heavy shoes on, and you could hear him walking throughout the house. He'd always say in his family the first one up gets the shoes. It might have been a joke but there was probably truth to that, too. That stuck with him, he'd always have his shoes on. I'd look at other friends' fathers and think 'You get home, take your shoes off.'"

"I don't remember ever seeing him reach down to put his shoes on or to take them off, he wore them all the time, even at my mom's during Sunday dinners," remembers Kenny Stuart, who will never forget the smell of the cigar that stuck like a cologne to the grandfather they called "Popeye." "He almost always had a cigar in hand. I remember driving to the cottage with him, he'd be puffing away on this big stogie with the windows rolled all the way up and the air-conditioning on."

But if you were a woman, you better not even dare ask Popeye for a puff of his Peg Top. "He certainly didn't like seeing women smoke," Kenny recalls. "'What are you doing!?' he would yell. 'That's not a ladylike thing to do.'"

While cigar smoke seemed to follow Popeye, so did cards and booze—especially at the cabin. Saturday morning would start with a Bloody Mary before horseshoes and time on the beach. Toe eventually bought a boat and would take his children and, later, grandchildren waterskiing. But being cut-off from the outside could backfire—guests would sometimes arrive unannounced. With no telephone to serve as a warning, his older brother Leonard would pull into the driveway with his wife, Irene, and six children spilling from the station wagon, to the ire of Betty. "My mother would go absolutely nuts," Bruce remembers. "Until one point she said, 'They come, I leave.' But that's the way he wanted it. No phone, so you can't bother him. Total privacy."

Betty did enjoy the company of Toe's older brother Tom and his wife, Isabel, and their family, as well as visits from her own family, where the endearment was always mutual.

When the Blake brothers did unite, it often led to eventful reunions. "They weren't drunks, but they were *happy*," Stephanie Blake says. "They would all fall asleep from the drinking. But they worked hard so they were tired, and the alcohol probably didn't help."

"One Sunday afternoon in the summer, we dropped in on Toe's cottage for a visit. There was Blake, Bill Durnan, Murph Chamberlain, and all of them were half in the bag," Dick Irvin Jr. remembered. "When we had our housewarming party in 1952, all the guys were there, enjoying the party. My dad never had a drink or a smoke in his life. Yet the guys he became friendly with on the team were all the guys who drank. Blake, Durnan and Chamberlain. I could never figure that out. Anytime he would get together with the boys, those were the guys he seemed to drift to and get together with. They really respected each other."

Toe did cut loose, a little, at the lake. His great sense of humor would emerge after a day with the kids; taking them for ice cream after spending the day horsing around on the beach brought him joy. He could sit in the lawn chair outside for hours, as long as there was a card game going and a gin and tonic or Manhattan in his hand. A startled Bruce and cousin Margaret would sometimes be shaken from their work of setting up camping gear by the former miner's enormous hand slamming down on the table in frustration. But there was none of the fury, cursing or rage he displayed with the newspapermen he played hearts, crib or gin rummy against during those 20-hour train rides to Chicago. On the banks of Missisquoi Bay, he rarely got agitated. "He knew he had another hand coming," Bruce says.

Despite the recent postseason failures, Toe had guided his beloved Canadiens to five straight Stanley Cups while also operating a successful tavern in downtown Montreal. He was the father of three healthy children and was married to a wife who was devoted to him and his every need. But all of that would seemingly matter less and less as Labor Day weekend rolled around and a new season was on the horizon.

Toe was eager for training camp to begin prior to the 1962–63 season. There was no room for letting up, and when a player did, Blake let him know about it. If a veteran did not arrive at camp in shape, Blake was going to make sure he finished it in peak condition. Ticket prices had gone up to $4.50—still the league's cheapest—and the city's fan base was beginning to become restless after another season without the Cup.

As the new season progressed, Toe grew infuriated as his mind zeroed in on the team's faults. How could a player use fatigue from a 20-hour train trip as an excuse when his body had been making that same exact trip for years? While other teams had begun flying between cities, Blake kept the team moving on the rails. When the team won, he could settle into his berth and play cards, do the crossword, read the dailies. When they lost or were dealing with injuries, he shuttered himself in to ponder the necessary changes. The fear that the players he put so much trust in were running out of steam was only compounded by a third-place finish. It was the worst season of Blake's coaching career. Imlach's Maple Leafs dispatched the Canadiens in five games—the club's worst playoff performance under Blake. His players were infuriating him. Plante had lambasted his teammates after a 3–1 defeat in Game 1, ticking off the teammates, coach and upper management.

Blake loved Plante the goaltender—"the best I ever saw"—but couldn't stand the person. Plante was full of surprises: he'd arrive on game day and say he couldn't play because of his asthma. The goalie even managed to have Blake change hotels for him in Toronto, moving him from the Royal York to the Westbury when Plante said the Royal York's bedsheets caused his asthma to act up. But then Toe ran into him later—with a girl on each arm. Plante told Toe they were his cousins—"I've got cousins in every city," said Plante, whose position was secure because backup Cesare Maniago was not a suitable number one shot stopper. "Sure they are," said Blake, who then promptly moved Plante back to the Royal York.

"That son of a bitch is driving me nuts. I never can be sure when he's playing, but he always ends up playing," Blake once said. "I don't know how much more of this I can take."

Geoffrion was also threatening the balance of the dressing room by kicking up a fuss when his teammates preferred Beliveau to him as captain. Blake was forced to intercede, taking the matter to Selke, but also letting Boom Boom know exactly where he stood as he manufactured friction in the team.

"What's Geoffrion ever done for us in the playoffs?" asked

Blake, who would move on from Geoffrion after the 1963–64 season, when the Hall of Fame forward missed a pregame team meal.

The players Blake believed in were becoming greedy, and his team looked soft. His passion for physical, fast-paced hockey was not translating to his men. *If I were playing today, I would clean up, score so many goals, the way the defenseman let players walk into their zone,* he thought. "What these guys need is a lot of prayers and a change in attitude," Blake told reporters after the Game 5 loss to Toronto, alluding to a newfound defeatist attitude.

"The team wasn't physical enough. How can you be out on the ice for 60 minutes and not hit anybody?" he reportedly mumbled to J.C. Tremblay. "There are some players on this team who haven't hit anyone in years." Rugged players like Al MacNeil, Lou Fontinato and Jean Gauthier had left the team—and had taken a big chunk of the Habs' most physical play with them. Blake was not religious, but if there were hockey gods, he was asking them to restore the team's play to a few years prior, when the boys he had relied on every night were in their prime. Blake remembered how his old coach Dick Irvin had told him when he turned 30 that he would have to drive harder just to break even. It sounded silly at the time, but now Toe saw how right he had been.

The fun never really seemed to return for Toe. It had been three seasons since he had drunk champagne from the Cup or invited his boys to the tavern for a celebratory beer. "I want to live the way Toe Blake used to live," he said. The realization of how good he had had it and how arduous the road to achieving success was now becoming clear. If the players' attitude wasn't right, was he no longer able to reach them? The game was changing—times were changing. Players were investing more of their time in developing off-ice professions for when their playing days ended. Dickie Moore had started renting construction equipment and owned a number of Dairy Queen franchises.

Geoffrion owned restaurants. Donnie Marshall had gas stations in his portfolio.

Blake, whose sole focus since the age of 12 had been hockey, knew when a coach could "no longer motivate his players, it means he's done."

• • •

The summer of 1963 wasn't the first off-season where reports of retirement swirled around Toe, but it was the first time Blake seriously considered it. Despite the nosedive, peers such as Rudy Pilous of Chicago and Milt Schmidt of Boston continued to commend Blake's work. But changes were necessary. Blake felt it, and Selke acted on it with a blockbuster seven-player trade in June 1963. Selke sent Jacques Plante, Donnie Marshall and Phil Goyette to the New York Rangers for Lorne "Gump" Worsley, Dave Balon, Leon Rochefort and Len Ronson. The trade left Canadiens fans and Plante alike stunned, considering the six-time Vezina Trophy winner was thought to be untouchable. The trade was as shocking to Worsley, who wasn't completely convinced even after a neighbor repeated the news to him three times.

"Why the hell would I believe him?" Worsley said from the backyard of his Montreal home, where he sat in the summer sun, nursing a hangover. Worsley was already so discouraged from playing under Phil Watson that he had taken to challenging the coach's authority by drinking right after practice at the 322 Club, which sat directly across the street from the old Garden on 49th Street. So Gump was happy to go home to his native Montreal. He was a product of Pointe-Saint-Charles, a working-class area focused around the CN rail yards where it was not uncommon to receive a lighter for your 16th birthday. He was quick to reply "the Rangers" when asked which team had given him the most trouble in goal. Montreal fans were skeptical, however, with Beliveau coming off his worst season as a professional. Even the Canadiens captain joined his coach in spreading rumors of retirement.

"When the team gathered at training camp all that was left of the old, victorious outfit was a fat book of memories, a couple of has-beens, a flock of untested rookies, and some nondescript players acquired from New York," reported *Sports Illustrated.*

The newspapers picked Montreal to squeeze into the playoffs by finishing fourth. Imlach predicted Montreal would finish out of the playoff. "Why don't you quit, you bum?" one fan wrote to Blake.

"What's Wrong with the Canadiens?" *Sport* magazine decried. "Without the Rocket, Plante, Moore, Harvey, Montreal's hockey dynasty is decaying."

"I promise you this," Blake told *Le Soleil* newspaper. "When the hockey season comes around, expect me to be as hard on the players as I possibly can. They won't be dancing waltzes during practices anymore."

Gump pulled a hamstring early in the season to leave 5-foot-6 Lachine native Charlie Hodge—"the most nervous kid in hockey," as described in *Thunder and Lightning*, a biography of the Canadiens written by John Ferguson—as the number one goalie. Gump would even be put on waivers and made available to any team for $20,000 the following off-season. No suitors took a chance on the 35-year-old.

Following training camp, Blake told reporters he expected his team to challenge for the Prince of Wales Trophy. The addition of a few rookies would push the experienced players. Terry Harper and Claude Larose provided a physical element, while Jacques Laperriere would go on to win rookie of the year. But most notably, the addition of Ferguson had provided Toe with the exact invigoration he was looking for—on and off the ice. Blake had personally scouted Ferguson. He was the prototype player, a man who hated to lose just as much as Blake did. Seeing teammates chatting with an opponent at center ice in the warm-up provoked Ferguson to fire pucks at them in disgust. Blake paired Ferguson with Beliveau and Geoffrion after Toronto had manhandled his group in the playoffs.

Ferguson repaid Blake's faith just eight seconds into his debut at the Boston Garden by taking on notorious brawler Ted Green. Ferguson also finished his debut with two goals. Beliveau, who had arrived in camp in better shape, rolled back the years some with his inspired play. Balon proved to be an aggressive force and utility player, plugging in to kill penalties and fill in for injured players. Harper and Laperriere anchored a bullish defense that leaned on opponents without needing to come to fisticuffs.

The smile began to return to Toe's face as he watched his men hit each other in practice. Sometimes they even fought. But none of it carried over into the dressing room. Blake was beaming when Geoffrion blasted a slap shot past Plante in the Habs' first post-trade meeting with New York, after his former goalie had said the Canadiens were coming apart at the seams.

By Christmas, the team was as high as second in the standings.

Still, Toe fretted.

• • •

Bruce's teenage years were marked by wonder: What particular play or result was Toe worrying about today? Bruce could only guess through what he overheard his mother or sisters murmur, or what the kids at school and the skating rink said after reading the papers. The frustration was obvious when Toe accompanied him to Bruce's own hockey games. Toe was swamped by the goodwill of children and parents who greeted him with smiles as he settled in to watch his son's peewee team play. But when one father of a larger boy yelled at his son to "Hit 'im! Kill 'im!" with Bruce in his sights, Toe politely leaned over to the vocalist and affirmed with the shake of a fist: "He hits him, I hit you." Toe had already let his guard down with Mary Jane; he wasn't going to allow it with Bruce now.

That attitude carried over into the Canadiens dressing room and onto favorite whipping boys such as John Ferguson, Red Berenson, Jean-Guy Talbot and Ralph Backstrom. Ferguson could withstand it, and Blake knew he could take it. Berenson, meanwhile, was a college kid wearing a helmet—both sour points in Blake's books.

"When I came out of college, I think Toe looked at me sideways," Berenson says. "I don't think we ever hit it off until I had my coaching career. It wasn't a bad relationship; it was just we didn't have a relationship. If you were one of his best players, you loved him, and if you weren't, you didn't."

Berenson wasn't sure Blake's intended message always got through to his players, even if they provided results. "He was an old-school coach who didn't provide a lot of dialogue to the younger guys. You just did what you were told, and you better listen," Berenson says. "You had to do everything you could to play and just to dress. There was a lot of pressure on the fringe players like me—if you played, you had to play well. But we all wanted to play. No question he knew what he was getting from the older players, so he trusted them. I was just thrilled to be there. I had a lot of respect for the organization."

The players often bet who would be Toe's target for the night, with practical joker Backstrom emerging as a top candidate and sometimes touching a nerve with his criticism. Once, after Blake had left the room with a slam of the door, a furious Backstrom grabbed a skate and harpooned it toward the exit. The blade stuck, and the skate dangled from the door frame. Blake stopped in his tracks when he heard the thud, a smile spreading across his cheeks before he carried on in stride.

Blake was happiest when his players were angry—there was no risk of complacency creeping into the team. When Backstrom was handing out cigars in celebration of the birth of his daughter

Diana, Blake chimed in, "Maybe now you'll get off your ass and play hockey." Not even Jean Beliveau was spared. Blake once left Beliveau, who was returning from a hand injury, on the bench, to send a message and challenge the lethargy he thought had taken hold of his team. That Beliveau hadn't been able to overcome the pain of injury was unacceptable. As the all-time great sat, Blake heard it from the Forum crowd and Senator Hartland Molson, seated right behind him. Blake could cross the line, but it derived the desired results. He'd even once criticized Beliveau—much to the player's chagrin—about celebrating a hat trick when the Canadiens captain should have scored six or seven goals. "But this is one of the reasons why the players admire him," *Le Soleil* wrote. "Defeat weighs heavily on the shoulders, which makes it necessary to chase by any means necessary."

And he was forgiving in other ways, never checking on players for curfews, instead leaving those duties to his captain Beliveau, who led by example and made Toe's job easier. Toe had just one rule: never drink a beer in the hotel where you are staying. He would buy cases of beer to bring on the train instead. The spirit inside the club improved tremendously, with the family-feeling Blake longed to create finally settling in due to the influence of Beliveau, Backstrom, Laperriere and Ferguson. Ferguson recalled one dinner when players suggested No. 6—Backstrom's number—should pay the bill at a banquet the team was attending. Backstrom was quick to point out that the player who wore it before him should pay—the absent Floyd Curry. Blake joined in the fun to suggest whoever wore it before Floyd should be on the hook, which was ultimately himself. Backstrom responded: "Before you they used Roman numerals."

"You look forward to going to the rink, eh? You like the way the guys hang together. I mean, you don't hear guys bitchin' at guys in the dressing room. The big stars are all part the team, you understand me? Like Jean Beliveau, there's a big man, eh?" said Worsley, who pronounced Beliveau's first name as *John,* in an interview with *Maclean's* magazine. "When we're on the road Jean says 'let's all go,' and he means it that everybody goes out some place together after the game. It's en masse. Not the big stars in their clique, and the lesser lights to find their own way; it's everybody."

The new energy inside the team was undeniable, and by February the Canadiens had tied the Chicago Blackhawks for first place. Montreal fans were buzzing, supporting this mix of veterans and youngsters wholeheartedly. The Habs beat the New York Rangers at Madison Square Garden on the final day of the season to win the Prince of Wales Trophy by a single point. Beliveau won the Hart Trophy, Hodge the Vezina and Laperriere the Calder. Blake was named coach of the year by *Associated Press* and *The Hockey News*. But the accolades did not intimidate "Punch" Imlach and the Leafs.

• • •

Imlach and Blake enjoyed a respectful but feud-filled rivalry. Their personas and personalities were very different, but there was one quality they shared: contempt for losing, especially to one another. They had first met when Blake was coaching at Valleyfield and Imlach managed a Quebec Aces team led by Beliveau. Blake enjoyed a slight edge in their head-to-head matchups, with the Canadiens winning four of the seven playoff series between the teams. When Imlach took over the Leafs in 1958, Blake already had three Cups to gloat about. That didn't stop Imlach from predicting victory in the 1958–59 final, which the Leafs ultimately went on to lose to the Canadiens in five games.

Punch loved to make predictions, to call the Canadiens overrated and to talk up his own exploits. Blake snapped back with pokes at Punch's boring and unimaginative playing style, including defensive zone traps that, he told *Samedi-Dimanche*, "chased everyone from the Quebec Colisée." Punch would often single out players and personalities in a bid to unhinge Blake's locker room, including teasing the idea of signing Beliveau away to play in Toronto. "Imlach was nasty in his own way—he had a way of getting under Toe's skin, it cut through him," Stan Fischler says. "He was much better with words, a better wise guy."

"Imlach reminds me of the guy who goes to the race track and buys every combination on the daily double," Blake once said of his rival. "Then, after the results are in, he sneaks away into a corner, tears up all his losing tickets and rushes back waving the winning ticket." One newspaper said the pair were ready "to bury the hatchet—but only in each other's head."

Imlach's bid to unsettle the Canadiens with his playoff prediction in 1958 was the root of their discord, with the Leafs coach going on to suggest the Canadiens would struggle during the season. "Normally, I wouldn't bother with Blake. But sometimes he irritates me. He's the world worst front-runner," said Imlach, who took satisfaction in goading Blake.

Ahead of his own 1960 Stanley Cup loss, Imlach said, "Each spring (Blake's) depressed by the approach of the inevitable. The longer he coaches that silver-plated length of stovepipe, the closer comes the day when he must give it up. And so, he nurses his misery from April to April. Two score years from now, Blake will be a wreck. You can picture the man tottering toward the old age pension payoff window with that unsightly chunk of metal strapped to his back."

Imlach seemed clearly frustrated at Blake's treasure trove of players and the Canadiens' supremacy during the late 1950s. But their predicament was similar, with both coaches feeling the strain of anxiety and needing annual health checks by club physicians to ensure they were fit to continue coaching. Imlach even missed several months due to exhaustion.

Their professional tactics differed, however. Imlach tried to motivate his players with money, literally throwing it on the dressing room floor before a playoff series victory over Chicago. Blake responded to Imlach's jabs by pointing to his team's successes. "It wouldn't work for me . . ." Blake told *The Hockey News*. "Our guys don't need money any more. What I might do is try throwing the Stanley Cup on the floor. All we want is the Cup."

Despite their public feuding, inside the Canadiens dressing room Blake rarely referred to Punch by name. "I always thought Toe was a way better coach than Punch," Terry Harper says. "Punch seemed erratic as hell. He wasn't a guy who really stood up for his guys like Toe did. That's why I thought we'd beat them. Talk about Punch? He did not. He talked about their players . . . It was all about Mahovlich, Horton, Stanley . . ."

As the 1960s progressed, Imlach could sense his Leafs were catching the Canadiens. With the Rocket, Plante and Harvey gone, the Canadiens' aura of invincibility had faded, and Imlach implored his players to take advantage of a rival that was "done."

Imlach started his mind games immediately to begin the 1963–64 season, suggesting the Canadiens would not even clinch a playoff position. But instead the Canadiens won the league to set up a playoff rematch with the Maple Leafs. Imlach sequestered his team in the Detroit suburb of Dearborn and put them through intense, full-blown physical practices, with Leafs goalie Johnny Bower forbidden his usual time to sneak in cheeky drags of a cigarette from the bench. Blake put his players through light practices in Saint-Jérôme, 45 minutes north of Montreal, amid the posh surroundings of the Alpine Inn, where curling was offered as a distraction. "Take it easy, will you. Let's all relax. The program is to take it easy," Blake told reporters while puffing away on a cigar. "We're going into this series in a much better frame of mind. We're up for this series but it will be tough."

Both coaches employed strategic changes in the way they approached another showdown: Blake mellowed and Imlach shut up. "If I talk, I get into trouble. And if I don't talk, I get into trouble. So what's the use?" Imlach said.

An aggressive series saw the teams split the first two games at the Forum. Montreal lost Beliveau to a knee injury in Game 3, but the Canadiens managed to overcome the setback and move within one victory of returning to a Stanley Cup Final for the first time since 1960. Imlach had employed some unorthodox methods to rally his troops during the series—watching the film *One Man's Way*, about the life of Dr. Norman Vincent Peale, an American minister who was known for popularizing the power of positive thinking; Imlach had given each player a copy of Peale's book after learning Montreal's Bobby Rousseau had read it before scoring five goals in one game. After the Leafs tied the series at 3–3, Blake was diplomatic about his team's chances, while Imlach pronounced his team was "going to win a hockey game."

And they did, finishing off this angry series and silencing 14,541 spectators inside the Montreal Forum. Dave Keon's hat trick guided the Leafs to a 3–1 win and a third straight final. After the final whistle, when the players had filed into the dressing room somberly and Blake had shaken hands with Imlach, the Canadiens coach retreated alone to a side room inside the locker room. It was his first taste of defeat in a Game 7—as a player or a coach. Blake was left mystified again—he had been certain his players would rally back for the equalizer when they were down 2–1. But, as in recent years, they hadn't. The silence was overwhelming. Disappointment hung in the air like those soiled jerseys the players hung off the MSG water pipes—an unassuming piece of scenery to the people inside, but those who walked in found a room cloaked in foul odor. The feeling winning brought with it was like a distant memory.

CHAPTER 10

CARETAKER COACH

IT WAS CHRISTMAS DAY, and the Blake sisters were at each other's throats. Joan and Mary Jane went back and forth, arms waving to emphasize their argument. They had both enjoyed a few drinks, which upped the viciousness of their insults. The children sat around the table in silence, the younger ones growing visibly upset. Bruce slumped into his chair, accustomed to the drama unfolding at the dinner table. Bruce eyed Toe, sitting at the head of the table, face slowly changing color as he joined in.

As always, Toe went to Mary Jane's defense. Joan, whose relationship with her father had always been fraught, seized on this. Toe was inclined to protect Mary Jane, his little girl, the one who had gotten pregnant at age 16 with the first of four kids. Toe preferred to go for Sunday dinners at Mary Jane's in Lasalle, on the outskirts of Montreal, even if Joan and family lived closer. Some said Mary Jane had been running with the wrong crowd. Her husband, Roddy Stuart, who was now working as a waiter at Toe's tavern, soon joined in. Joan's husband, Keith, was anxious about entering the fray. Keith and Joan lived down the street on Wolseley Avenue, just a few blocks away from the Blake family home on Sheraton Drive. The physical proximity belied the vast gulf between Toe and his eldest daughter. Keith McDonald, a well-built advertising executive whose major account was Yellow Pages, loved to cycle, ski and golf, had always enjoyed the company of his father-in-law and did not want to interject and introduce an unwanted dynamic into their relationship. They talked hockey with ease, with Toe happy to indulge Keith in stories of his Montreal Canadiens days. But even their relationship was becoming compromised as Toe got hold of whispers that Keith was using his father-in-law's name to advance his own interests. Keith held back tonight, and Joan was handling herself aptly.

There was always something going on between Joan and Mary Jane. Joan was nine years old when Mary Jane was born on December 28, 1945. Toe's gaze protectively turned toward the new addition to the family. Maybe, in the little time he had at home, Toe gave more of his energy to his newest offspring. Toe always seemed to defend his younger daughter—*the one that terrorized me as a teenager,* Joan would remember; the one always doing her best to disrupt Joan's teenage life. The age difference meant Joan was often left to babysit Mary Jane, who took pleasure in making her life hell. And yet here she was, Daddy's girl.

Joan was closer to her mother, Betty, who was home every night to welcome her back from school while Toe was playing for the Canadiens, and later when he toiled behind the hockey benches of Valleyfield, Shawinigan, Chicoutimi or wherever the next game was played. Before he knew it, Toe was waving to Betty and Joan up in the stands on a regular basis as his oldest daughter began accompanying his wife to the Saturday night games at the Forum. She may have even been there the night Betty engaged in a heated argument with the parents of Bobby Hull, who were cheering a little too loudly for the Chicago Blackhawks star from a seat among the players families.

While many knew Toe had a family, Joan was the physical proof of it, having reached her 20th birthday soon after Toe won his first Stanley Cup as coach. She was photographed alongside her parents during these years, sometimes looking more like Betty's younger sister than daughter. Joan also found herself in the papers because of her father's fame, including in the society pages after her wedding to Keith L. McDonald on May 17, 1958. Canadiens players and executives attended the union at St. Malachy's Church that Saturday morning; the *Montreal Gazette* described Joan wearing a gown of white bombazine with Guipure lace and embroidered with seed pearls; it had a portrait neckline, draped sleeves and a hoop skirt. She carried a bouquet of pink baby roses and stephanotis and wore a short veil of tulle illusion held together by a bandeau of lace and seed pearls as her father walked her down the aisle. Mary Jane, 12, was a junior bridesmaid, wearing a white Juliet cap over pale yellow taffeta and carrying cascade bouquets of pom-poms. Betty wore a model gown of beige silk with a similarly colored picture hat and a corsage bouquet of talisman roses. After the exchange of vows, the wedding party moved past the white gladioli to the Queen's Hotel reception. These were some of the happiest moments for the Blakes, even if Joan had swallowed her pride and allowed Mary Jane to be a bridesmaid.

But tonight, Bruce could see this exchange was not going to end well. He slinked off to his room to find his guitar. Joan and Mary's kids, the impetus of this argument, were excused with the quick nod of a head that allowed them escape into the basement. The grandkids were close in age but had little in common. In the basement, they were surrounded by photographs of Toe's days with the Canadiens as a player and coach, and the club insignia was everywhere you looked: on glasses, banners, caps and cups. When the Ping-Pong ball flew off the table, it was liable to hit one of the few trophies that had not been stolen, or the poker table in the corner, or the television that somehow seemed to have hockey playing on a loop. The basement was where the children gathered the odd time they all came together to visit their grandparents, while the parents mingled with drinks in hand upstairs until the Chinese food order from Ruby Foo's arrived. They marveled at how Popeye's mass of fingers could ever manage chopsticks without snapping them in half. But not on this Christmas night. They retreated below as Popeye's head swelled and his fingers bulged, ready to be brought down, seemingly through the table. Toe was not an outwardly affectionate grandfather, but the grandchildren could feel his love and his presence even if they could not always coax many words from him. He always treated them with boxes of Laura Secord chocolates, wrapped and presented for special occasions or for a surprise pop-in visit. Sometimes he would bring signed hockey sticks. But when Toe's fists came down on the table, the force of impact caused all bickering to cease.

"Dad could only take so much, and then, poof, he would explode," Bruce remembers. "And you couldn't see it coming most of the time. He'd be up in a rage and you'd think, *What the fuck just happened?*"

Now Toe was roaring alongside Joan and Mary Jane, with Betty, whose health was weak, watching, saving her energy for more important fights. This Christmas soon came to a crashing halt.

"You can go ahead and fuck off, Toe!" Joan yelled, to the surprise of all at the table.

"Get the hell out of my house!" Toe retorted, sending the McDonalds home. The box of Queen cigars his grandkids Judy and Blake had brought for Popeye sat wrapped underneath the Christmas tree. From downstairs, Bruce heard the slam of the door and Mary Jane continuing to shriek. As the drama ended, Toe buried his head in his hands before slowly dragging his face up and out into the light of the lamp above. He looked across the table at Betty and probably thought, *Christ, how the hell did it come to this?*

• • •

Toe Blake went into the 1964–65 NHL season under some of the greatest pressure of his life. The "caretaker coach"—as he was labeled by critics—was petrified of enduring a fifth straight season of Stanley Cup disappointment. Toronto had been crowned champions for the third straight year, a run that not only rankled the Montreal fan base but infuriated Blake as Imlach rubbed his nose in it. Blake's disdain for the Leafs stretched back to his playing days. Once, he preferred to go barefoot than sport Toronto socks when trainer Hector Dubois was unable to find an alternative. Another time, police pulled Blake over for speeding in his Thunderbird, with Betty and Mary Jane's kids along for a ride. His grandchildren kept Toe from blowing his top as the officer said, "Don't be too hard on the Leafs on Wednesday" and handed him a ticket. Blake went down to city hall to pay the fine and left a toy monkey wearing a Maple Leafs jersey for the officer: "Canadiens colors? Never on a monkey" Blake would say.

Blake figured another disappointing campaign could spell the end of his time in charge, especially following the sweeping off-season changes to the front office. Frank Selke and Kenny Reardon were gone; Sam Pollock had been promoted to general manager. But one of Pollock's first tasks was to put Blake's mind at ease and make it understood the organization backed him. The signing of defenseman Ted Harris, an American Hockey League journeyman who would develop into a Second Team All-Star under Blake, helped. A product of Eddie Shore's Springfield Indians, Harris immediately impressed Blake with his physical play and became a stalwart on the blue line. Harris's arrival was encouraging, but the drag of playoff sorrow Toe felt was compounded by personal worries: Betty, his wife of 20 years, had been diagnosed with cancer.

Little terrified Toe like cancer. On the ice, there was always a tactical solution to an obstacle. There wasn't a foe Toe couldn't wrap his meat hooks around and shake into submission. The barrel-chested Blake had once stood up to the heavyweight champion of the world. But cancer now left him hamstrung, unable to defend his wife against an invisible opponent.

Betty had recently convinced Toe they should move out of the duplex on Ponsard into a real home—he was the coach of the Montreal Canadiens, after all. It seemed like a good idea, even if both Joan and Mary Jane were already out of the house. Toe paid $40,000 for a place on Sheraton Drive that backed out onto the fifth hole of Meadowbrook Golf Club. But the two-storey house began to take on the air of a mausoleum after Betty's diagnosis, with Toe and Bruce surrounded by new furniture and appliances as Betty rested in a house that ultimately came to represent her illness.

Toe's father, Wilmer, had succumbed to cancer, his final days lived out at in a hospital bed before his death in 1950. Toe did his best to return to Coniston—his parents having moved to a new home on Caruso Street in the 1940s—to offer comfort in those dying days. Toe described his father's passing at age 76 as "like a ship going out to sea." Arzélie died four years later, at 78, after Alzheimer's, a disease that would chew up and spit out several of the Blakes, took hold of her. In 1954 Toe would again return to Coniston to help comfort his mother in her final days (she stayed with his brother Leonard to the end). "Toe came and everything stopped. Nothing else was important in his life, he was there to look after her," Stephanie Blake remembers of Toe and her "Mame." Both Wilmer and Arzélie lay together at St. John's cemetery in Garson, Ontario.

Now Betty's diagnosis shook Toe to the core. "They adored

each other. They would do anything for each other," Stephanie says. "They loved each other, it was a very happy relationship. Betty was included in everything. She'd tease Toe; she had a lot of fun in her; she was a very present and happy woman. Toe came first—the kids were important and not neglected, they were very loved—but Toe came first . . . He was very important to her and her to him. They were in love—it was beautiful, really beautiful, to see."

Toe became a mouse when accompanying Betty to the hospital for visits with Dr. John Palmer, a tough Scotsman with a grating demeanor that intimidated Blake. Or perhaps the entire scenario is what intimated Blake, thinks Dr. David Mulder, then a Montreal General Hospital surgical resident who accompanied Toe and Betty for some of those initial hospital visits. Blake met Mulder when Pollock hired him as a "cut man" for the Junior Royals. Mulder was paid $10 per game—amounting to $130 per month—to sew up players during the season, often stitching up to six players a night.

"From the way he treated players and everyone else around him, I was afraid of Toe," says Mulder, a pioneer in trauma care at Montreal's McGill University Health Centre. "But he was a gentleman off the ice, a teddy bear. Toe was a very open, communicative guy—away from the arena and the pressure of the game. He recognized me from the Royals, and when his wife was ill with breast cancer, he asked me for my help. He was as tough a man as he was shy—he wouldn't ask Dr. Palmer anything. I think Toe was afraid of Dr. Palmer. So Toe would say to me 'Hey, Doc, can you help me talk with Dr. Palmer?' Maybe he didn't want to hear bad news. So he was very grateful I was there. He was terrified of the word *cancer*."

When the new season got under way, Toe found himself mired in an emotional juggling act that saw his personal life eclipse his professional life for the first time. He was running a successful tavern, too. Mulder remembers moments at the rink when Toe was seemingly able to shake off the stresses of home, albeit briefly. On Saturday mornings, after the team had finished their morning skate and cleared out, Blake sought out Mulder to talk about Coniston, knowing the young resident had worked summers at Inco's Copper Cliff mines. "Who worked the mine shaft where you were? Who was the manager?" Toe would ask. "Did you meet this foreman? What about that mine shaft operator? They are good people from Coniston, despite how tough it was growing up during those days. That's why I am how I am today."

Toe sympathized with younger men and women who were beginning their careers, giving them extra attention to try to help them succeed. Mulder remembers Toe taking a fancy to his work one afternoon during an appointment with Dr. Palmer. Surprised at how little the surgical residents earned, Toe immediately found a way to help them out. "He said, 'Bring as many residents as you want down to the Tavern on Friday night to drink as much beer and eat as many pigs' knuckles as you want.'"

Blake also schooled Mulder on secret get-rich-quick tricks regarding the lottery. "Hey, Doc," Toe would ask, "you ever buy a ticket?" Mulder had little extra income to throw at lottery tickets. "You can't win if you don't buy one, so I'm going to let you in on a little secret on how to win. Take a one-dollar bill, look at the serial number, and one week you take the first six numbers and the next week you take the last six numbers—you win all the time. I did it and won $20."

Despite the camaraderie, Blake's displays inside the locker room and behind the bench reminded Mulder of the burden he lived with as coach of the Canadiens. "He was always yelling and telling the players what to do and where to go. One game they were losing—and he hated to lose—so in between the periods he kicked over a stand that had quarters of oranges cut up for the players to give them more energy. One minute you were his friend, and the next minute he was walking down the aisle, crashing sticks, slamming the door. Boy, he hated to lose . . . The whole attitude was: winning was the only thing."

Mulder was among a number of staff, players, pressmen and fans who watched Blake grow more irritated during the seasons between Betty's diagnosis and his retirement. The locker room had never been a problem under Blake, and it never would be—the current crop of players took Blake's tactics and showmanship in stride. They often had to jump onto the ice to keep their coach from jumping on a referee, or hold him back as he unleashed a right hook toward a fan in the stands following a defeat.

Dick Irvin Jr. had the awkward task of collecting lineups from Blake and delivering scoresheets after the game. Blake didn't have an office, just his own little cubby where he'd hang up his coat and jacket, and a little bench to sit on. "After a home loss, you walk into the dressing room and you could hear a pin drop," Irvin Jr. said. "Blake would be sitting on the edge of a table in the middle of the dressing room, head down, staring at the floor, no one saying a word. I would come in, hand him the paper and he wouldn't even look up—he'd just take it from me and I'd walk out."

Toe could burst into the dressing room moments into the intermission, pacing back and forth in front of his players, muttering, "Fuck, fuck, fuck." Then he would suddenly stop, turn toward the door and walk out. The players would look at one another, some muttering and others thinking, *Holy shit,* as they tried to comprehend their leader's message.

"Other times," Terry Harper recalls, "he could sense when the team was uptight and he'd come in and say, 'You read in the paper where they said where you guys are so tired you can't even make it to the game?' And he'd walk up and down in front of us with a stick in his hands, slouched over like he was so tired he could barely stand up . . . And he got everybody roaring laughing, you could hardly sit in your seat you were laughing so hard, the way he put on that little show. The team would go out and be flying again. He had that sense of whether the team needed to be beat up on and pushed or brought down because they were too tight."

To the casual observer, Toe displayed little of this humor while prowling the bench. Every game was akin to the storming of Normandy, with Blake, the general, keeping his troops on their toes with steady, pacing footsteps and cursing behind them, alternating between despotic and desperate. But Toe couldn't jump out there and alter the game himself, just as he couldn't fight his wife's cancer. "It's the way I am. It's the only way I know how to get there," said Toe.

The 1964–65 season might have been the finest of Blake's coaching career. He guided a team few picked to contend to a second-place finish and a first Stanley Cup since the record run. This despite Montreal's goaltending tandem of Charlie Hodge and Gump Worsley surrendering 185 goals, the departure of Boom Boom Geoffrion and a season-long injury to Gilles Tremblay. Toe also came into the new season frustrated by an injury picked up after a piece from his lawnmower came unstuck and pierced his knee joint, sending him to hospital.

"My first Cup was the greatest because no one thought we could beat Chicago," Ted Harris remembers. "But we just stuck together and played as a team. Especially since Chicago was loaded with damn good players and were expected to win."

"More than any of his five previous championships," wrote *Sports Illustrated*, "this one was almost completely the handiwork of Blake, a short, corpulent, interminably irascible man who gives the impression he would like to hit anybody in the mouth who dares voice a dissenting view."

That dissenting view was always furnished by the press in Blake's mind. "I can't imagine Dick Irvin or Toe Blake having a press conference after every single game like today," said Irvin Jr., who started covering the Canadiens for CFCF Montreal TV in 1961. "They wouldn't even go near anybody after a game. To think of them having to stand up in front of everyone and explain why they did what they did—they would never do it in a million years. It makes me laugh just thinking about it."

"I'd say that the toughest job for a coach today is handling the press after a game," Blake told *Sports Illustrated*. "Particularly when you lose. You have to be a politician and a diplomat. They're all looking for an angle. That's what they call it. An angle. I tell you it's wicked."

It seemed only fair for Blake, prone to violent outbursts, to be indignant toward the press. "All you guys with your fuckin' black boxes..." he would mutter in reference to their tape recorders. Some days, after practice, Toe wouldn't even be done shaving when a pack of newspapermen swarmed around the bathroom mirror in the locker room. With shaving cream still on his face, Blake was at the ready and would respond to individual questions by pulling a clipping of a report by that same correspondent from his pocket blazer. Blake's contempt prompted him to dare the media to heed his call and relay his message. "I'm not going to say anything about the referees, but now I'll see if you've got the entrails to say anything about it!" Blake said that spring during the Stanley Cup Final against Chicago.

Dick Irvin Jr. went on to become a play-by-play announcer for CBC's *Hockey Night in Canada* broadcasts, but he could never put a finger on how to read Blake. Toe's foul temper and language were consistent, but you never knew who they were going to be directed toward on any given day. The *Toronto Star* used to send out a questionnaire to all the coaches in the league, asking for their opinion on a variety of topics, from best skater to stickhandler to best shot. The last question was about the best referee, and Blake answered by writing, "None—all bad." Blake's friendships with many of the pressmen he had played cards with on the long train rides deteriorated when the winning stopped. And when he used to previously play cards with some of the players, now he played with none since he worried it gave off the impression of favorites to the team. Blake was further isolating himself.

Going into the 1964–65 season, for example, Blake's friendship with Jacques Beauchamp of *Montréal-Matin* was over. He had taken exception to Beauchamp's decision to publish his criticism of referee Eddie Powers the previous season. "They'd be better off investigating the conduct of officials who handle themselves in such a way you'd think they bet on the outcome of the game," Blake had reportedly said. Toe insisted his diatribe had been taken out of context and delivered off the record. Powers ultimately sued Blake, Forum management and *Montréal-Matin* for damages. The case was settled before a trial took place more than a year later. Beauchamp, one of Blake's biggest backers, was suddenly no longer at the card table alongside the *Montreal Star*'s Red Fisher and Pat Curran of the *Montreal Gazette* for those long train rides, or in hotel rooms during the slow buildup to the evening game.

On one occasion, Fisher revealed he had a scoop set to be published and informed Blake. Blake brought his hands up to his temple, leaned forward in the chair and lowered his head between his knees to stare at the floor for several moments before starting to rock slowly back and forth. Fisher had seen Blake at his most vulnerable and desperate yet never relented. Unsurprisingly, Blake and Fisher's relationship was next to fizzle, when Blake threatened to "biff" Fisher in front of the Forum press corps over a story. Blake had been driving Betty to the hospital for her treatment when Fisher called for comment on the article and was brushed off. The pair didn't talk for eight months and went to great lengths to hide from each other. One would see the other in a hallway and turn and go the other way.

"We were laughing like hell about it," Irvin Jr. remembered. "Hiding from each other in hotel lobbies, acting like kids, children. They were inseparable for years. They'd play cards morning, noon and night on the road and suddenly they aren't speaking to each other—go figure. Grown men."

The 1964–65 season started off like any other, with Blake

pushing his players hard to get off to the good start he always wanted, to get a good lead in the standings early on. The players responded by going into November undefeated. Blake normally let up a little bit on his players come December, toning it down over Christmas before ramping it back up after the turn of the new year. When the Canadiens played a Christmas Day game on the road, Blake's yuletide cheer would appear as he moved between train cabins to offer his players a glass of rye.

"He realized you can't keep the intensity for 70-plus games. So he'd kind of back off and ease up a little bit. He liked to get off to a good start as it would give the team and individual players some early confidence," says Harper. "Come middle of January he'd start again, cracking down with tougher practices, working on things that weren't working a lot harder for the push to the playoffs."

Without access to statistics and in a data-limited era, Blake kept his own records, tallying individual and team numbers to help his analysis of matchups. The 53-year-old Blake used to pore over the game sheets to see who was on the ice in certain successful or unsuccessful matchups to get an edge over opponents. Detroit and Chicago had been particularly tough to beat that season—Chicago scored a 7–0 victory toward the end of the campaign—so matching up players and getting the right lines out on the ice at the right moment was important. Scotty Bowman had just been hired as coach of the Junior Canadiens and he made a point to go and visit Blake in his corner office upstairs at the Forum for one hour every Friday before Blake had to rush over to the tavern.

"He was busy getting his team ready, but he still welcomed me. We talked about the game, we talked about the league, my team, and he would ask me about my players," Bowman says. "I'd ask him questions like, 'Toe when you're going to play a team that is a lot stronger than you, what forechecking system would you use?' A lot of times when I asked him a question, he would stress 'You have to make your own decision about what the answer is'. He never wanted to interfere much. But then I would say, 'Well, what would you do?' On this occasion, he asked me if we had had much time to practice. I told him we had 10 days. He went to his paper and he showed me three different systems. 'But you have to pick which one you want to use and you'll have to practice it,' he told me. Practice was important to him. He told me when you're practicing line rushes against defensemen, stress to the players how important it is not to go offside: 'It's like going over a cliff—don't even make it close so the linesman can call offside.' He explained the systems to me and said, 'You'll have to figure out which one you like the best and use that one'."

Those systems had served the Canadiens well during a season in which captain Jean Beliveau struggled to get going. Blake's belief in team play inspired defensive players like Claude Provost to contribute, and the right winger led the team in scoring. Beliveau, who managed 20 goals, finished fifth. Pollock's trade of Bill Hicke for Dick Duff just a few days before Christmas proved to be a coup, as the New York Rangers right winger quickly gelled into a Canadiens lineup that went on an 11–2–2 run through to the start of January.

"I got a big break coming to Montreal and getting a chance to play with Beliveau," Duff said. "The players in this team have a real good spirit, they really enjoy playing hockey; I think it brought back a little fire in me. I'm pretty sure it did."

After two straight playoff exits to Toronto, that fire helped the Canadiens reach their first Cup Final in five years, at the expense of Toronto, as Provost scored the overtime winner in front of 14,702 at Maple Leaf Gardens for a 4–2 series win over their recent bogeymen. "You know, I've always said the winner of this series is going to win the Stanley Cup. This club has never quit," Blake said, qualifying his squad as one of the "fightiest" he'd ever coached. "I think they have a good chance. (And) if we meet Chicago, we have the extra home game."

That extra home game proved the difference after Chicago beat Detroit in seven, thanks in part to leading playoff scorer Bobby Hull's eight goals and five assists. Stan Mikita's "Scooter Line" was also contributing, with a hand in nine of Chicago's 23 goals in the series. Chicago's last Stanley Cup had come in 1961, when the Blackhawks ended Montreal's record run of five straight. Now they looked the favorite to stretch the Canadiens' run of futility to five years. Blake decided Provost would shadow Hull. "Crowd Hull," Blake told Provost. "Lean on him. Follow him around like a busted garter."

Blake selected his goalie for Game 1 of the final just prior to game time, with Charlie Hodge getting the nod since Gump was battling the flu. But moments before the start, Blake surprised everyone by giving Worsley his first ever start in a Stanley Cup Final series. "I just changed my mind," Blake said, "just like a woman."

Yvan Cournoyer, meanwhile, was much maligned by Blake early in his career. His inexperience, softer personality and lack of defensive awareness frustrated Blake, who started by using him mostly on the power play, to the derision of the Forum fans, who Blake used to shake his fist at as they called for the speedy forward known as the Road Runner. But Cournoyer came good in the opening game with the winning goal, Provost limited Hull to one shot and the Canadiens were on their way to 2–0 series lead thanks to home ice advantage.

Getting ahead 3–0 in Chicago was always going to be ambitious. The Chicago Stadium spectators made a difference; the location of the old building on West Madison Street, in one of the worst parts of town, accentuated the bloodlust the home fans could display. When they got mad, some fans among the capacity crowds of 17,200 would fling ball bearings or the folding chairs they sat on onto the ice. The Blackhawks welcomed back defenseman Pierre Pilote (injured left shoulder) and forward Ken Wharram (left knee) thanks to the application of dimethyl sulfoxide (DMSO), an experimental veterinary drug that was a natural by-product of wood-pulp manufacture and used as an industrial solvent, paint thinner and additive in a number of chemical products. The FDA would ban the drug later that year, but at the time it helped these two key players heal enough to return to the lineup. Chicago won 3–1 to get back into the series and also forced Worsley from goal with a torn muscle in his right thigh. With Hodge in goal, the Blackhawks won Game 4, 5–1, to even the best of seven final.

Montreal routed Chicago 6–0 on home ice before succumbing to two late goals to drop Game 6, 2–1, with the finale set for the Forum. Blake had lost his only previous Game 7.

The Canadiens returned to their mountain hideaway in Sainte-Agathe prior to the season's last game. Toe was saying very little in the buildup to the winner-take-all contest, caught up in his own thoughts on how to ensure his sixth Stanley Cup after a decade in charge. Provost—or Joe, as he was called by his teammates—had done a tremendous job, sacrificing his offense to keep Hull at bay. Hull scored only two goals through six games and would register no more. Ferguson, meanwhile, had done an excellent job shadowing Eric Nesterenko when asked. Blake had an inkling and called on Worsley to ask how he was feeling.

"Not bad," Worsley said.

"Okay," Toe said, "I'll check you later."

Worsley made the 60-mile trip to the Forum to go through exercises on the Forum ice. Toe had accompanied him and keenly observed the goalie's workout before the pair returned to the team in the Laurentians. When the Habs returned to the Forum for the game, Worsley went to the Forum lodge to give his wife, Doreen, her game ticket. Worsley sat down to shoot the breeze, figuring Ernie Wakely would dress as Hodge's backup. Then Canadiens trainer Larry Aubut walked in.

"Hey, Gump, you're playing tonight," he said.

"Yeah, sure. How about a cup of coffee, Larry?"

"I'm not kidding," Aubut said. "You're in the barrel tonight."

"Who said so?"

"The Bird," said Aubut, using another one of Blake's monikers.

Blake's last-minute decision bolstered the team, and he didn't need to say much before the start to motivate his squad.

"I'm not going to talk about individual players . . . I'm not going to mention Ken Wharram and I'm not going to mention Stan Mikita," Blake said. "I'm not going to mention Bobby Hull, or any of them."

Montreal couldn't have started better, as a Dick Duff pass went off Beliveau and past Glen Hall 14 seconds into the game, and Worsley saved 20 shots as the Canadiens cruised to a 13th Stanley Cup with a 4–0 triumph.

"We've won six Stanley Cups since I've been coach, but I can honestly say that none of them has given me the satisfaction that this one tonight has," said Blake. "We had a little trouble this winter but it didn't creep into the club. This is one Stanley Cup I will never forget."

Organist Léo Duplessis played "Auld Lang Syne" as the players from both teams shook hands. A large portion of the 15,740 Forum fans, who'd paid between $2 and $2.75 to see the game, flooded the ice, with kids scrounging for sticks as the team trainer tried to hold them off. That didn't stop Worsley from autographing one youngster's find. Duplessis swung into "Prendre un p'tit coup" when Toe was hoisted above the Cup onto his players' shoulders to waive his famed fedora in celebration, with J.C. Tremblay snatching it away to toss it into the air. Somehow, the fedora was back with Blake in time for the presentation of the Cup. After Beliveau, who had won the inaugural Conn Smythe Trophy as playoff MVP, had skated around the rink to "Happy Days Are Here Again," the team retreated to the locker room to chants of "Les Canadiens sont là." As the players entered the room, each was handed a bottle of champagne while cases of beer were readied, and the contents of both were used as shampoo. Gump, who nervously puffed away on a cigarette in the dressing room, didn't waste his, except for offering Quebec premier Daniel Johnson a swig; the politician complied by hogging it for a little longer than the goaltender would have liked.

Following the match, Blake took the time to list each player's qualities and how that player contributed to the triumph. He also explained his decision to ride Worsley instead of Hodge. "Charlie had played two very good games, but in a game like this I thought Charlie might be a trifle little more nervous. They say Gump has no nerves at all. We tried him out yesterday in practice and he was doing very well. I've been worried ever since that game in Chicago about making the change."

Blake and Beliveau were then peppered with questions about retirement. "There's more chance of Beliveau coming back than me. Sure, all this is great, but it's not always like that," said Blake, the first NHL coach to win six Stanley Cups.

Holed up in Toronto's Royal York Hotel earlier in the season, Blake had made a clear pronouncement about his future to his card-playing partners of the press. "All right. I'll bet $1,000 right now that if we finish first and win the Stanley Cup, I won't be back as coach of the Canadiens next season," Blake had said. "I've found the pressure worse this year than ever before. I've had a hard time controlling my temper at times, especially when the team was in a slump and there was a lot of second-guessing by the fans and the press. I had problems saying the right thing, so as not to hurt any of my players, and everything I said seemed to be twisted the wrong way. My wife and I are going on a holiday away from everybody for a few weeks. I'll take time to think about it and then make a decision."

Meanwhile, Betty Blake couldn't help but smile after the victory. Toe had done it. She knew how important this championship was for him—for them. And those Hulls weren't cheering anymore.

CHAPTER 11

THE TAVERN

"Where Sportsmen Meet."

THE SPECULATION OVER TOE'S future lasted less than a month: he returned from vacation to sign another one-year deal on May 31. The 52-year-old's concern over his health included worries about a stomach disorder, but he ultimately decided he was "fit as a fiddle" and fine to return for another season. Molson and Pollock were relieved Toe would return. "If I wasn't coaching, what else would I do?" said Blake, who celebrated the deal by chartering a plane with friend Ron Lister to go fishing.

With the stress of winning having abated for a few months, Toe was in excellent health. The team's post–Stanley Cup ritual visit to his tavern was finally revived after four years. "After we won the Stanley Cup and the parade started, that's when he finally exhaled," defenseman Terry Harper remembers. "Come on over to his bar and have a beer. That was a real exhale." The visit to 1618

St. Catherine Street West was perhaps the only time during the season that Blake and his players mingled off-ice.

"Toe never said a damn word to me," Ted Harris says. "The most I talked to (him) was after we won the championship and he had us to his tavern. That's when he said the most to me."

Marcel Bonin, who had played for Blake from 1957 to '62, remembered a noticeably less agitated Blake at the tavern, too. "After we won the Stanley Cup, he'd invite us to the tavern and he would be so relaxed, one of the best men in the world. He wouldn't fraternize with the players during the season, but after that he would."

While Rocket Richard and his brother the Pocket Rocket also owned taverns in the city, Toe Blake's Tavern—"where sportsmen meet"—had been the unofficial home of hockey and sports in Montreal since opening its doors in 1952. It was easy enough to pick out with a glance above the throngs on Montreal's busiest shopping street—a flashing neon sign shaped like a hockey stick and puck pointed the way. The waiters wore red jackets over white shirts with an open collar, or occasionally a bow tie and black trousers. They blended into the decor, where men sat at wood tables in round-back seats for slim glasses of Molson or Labatt beer. Taverns were one of the few all-male preserves in the city, and the Montreal tavern was one of the last in the Western world that segregated the sexes. No women got past the doors, save the Salvation Army nuns who occasionally passed through for donations. Dimly lit, with televisions perched in corner nooks, the walls of Toe Blake's were decorated with caricatures of famous hockey players like Lionel Conacher, Howie Morenz, Eddie Shore, Wilf Cude and the Old Lamplighter himself. The portrait Blake received as a gift when coaching at Valleyfield could be found upon the wood-panelled walls, where a poster of the Forum's seating plan also held prominent space.

When the team visited, after greeting patrons and signing autographs, they were ushered into Blake's private office at the back. They squeezed 20 men into the tight space, and the cramped confines accentuated the boisterous atmosphere. Blake would even share a beer with his players, something he normally reserved for close friends or, more rarely, favorite customers. Harper remembers his excitement at his first visit: "There was mystique because you only got to go there when you won the Cup! You got to see what the inside actually looked like. I would never have gone in during the regular season. Toe had many unwritten rules—and that was one of them: do not to even think of going in there until being invited after winning the Cup."

Bruce Blake remembers that "Tavern-Keeper" was listed under "Occupation" in one of his father's passports. "If he wasn't coaching, he was at the tavern," says Bruce, who was just six in 1956, when he first started visiting the tavern on Sundays—the only day it was closed to the public so Blake's acquaintances would show up to play cards and have a drink, with a bottle of scotch normally close at hand. "There was no music, just the crowd, the people. There was sawdust on the floor if the cleaner hadn't done a good job. My sister Mary Jane and I drank ginger beer and would run around the place looking for money on the floor while my father finished paperwork in his office. You'd find all kinds of stuff: false teeth, barf, money—if it was a dime, you could buy some peanuts from the peanut machine."

Blake's clients were generally people who worked in the city center—of both the blue- and white-collar variety—area residents and, of course, hockey fans. The locals would rub shoulders with visitors from Boston, Toronto or any other city whose team was visiting. The tavern cut across social barriers to include police officers, executives and men just looking for a place to get together and drink and, maybe, break into song. Beer was 10 cents, a draft lager was 25 cents and a prime rib steak cost $1.20. Every day at lunch, Toe Blake's Tavern served 450 meals.

"A man comes in, he knows what he wants," said Emile, the tavern's chef, in a documentary about the city's all-male preserves, including Toe's. "Rib steak with French fries, medium. While if a lady (were to come in, hypothetically), she might say a rib steak medium, French fries, I don't want coleslaw but some tomatoes, I would like it very lean. They are much fussier than a man would be. As long as he has a full plate of tender meat, he is satisfied. I much prefer to serve gentlemen than ladies."

Some women were happy to let their husbands waste away their hours drinking beer with the boys—but not all women. "(Taverns) should be abolished because they bring to my mind the smells of stale beer, bad conversation and all the husbands getting drunk together," one woman of the time said. "I hate taverns, I think they are absolutely impossible! All these men go into these dark holes, it's reminiscent of the womb. They're just like small boys who feel they need some place to hide. When they finish drinking all this stuff they go home and scream at the women anyway. He's supposed to be in the house at a certain time and if he goes to one of those places, he won't come home."

For Terry Harper, it was a pleasure to meet all these people. "All the regulars are there, those were real hard-core fans in there. So it was a real thrill to go over there and have a couple of beers and mostly talk. Talk about having attention paid. We were spoiled rotten."

Blake was loose with the boys inside the tavern, but never loose enough to discuss himself or his own playing career. The only hockey moments that were rehashed were those of that season past.

Later in life, Bruce and his future wife, Julie, would walk over to the tavern on Sunday afternoons to meet Toe, who would graciously invite them out for dinner, always on him. "Toe was always very generous," Julie remembers, "and everyone would be fawning over him, from the waiters to the public. People would be coming up to him at the table for his autograph—even if he's having dinner at his table with his son and his girlfriend. He was always so gracious and willing to speak, to tell a little story, and that's when I became more in awe of him. Bruce came to pick me up once with a girlfriend of mine to go to his house to watch the game, and she was really into hockey and a Boston fan and she was wearing a Bruins jersey. But he took that with a grain of salt and took us out for dinner to Bar-B-Barn that night."

The warm and cordial atmosphere of Toe's continued to welcome Montreal's Stanley Cup champions until it closed its doors in 1983.

"The latest rumors going the rounds may be the Endsville from which there is no return," wrote *Montreal Gazette* columnist Tim Burke a few years prior to the closing. "I speak of an impending disaster. Not fire, flood, famine or death or anything that trivial. But the demise of Toe Blake's Tavern! *De profundis.*" A picture captioned "Toe Blake in grouchy mood" accompanied the story. "Tear down Toe's and you rip a little out of all of us," *The Gazette* continued.

The Grey Nuns had owned the block for a millennium before selling it, which shuttered not only Toe's but several other local favorites like the Donut Bar, Le Briton restaurant, the Leader Pool Room and Steinberg's grocery store. The Leader Pool Room was how Toe came to know the spot where he'd eventually open his tavern—he shot stick here after being banned from the Forum's poolroom for using foul language.

Toe was offered the option of relocating to the second floor of the new building, but then he would have had to operate his establishment as a brasserie or, effectively, a mixed-gender bar. Toward the end, Toe would go into his tavern some nights to find the hall empty and the manager asleep. The doors closed for the last time on November 28, 1983. At least 200 people attended the auction of the bar's contents several days later, including many women who just wanted the opportunity to finally step inside. Dickie Moore spent $170 for a table and four chairs that he promised would get a place of honor—"Toe's corner"—at his

Arundel golf club. "He didn't have much to say. This is a sad day for him, and I feel for him," Moore said.

Blake kept much of the hockey memorabilia within the walls of the tavern, including hundreds of hockey caricatures, paintings and photographs. They all sat in storage, even after Blake offered them in 1985 to the Hockey Hall of Fame, which refused them for lack of space. Among the artifacts now lost or spread among family, friends and others were 50 caricatures of players from the six-team era drawn by cartoonists Lou Skuce of the *Toronto Star* and John Collins of the *Montreal Gazette*. The value of these caricatures in 1985 was $50,000 after Blake paid more than $100 for each. Curator Lefty Reid couldn't guarantee that the Hall of Fame could display all of the images at once, which was Blake's wish if he were to donate them. The Montreal Canadiens discussed acquiring Blake's collection, but that never happened. "They're terrific pictures. It wouldn't be right to sell them to individuals. I would never think of doing that," Toe said. "I'm hanging on to them. I want to do the right thing." The combative Blake was as mysterious as ever when asked about the future of the art if no suitor was found: "I might even go back into the business myself."

CHAPTER 12

LAST CUP

"There's been only one rap against him—he has never learned how to lose."

—*MONTREAL GAZETTE*

THE CLUB HAD JUST won a 14th Stanley Cup, yet the buzz in the championship locker room was fading. Players who had been pitching back magnums of champagne suddenly hesitated, dropping the bottles from their lips to focus an attentive gaze toward the center of the room. Some players had heaved a radio announcer and a sportswriter into the showers and were hunting new victims, but now they noticed a change in the mood. They composed themselves and gathered closer to the crowd. Some eyes began to swell with tears, some filled with affection and others just stared ahead out of respect.

Toe Blake had won an eighth Stanley Cup to close out his 13th season at the helm—but now it was time to go. He had to go, he thought as he nervously played with his tie and—for once—struggled to say the words that had always seemed poised to leap from the tip of his tongue. He was now 56, and the pressure had gotten to him; the grind of being a one-man coaching staff had taken a toll on everyone around him, from the players to his family. He wanted to spend more time with Betty, see his grandchildren more often. Expansion had brought planes, unknown cities and none of the comforts of those long train journeys. The flab around his midsection had expanded and his doctor was concerned, asking him to watch his diet. His hair was graying from those eternally tortuous afternoons building up to games. His nerves had felt frayed for years, but now he found himself trembling hours before the start of the game. He was shaking like a leaf from the moment the team had won his ninth Prince of Wales Trophy as coach. *How can I continue doing this if my nerves can't hold up?* He had been as nervous as a rookie during these playoffs. In the fifth game of the semifinal against Chicago, his anxiety had overtaken him; he'd felt lost. *Where the hell am I,* he'd wondered from behind the Forum bench. He turned to his right to find someone at the end of the bench who didn't belong. He called the steward and asked him to take this stranger to his seat. Gump Worsley and the man in the red jacket looked at each other, puzzled by Blake's request to remove a player he had coached for five seasons.

Blake readied himself to speak to the men who had given him everything at the slightest bark of his tongue. President David Molson and general manager Sam Pollock had known the announcement was coming, and Toe had let Gump know before the start of the first-round series against Boston. *I know I'll regret this*, he'd said to himself; *hockey has given me everything. Maybe I'll come back one day. I won't say I'll never come back. But I have no choice, I have to quit.*

The newspapermen and TV cameras jostled for position around players, staff and management. Toe gazed around the room, and nervousness suddenly enveloped him. He clutched his trusted fedora as he summoned up the will from deep within to utter words he'd never imagined he could actually say. He wiped champagne from his face and cleared his throat before apologizing for stealing away some of the spotlight from the Stanley Cup triumph. And then he retired from hockey.

"This has been the greatest but also the longest and the toughest season in 13 years behind the Montreal bench. I just can't take it anymore—the tension and the pressure are too much," a suddenly sheepish Blake muttered. "I'd like to coach for 100 years—it's the only thing I can do—but I just can't take it anymore. Maybe I can't live without it but, for my health's sake, I have to try."

The gravity of the news shocked the Canadian public, with some tuning their radios or TVs to another station after the announcement to confirm the news wasn't phony. The locker room buzzed. There was surprise, disappointment and even relief. The surprise wasn't so much about what he'd said—it mostly came from the timing. Bruce arrived in the locker room to find his father shaking. Maybe Betty had known, but no one else in the family had been aware of Toe's intentions. Still, as he took a swig of champagne from the Cup, Bruce wasn't surprised.

"I wish it wasn't true. I never met a man with such an intense desire to win," Ferguson said. "If I had to single out the greatest of his qualities that would be it: his desire . . . it affects all of us."

"You could fill the job but you can't replace Toe . . . not with 15 guys," Worsley said. "It's a tough act to follow. Yeah, like trying to sing after Sinatra. Only that's a one-nighter. You'd have to follow Blake all year."

"He built a great team by insisting on perfection. He wouldn't even tolerate a nonchalant practice, and a mediocre performance during a game even less," said the Pocket Rocket. "It's a heavy loss for the Canadiens and for hockey."

"I'll believe it when a new coach is hired," quipped favorite whipping boy Ralph Backstrom.

• • •

Toe stormed along the hotel hallway, banging his fist on random doors as a harmony-heavy rendition of "By the Light of the Silvery Moon" bellowed out around him. "My guys have a big game tomorrow night. Knock it off!" But he was drowned out by a new chorus coming from another room, this time "Sweet Adeline."

The Canadiens had lost the first two games of the 1966 Stanley Cup Final to the Detroit Red Wings on home ice, and Blake was concerned. He'd moved the team from its normal downtown hotel to one in the Detroit suburb of Dearborn. Blake had been booking accommodations for his payers for nearly two decades, but he'd never before booked his team into a place hosting a barbershop quartet convention. At least he wouldn't have to pull himself out of his room for the midnight curfew check, as he was already running the halls. While the players knew never to drink in the hotel lobby, they also knew if they had been out it was best to come back after 1 a.m., when "the Bird"—a nickname Blake had earned for his resemblance to future Minnesota North Stars coach Wren Blair, who was known for berating officials and wild actions behind the bench—was already asleep. But Blake didn't have to monitor as much with a captain like Beliveau leading by example. Though he knew his guys could occasionally go overboard, he didn't really care as long as they played their best and didn't embarrass the club. But here in Dearborn, the birthplace of Henry Ford, Blake was struggling to maintain order with a must-win game at hand. The Canadiens had followed their unexpected Cup triumph of 1965 by winning the league the very next season. Worsley and Hodge rebounded from an unimpressive season to share the Vezina Trophy. Jacques Laperriere had secured the James Norris Trophy as the league's top defenseman. Now, the final—and most important—prize was suddenly in peril.

"You didn't realize how important the little things he did at the time were," remembers Terry Harper. "He didn't start the season by talking about winning the Stanley Cup, that's not what he would talk about. He'd talk about winning the Prince of Wales Trophy, or the Vezina. It was a more measurable goal that you could think about doing, and it would take the pressure away from us. All through the season he had little goals, per game. When you have these little goals that are close you can measure yourself and your improvement. They were goals you could achieve. And it gave the team more confidence."

Those goals included in-game performances that revolved around the team—never one player. Beliveau may have been the unquestioned leader on and off the ice, but the team captain did not have to do it all. Bobby Rousseau led the team in scoring that season with 30 goals. Gilles Tremblay, who came into the league as a defensive specialist, ended up contributing 27 more. "He transformed my game, told me I couldn't just be a defensive player but better balanced," Tremblay told an interviewer during a 1972 event in honor of Toe. "Even if you are the best defensive player, if someone comes along that can score goals, you will be toast."

While the players bunked down and did their best to ignore the barbershop sounds, Toe slammed his hotel room door shut and slumped into the chair. There would be little sleep on this night now that he was alert, his mind racing over what his lineup would look like for Game 3. The Canadiens had finished eight points clear of Chicago in the regular season, then swept Toronto in four games. Back-to-back losses on Forum ice had now put them in a precarious spot. Blake was already battling frequent and persistent headaches, shutting himself in whenever possible. Eventually, he turned on the TV in an attempt to give his mind some rest. But just when he started easing into the show, his eyes widened as he played out the next night's action in his mind.

Following the 5–2 loss in Game 2, the *Montreal Gazette* had quoted Toe as saying, "It's bad enough just making mistakes but how-in-hell can you expect to stay in the game when you've got guys just running away from the puck in their own end. We had 15 guys out there who couldn't do anything."

The mental errors were clear; the focus was not there. Red Wings goalie Roger Crozier had been sensational and further frustrated the group. Blake's team would have to become only the second club, after the 1942 Maple Leafs, to recover from an 0–2 deficit to win the Cup. Blake had acted straightaway after defeat, recalling Leon Rochefort from the Quebec Aces to replace Claude Larose. Center Dave Balon was itching for an opportunity. *Maybe I'll try him with Rochefort and add Cournoyer to their line for goals,* Blake thought. Beliveau, Provost and Larose had been the team's best line, and that wouldn't be altered. Before he knew it, sunrise was encroaching outside his window, ready to disrupt the few moments of calm he still managed to enjoy.

"Dirty Dora!" Blake yelled as Norm Ullman moved Detroit ahead 1–0 after just 280 seconds, the startling clap of his hands coming together enough to make a spectator in the front row jump from their seat. Blake immediately relegated Rousseau and Duff to power-play duties and moved Ferguson and Roberts into their spots either side of Backstrom. He knew he had to keep Beliveau's line humming to have any chance. Balon came through with a tying goal before Beliveau led the visitors into the first intermission with a 2–1 advantage. Blake didn't point any fingers, but his message during the intermission was clear.

"Toe came into the dressing room and he did a little dance up and down the middle, and he said (in a girly voice), 'You don't touch me I won't touch you,' and he had us all laughing," defenseman Noel Price remembers. "But then in the first shift,

Beliveau went out and nailed somebody. And the rest of the team just followed after that."

The Canadiens outskated and out-hit the Wings in a 4–2- win Blake hoped would swing the momentum their way. Blake couldn't wait to get away from the singing in Dearborn. He moved the team to a hotel across the border in Windsor, Ontario. Despite the victory, he could sense the squad was still tight. So, he gave the players $200 and told them to go out and let off some steam at "an out-of-the-way place, so the people don't recognize you." The trick worked. The Canadiens evened the series. And now that his team had a handle on the final, Blake could afford to stick with his trusted players.

"That's kind of Toe Blake's thing—he wouldn't make a change, he'd say, 'These are my guys, they can do it, let's not panic, let's not change things, these guys will do it—they've done it before and they'll do it again for me,'" Harper says. "Once you were on his team, you played for him. You would have to die before he would finally change you for someone else. That was a real incentive, it made you want to work harder for him."

The team was on the cusp of a clinching second straight Stanley Cup come Game 6 back at the Olympia. Detroit scored midway through the third period to tie things up. Blake showed little emotion as the PA announcer came on the microphone to announce the goal. Instead, he looked down his bench and back out to the ice. He buried his hands deep in the pockets of his dark suit as he paced behind his players, head down, hoping it would submerge the Detroit momentum. He fidgeted, trying to find a new place to store his hands. He paced, revealing none of the strain within as the stewards raced to clear the ice of programs. "He always let the guys play, but he walked up and down that bench," Price remembers. "He must have walked a hundred miles each game."

J.C. Tremblay's long, elegant strides meant nothing when the defenseman lost the puck near the Canadiens zone. An exasperated Blake ground his uneven teeth, clenching his jaw as tight as his fist. "Tremblay should have been looking to head-man the puck up to one of his wingers along the boards, ready to break out," he muttered to no one. A Worsley kick save denied Gordie Howe before Provost missed an open net at the other end. The horn blew to signal overtime.

Toe emerged from dressing room to start overtime and walked on the ice along the boards to the bench, occasionally sliding either to check the ice, to get there faster or just for the fun of it. His expression was one of indifference. He looked unruffled and unconcerned, as if he had the full confidence that came with the experience of being in this spot before.

Overtime was under way as the TV feed cut to Toe, hands on hips, watching the action while he smacked away on chewing gum. It could have been pre-season, judging by Blake's expression—a man still so confident in his team's ability to pull out impossible Cup win after Cup win. The winning goal came quickly, at 2:20 of overtime, when Henri Richard finished off a give-and-go by sliding into the goal with the puck alongside.

Blake noticed Detroit's players encroaching on the official, looking to have the sudden, unexpected goal waived off. "Get out on the ice! Get out on the ice!" Blake yelled, motioning and physically pushing his players over the boards to celebrate. The victory was so unexpected that team trainer Lucien Desrochers hadn't brought champagne, so there was no bubbly inside the delirious dressing room. The players were on the train with the Cup an hour after the game, bound for Montreal, where 500 fans awaited upon their arrival at Central Station. Half a million people would line the 10-mile parade route, which closed with mayor Jean Drapeau presenting the team with a six-month entry passport to Expo 67. Blake would be inducted into the Hockey Hall of Fame later that summer.

No one had lifted the Stanley Cup as often as Blake—10 times in total and in nine of the Canadiens' 14 triumphs so far.

Still, the 53-year-old made it sound like it was enough. "This is not a very good time to say it. But I called the shot when I told Henri he was going to get the winning goal. I guess it's time to quit when you do things like that," he said.

Blake's yearly flirtation with retirement would continue until he returned from a holiday in Florida with Betty. His wife had been in better condition and hadn't relapsed following her mastectomy. "They must be hoping I retire," he'd said of his opponents, suggesting he'd be watching the games on TV next. But on June 29 he signed another one-year deal to lead the Canadiens. Asked which of his Stanley Cup wins could be considered the most important, he replied: "The eighth."

• • •

In nine trips to the Stanley Cup Final, Blake's Canadiens had lost only to the Toronto Maple Leafs, in 1967. Blake characterized it as the hardest defeat of his career. That year, the Canadiens swept the New York Rangers in four games to reach a third straight Stanley Cup Final, which they opened with a convincing 6–2 victory over the Leafs. Blake was surprisingly upbeat heading into the second game, despite Punch Imlach's promise to make the Canadiens "cry before it's over."

Despite Imlach's typically pugnacious prognosis, Blake was not about to waver in the face of yet another of his rival's typical jousts. "What else can I do? I can't start experimenting and making changes now," said Blake, who was already employing a 21-year-old rookie goalie named Rogie Vachon in place of injured veteran Gump Worsley. The Leafs responded with two straight wins, including a 3–2 double overtime victory to take the lead in a series that had quickly morphed into a veteran classic typical of the Original Six era.

"It was a remarkable effort by both teams. A playoff game we rarely get to witness," said Blake, respectful of the gravity of the series. In contrast, Imlach, according to the *Sherbrooke Daily Record*, was "whooping it up and needling Montreal sports writers."

The Canadiens responded with a victory in Game 4, but an exasperated Blake could only watch as Terry Sawchuk replaced the injured Johnny Bower in the Leafs goal and backstopped Toronto to a 4–1 Game 5 victory. All signs pointed to Blake going to the 38-year-old Gump, the player who had done it before, the one Blake could trust. Blake even took a page out of Imlach's book and predicted victories for his club, although there was little else he could really do with the season on the line. Still, it was not like Blake to speculate in any form. "Home ice won't be a factor until the seventh game. That's right, only in the seventh game when we win the cup," said Blake, who brought Worsley into a game for the first time in seven weeks in a bid to prepare for the critical Game 6. "I tried everything. Nothing seemed to help."

But Sawchuk was sensational again, and after it had clinched the Cup, Blake admitted Toronto had been the better team. But Blake's first defeat in a Stanley Cup Final as coach didn't stop him from hosting the annual trip to the tavern for beers with his players after the final and before they all broke for summer holidays.

When the Canadiens returned from their summer break, it was clear the game was about to change. The NHL had taken on professional sports' largest expansion by adding six more teams to the league: the California Seals, Los Angeles Kings, Minnesota North Stars, Philadelphia Flyers, Pittsburgh Penguins and St. Louis Blues. California, agents and spoiled players began to creep in and utterly change Blake's beloved game.

The Canadiens lost forwards Dave Balon and Leon Rochefort, defensemen Jean-Guy Talbot and Noel Price and goalie Charlie Hodge in the expansion draft. Changes were afoot inside the Forum as well as the home of the Canadiens saw major renovations. The interior columns were removed to offer clear and unobstructed views from every seat. Over 2,000 tons of steel was erected during the summer months for towers, seating galleries, roof structures and roof supports. The upper levels were more easily reached with the addition of escalators. The transformation felt like part of Expo 67, which had announced Montreal as a major international metropolis.

But the revamp did not sway Blake's misgivings after an uneven start to the new season. Blake erratically needled his players more often, calling them out in one sentence and protecting them in the next. "I haven't seen the 'Pocket' skate this well for a full practice since we started working out. Even on two-on-one situations he was digging. So if practices mean anything, I'll have to say that Richard will get two goals," said Blake after a bad loss in November, breaking routine with a prediction. "We need somebody like Richard to snap us out of this. No more than two of our guys are getting the chances, and they're always the same two—Cournoyer and Beliveau. The others aren't even getting close."

Toe wasn't the only NHL figure struggling with pressure during the 1967–68 season. Detroit goalie Roger Crozier, a Calder Trophy winner one season removed from his 1966 Conn Smythe win after the final against the Canadiens, had retired at 25 following a 9–3 regular season defeat. He could no longer stand the "pure torture" of hockey. A few days earlier, Toronto's Frank Mahovlich had walked off the team train into a hospital, suffering from "depression and nervous tension." The Canadiens feted their final Christmas with Toe at the helm in last place.

The Tricolores' miserable start to the expansion era had begun 12–14–8. No road trip quite summed up the season like their first visit to California, in November. The Canadiens lost 2–1 at the Oakland Seals before the Los Angeles Kings scored four unanswered goals in a 4–2 victory the very next night. Another dour defeat inspired further consternation in Toe, and a spectator named Bernard Weisman seized on Blake's misery. Weisman and his friend Norman Southerby had been heckling Blake at the Los Angeles Memorial Sports Arena, uttering taunts such as "Are you a sorehead?" and "Why don't you watch the game,

Toe?" Blake ignored them until Weisman moved forward and leaned toward the Canadiens bench. "What's the matter, Toe baby, you got rabbit ears?"

Blake's eyes widened as he turned to respond, motioning for Weisman to come down, closer . . . "Then you'll see what happens." Accounts differ from that point.

"The last thing I remember is being hit on the top of the head with a hockey stick," Weisman said.

One witness—Peter Tenen—confirmed that account, saying "Blake took a stick and swung it into the audience and hit Weisman," who fell down with his head "spurting blood" and screaming "my brains are coming out." Tenen said the Canadiens bench then started pummeling him with sticks, with Provost—identified by his No. 14 jersey—dealing a particularly vicious blow. Southerby suggested Blake's blow "was not injurious" but did describe a tomahawk chop descending on Weisman. Weisman said he spent 13 days in West Los Angeles Hospital with a six-inch scalp laceration that needed 23 stitches to close.

Bruce Blake remembers his father being concerned about the possibility of jail time but insisting he had never swung a stick at the man. According to Bruce, Toe picked up the stick as Weisman approached, but then sobered to the reality of the moment and realized what he was doing. Weisman then lunged at the 55-year-old Canadiens coach before stumbling over the seats to end up behind the Montreal bench on his hands and knees, staring at a crowd of hockey men. Blake stepped back, losing his fedora as three or four players jumped to his aid, pummeling Weisman with their sticks and their fists. Meanwhile, on the ice, the game continued.

The bedlam drew the attention of Los Angeles coach Red Kelly, who thought he spotted the 39-year-old Weisman take a swing at Blake and knock the Old Lamplighter's hat from his head. "Blake then came around with his fists and really corked the guy," sending Weisman back into the seats, Kelly said. Kelly didn't see any players hit Weisman with sticks, and "I never saw a stick in Mr. Blake's hand."

The judge initially dropped the 6-19 charge—assault with a deadly weapon—after Blake and Provost were questioned by Los Angeles police, including one who bore an uncanny resemblance to *Dragnet*'s Joe Friday. Blake and Provost were arrested on the Canadiens' next visit, in March, and Weisman and Mrs. Margaret Ottens filing a combined $655,500 civil suit. Ottens claimed to have suffered a concussion after one of the swinging sticks grazed her.

"Weisman assumed he was going to get several thousand dollars and the reason he offered me a cut was that I told him I made sure a few witnesses gave their names to the police," Southerby said.

According to Blake, Weisman "had been yelling at me all night but I didn't mind that as long as he stayed in his seat. He came down to the bench and knocked my hat off. Then I don't know exactly what happened. Before I knew it, my players were swinging their sticks at the man and he was going up the stairs with blood in his hand."

Judge Joseph Sprankle Jr. ultimately dismissed the case against Blake and Provost after granting a motion for a judgment of acquittal because of conflict of testimony. Bruce remembers Provost was "shitting his pants" before the final verdict.

"In view of the numerous witnesses on behalf of the defense to indicate Mr. Weisman was the aggressor—leaning into the box and taking pokes at the coach—that the action could very well be interpreted as defensive for the coach," Judge Sprankle said. "When I convict anybody, I have to be satisfied that if I'm going to send them to jail my conscience is clear. I couldn't do that in this case."

The case hung over Blake for much of the season. While it was ongoing, he was reportedly constantly on edge, blowing up at the press over the slightest thing. It may have been the low point of his career, as the club felt the need to organize a series of luncheons aimed at promoting better relations between the media and club management. Blake was boiling inside when he was asked to sit at a table alongside MC and one-time friend Jacques Beauchamp. President Molson felt better communication was necessary when he looked at Blake's reaction to questions about his breakup of the "Kid Line" of Jacques Lemaire, Mickey Redmond and Danny Grant following a 2–2 tie with Chicago.

"After working so hard, waking up in the middle of the night and all to study my lineup, this seemed like a stupid question and it still does," said Blake to the *Montreal Gazette*. "I had my own reasons for not playing Danny Grant and felt that I had figured everything out beforehand. These young fellows have a lot of promise but you can't expect the kids to carry the Canadiens. I'm not going to rap any of my players for the benefit of the press."

By the end of December, Blake was charging at referees, forcing players like John Ferguson to restrain him on the Garden ice in Boston as he berated referee Bill Friday over a blown penalty call. Beliveau, injured and sitting up in the press box, was forced down onto the bench to take over as Blake sat a few yards away, relaying signals to trainer Larry Aubut. He then waited in the rink corridor leading to the dressing rooms to ambush the officials with verbal abuse. Toe was fined $250 for his actions, and his conduct was labelled "reprehensible" by president Clarence Campbell.

Dick Irvin Jr. has particularly personal memories of this game because Beliveau's decision to play Lemaire on the power play worked out. Irvin's CFCF postgame report that evening opened with a quip about Blake not being there to see Lemaire's goal because he'd been thrown out of the game. Betty Blake took exception to this, and when the Blakes attended the subsequent Montreal Sports Celebrity Dinner—a charity gala hosted by Irvin that raised funds for the Montreal Children's

Hospital—she led Irvin into the mezzanine of the Queen Elizabeth Hotel to deride him over saying "such a terrible thing about her husband on the newscast." Toe watched, standing behind her and laughing. "She never spoke to me again for the rest of her life," Irvin recalled.

Blake never returned to another of Irvin's galas. The Rocket, Beliveau, Scotty Bowman, Guy Lafleur, Sam Pollock—many Canadiens legends were guests of honor, celebrated for their impact on Montreal sports. Irvin asked Blake to appear in ensuing years, when he was out of the game.

> We showed a film of the celebrity, and they would get up and say a few words, and he flatly, utterly, completely refused. I told him, "Look, Toe, you don't have to say a word," because he didn't want to speak. "Just be there; we'd like to honor you for your contribution to Montreal as a player and as a coach, that's all, just take a bow and sit down and we'll have a little film and wave at the crowd and that's it." He would never do it, and I was disappointed in that because I thought he deserved it. He never agreed to sit at the head table. If you didn't know him, you were left with the feeling he was a grumpy old man, which I don't really think he was. But why would he not be a little bit into it, I never understood.

Blake's avoidance of the limelight became more pronounced. Christmas came and went with the Canadiens in last place. The Blake home was not a happy place that year. Betty's cancer returned. She was no longer attending games, leaving Bruce to go to the Forum with whichever high school friend he wished to bring along. Joan and Mary Jane were at odds with one another, and Toe sat in the middle of it all. Blake ambled to the phone once Joan and the kids had paraded out, picked up the receiver and called his good friend Ron Lister.

Lister was Blake's curling buddy at the Caledonia Curling Club, and they also played horseshoes, cards and golf. Lister, a locksmith who had played hockey himself, socialized in Blake's circle with Red Storey and Danny Gallivan. Blake knew that with Lister there would be no hockey talk, only late-night card games and refills of rye. Sometimes Lister would open up the shop on Wellington Street so they could get a card game in away from everyone, with Blake flinging his cards or questioning a shuffle when things didn't go his way. Blake did everything by the book. Once, he forced a game of horseshoe to be replayed because the pins were two inches off. Anything to avoid losing. The shop was preferable because Lister's neighbors in Verdun almost always seemed to know when Blake was visiting, with queues forming down the block for a glimpse, a handshake or a story from the Old Lamplighter. Blake would never stay long on those visits. He chased his scotch and water with a rum after hanging up the phone. It was Christmas, after all.

He looked out the window to his backyard, toward the deserted fifth hole of Meadowbrook Golf Club. Betty was in bad shape, and here he was, all alone in this compound. His fist seized up on the glass as he retraced the argument with Joan. *Better to be alone before the booze makes me say something I regret,* he thought.

Toe's mind raced. *How could I have told the president of CNR to go to hell,* he thought, remembering one of the many front-row hecklers he had squared up to over the years. *Maybe that's where Mary Jane got it from, she's volatile like her old man.* The relationship with Joan wasn't great—it was clear she had always been closer with Betty—but they always made time for one another. Toe's life had always been hockey. Had he given so much to this love he'd neglected those around him?

"The most important thing a coach has to do is just more or less try to keep a happy family," Red Fisher would write in a final farewell to Toe. "The worst thing is when dissension creeps in, and it's especially bad when you're losing. That's when your work really gets difficult. You lose . . . and so many things start to happen."

Here, at 206 Sheraton Drive, Blake didn't have that winning feeling.

• • •

"All we have to do is win a few games in a row and we'll be right up there," Blake said as the Canadiens said goodbye to Canada's Centennial year. "Everybody wants to win. If they're not on top they start crying. But it's a little early to be doing that. I've been there. I know what it's like to become so despondent everything you do is wrong."

The team responded with a 16-game unbeaten run, including 14 victories. The Canadiens were back atop the standings, going on to edge the Rangers for the division title. They swept the Bruins and beat the Blackhawks in five games to set up a date with St. Louis in the final. It was the first Stanley Cup Final in the new era of extended playoffs. The expansion Blues, led by Scotty Bowman, included former Canadiens Doug Harvey, Dickie Moore, Red Berenson and Jean-Guy Talbot. But the NHL newcomers quickly found themselves in a 3–0 hole. Still, Blake came crashing into the locker room after the second period of Game 4, with Montreal trailing 2–1 on home ice at the Forum.

"Nobody remembers who came second" Blake hollered. He was seething after the home crowd had cheered St. Louis's goal. "Get mad! You're better than they are! Look up! Up!" And with that, the players raised their chins high, their gaze landing on pictures of Howie Morenz, Joe Malone, Newsy Lalonde and other Canadiens legends painted high on the locker room walls. One of those profiles depicted Blake.

Those portraits were accompanied by a famous line, lifted from the World War I poem "In Flanders Fields," by John McCrae: "To you from failing hands we throw the torch be yours to hold it high." The French translation read: "Nos bras lassés vous tendent le flambeau, à vous toujours, de le porter bien haut." Frank Selke had had it inscribed on the Canadiens locker room walls in 1952. In McCrae's words, he'd found a phrase that spoke to the legacy the players in that dressing room left behind. Blake had never had the opportunity to look up to this inspirational phrase as a player. He regretted that he had not been able to use it as inspiration out on the ice. He tried his best to ensure that the players around him understood this. "Nobody grabbed McCrae's quote like Blake," Dick Duff once said. "He always let us know that if we don't catch that torch, he'll light it under us."

The Canadiens went out and scored two unanswered goals in the third period for a 3–2 win and a 14th Stanley Cup. The excitement might have been too much for 59-year-old Chibougamau native Guy Valiquette, who succumbed to a heart attack in the south grays section of the Forum. Blake stood by as Beliveau, on crutches, addressed the crowd of 15,505, with the Stanley Cup parked on a table at center ice. Blake nostalgically gazed into the silver Cup—set to be inscribed with his name for a record 11th time—preparing himself for the inevitable announcement, in a slightly baggy suit that did not hide the extra weight he had put on in recent years. His face was tired, his age betrayed by the worry he had endured in recent years. "I had to quit," Blake said later. "It's a helluva game. I had to quit, but I won't say I'll never come back."

"This series has been one big disappointment after another for me," Beliveau said. "First the broken leg. Now Blake (retiring). He's been a great man for this team, a tremendous force which has driven us to success."

After the champagne baths and celebrative stogies, Blake packed his belongings into a trunk and headed for the door, his trusty fedora and jacket in his right hand, his head hung low as he made his way toward the exit. His players carried the celebration into the night while Duck shuffled up the road to the Montreal General Hospital to be with Betty.

CHAPTER 13

LIFE AFTER DEATH

"Black or white, Catholic or not, French or English, I have but one goal: to win games."

TOE EASED INTO POST-HOCKEY life more quickly than expected. He found comfort in his recliner, where Canadiens road games were much easier to stomach in a horizontal position with a drink in hand. Blake remained with the organization as the assistant vice-president to general manager Sam Pollock, who wanted a stern, experienced man around to help guide 30-year-old scout-turned-coach Claude Ruel. It was the first of many titles Blake would collect over his final 20-plus years with the organization: executive, advisor, consultant, representative to NHL committees, public relations, vice-president of hockey and even broadcaster. The club wanted to do good by Blake for his 26 years of service by keeping him in the know and on the payroll. Blake became an in-house elder statesman, an advisor without a portfolio, dispensing counsel within hockey operations.

"Dad," Bruce asked his father one day, "what do you do?"

"I'm not quite sure, Bruce. I go in and they ask me questions."

Toe's time inside the Forum executive offices diminished as he got older, but visits to his hockey home never stopped, even when Alzheimer's began to take a hold of him. He would meander down from his office on the second floor to observe practice, always trying his best to remain inconspicuous. That was easier when Beliveau was jogging laps around the ring of white seats above. Having legends like these just hanging around inspired the players, even in practice, with Chris Chelios "flying like hell" whenever Doug Harvey dropped into the Forum.

"In those days, that was part of the success of the Montreal Canadiens," says former Habs coach Jean Perron, who remembers his first visit to the Forum in the 1980s, when he strolled in to find Blake, Beliveau, Harvey and Dickie Moore on hand. "They all told me, 'Jean, we're around to give you a hand if you need it.'"

The family atmosphere extended from top to bottom, with Blake and others often dropping in on the locker room to rouse the team, lend a word of support or to just get another taste of that feeling from their playing days.

"I asked him for counseling—when you have a guy like Toe Blake around you want to know what he would do, what kind of evaluation he could make about our team. But he never wanted to express himself about that. He was not the coach and he wanted to respect that boundary," says Perron. "Every time I said, 'Toe, you watched my team last night, what do you think?' he said, 'All right, you are doing a good job.' I'd ask him to go into specifics, but he never wanted to go further. I would ask him questions and he would always say the same thing: 'Jean, your generation of hockey players and my generation of hockey players are two different things. The hockey that you play . . . my kind of hockey was different.'"

Blake spent the mornings in an office he shared with Floyd Curry before breaking away with his former teammate—or any other old-timer who might be around—for lunch at the Texan Restaurant around the corner on St. Catherine Street. Blake's picture was among the celebrity portraits lining the walls of a venue owned by a Greek named George. Afternoons were normally spent at the tavern. Toe could be a pleasant and generous lunch companion when he was in a good mood, which was the norm after retirement. He always took an aperitif before his meal, normally a Manhattan. Young Forum executives listened in awe as he talked, startled when his fist crashed down on the table to make a point. Toe did not speak much, and he did not need to for his point to come across. To someone who had never laced up the skates professionally, it was suddenly clear how little Blake needed to say to intimidate an opponent. The difference in generations was often clear; Blake could not always understand the approach modern players took to the game, and didn't care to.

"How the hell could he do that?" an exasperated Blake was often heard remarking from his designated press box seat number 69 high above the Forum ice. "How could you even think of doing that!?"

For many members of the press who had covered him during his coaching days, he was suddenly a delight to sit next to on bus or plane trips. He talked all sports, not just hockey, and sometimes even politics. Blake could still display the flashes of rage and intolerance that had accompanied him during his time behind the bench, but they were no longer full-blown episodes. When the Pocket Rocket called coach Al MacNeil "incompetent" during the 1971 Stanley Cup run, Blake took exception to the French press's portrayal of this episode as a decisive language issue for the club. "Black or white, Catholic or not, French or English, I have but one goal: to win games," Blake told a reporter.

Blake's health improved after he exited the day-to-day coaching grind. The ageing process almost seemed to reverse, and he suddenly looked closer to his actual age of 56. He was calmer, more relaxed—or as relaxed as he could possibly be. There were more dinners at the once-iconic Ruby Foo's, his favorite restaurant, where he would order drinks by the pair on busy nights. But if someone rubbed him the wrong way with their analysis of the Canadiens, a violent shouting and swearing match could still ensue.

"For the first couple of years after I quit I would get just as wound up in the seats as I did behind the bench. But it tapered off," he said in December 1968.

> I miss coaching, but I missed playing more when I stopped that. That was the hardest thing, retiring as a player. Jeez, that was tough. I played thirteen years for Montreal and I was one of five or six veterans who had been together a long time—guys like Durnan and Bouchard and Chamberlain—and I was the first to go, and it hurt me to go while they stayed on. I broke my leg bad and I had a good coaching offer and I had no choice, but once you've been a player, you never stop wanting to go on being one. You just don't know how much you'll miss it until you stop.
>
> What you miss most is being with the guys. You're part of a club. You're one of the boys. You're in there with the sweat and the suffering and the fun and the excitement. It's never the same when you're not playing. It's never the same as a coach. But as a coach, you're still close to the guys and part of the action. Even now, I travel with the club a lot. I'm still with the team. But it's not the same. I think I made the right decision. I'm

> feeling easier in a way. I can get through afternoons now. But thank the Lord I'm still in the game. I couldn't leave the game. I couldn't even say I won't coach again someday. I couldn't ever say that. The only thing I can say for sure is I'll never play again. And it hurts to say that, even now, all these years later.

Blake did get one last crack at coaching in January 1969, when Ruel stepped aside to let him manage the Eastern Team in the All-Star Game. Blake, looking grayer and thinner on top, hammed it up with Western Team coach Scotty Bowman in the days leading up to the game, flashing his spray of teeth for the cameras without conceding whether he would return. "No one can predict the future. This might be my last game. Yes, I said 'might' and don't you fellas try to make anything of it," he said, never missing an opportunity to take a poke at the press. "I'll play the lines the way they were picked. I don't want the hockey writers mad at me anymore." After the game ended 3–3, Blake insisted "this was my last game—for this year anyway, and don't ask me anymore."

The coaching cameo was a real treat for Blake, who clung to the hockey lifestyle however he could. Being around the players brought joy amid a time of turbulence, with Betty's health unraveling quickly after his retirement. Whenever the Canadiens asked something of Blake, he agreed. Pollock was pleased to have Blake around to help with Ruel, who spoke little English. Toe traveled with the team and helped Ruel with hotel check-ins, something his players hated to see. They expected a coach to reign supreme as Blake had. Blake did his best to stay out of Ruel's way. He didn't want to heap further unfair pressure on him, especially in that first year. It frustrated him to see the values he held so dear—of total, absolute concentration on game day—slip away after NHL expansion. Locker rooms were becoming looser, rookies would show up to practice unshaven, players were late for team buses and tip money for bellhops went missing. The class that used to come with winning the Stanley Cup was slowly fading before Blake's eyes.

At one point, someone in the Canadiens public relations team decided the tight-lipped 60-year-old would be a good fit as broadcast partner to color man Dick Irvin Jr.

"He hated every minute of it," Irvin remembered. "Maybe they wanted Toe to be there as moral support for Scotty (Bowman). It lasted about a month. I had to prod everything out of him. I think after one long west coast trip he didn't want to do it again. I told him just not to show up on the next road game and he didn't and no one said anything."

The Canadiens teams of the late 1960s and '70s were always strong, and there were always tough decisions to make about which player would sit out and watch the game from the press box. Blake would visit the dressing room after the game and search out a player who'd had a tough game or hadn't dressed and remind them there were better days ahead. "Just be ready and you'll get your opportunity," said Blake, an icon to these players and a positive influence that each coach—whether it was Ruel, Al MacNeil or Bowman—appreciated. Blake enjoyed speaking with them all—they were hockey men, after all. If he wanted more than a few words without embarrassing a struggling player, he'd wait until the locker room had cleared out before making his approach.

He did this with Ken Dryden in 1972 after the netminder conceded eight goals in one game against Boston. "Don't take this one home with you, Ken, leave it here. The only way is to completely forget about it. Don't think about it once you leave here," Blake said with typically wild, rabid look and a tone that indicated no response was necessary.

Blake was always worried about interfering with the coach's authority and tactics. "You have to do what you think is right," Bowman remembers him repeating.

In the 1980s, Blake continued to visit the dressing room and remind players of McCrae's famous words, the expectations that came with being a Montreal Canadien, that the club had to be the example for the rest of the league. "You haven't won anything yet" he reminded the players after their first-round playoff sweep of Boston in 1986.

At home, it would normally just be Toe and Bruce with the TV set on the hockey game, the two of them playing cribbage, bridge—all the card games he had spent so many hours playing. Betty was often too weak to participate and often bedridden after another round of chemotherapy. Mrs. Salter continued to cook and clean and keep the boys company. Toe didn't talk much hockey. But Bruce remembers his father loosening up as they got older, even in those tense final years as coach of the Canadiens. Father and son would sit and discuss the game at the card table, and those conversations would become easier in later years when Bruce began to get serious with his girlfriend, Julie.

"As I got older and more knowledgeable, I would ask him about this guy or that guy," recalls Bruce, whose father was slowly opening up in post-coaching life, often engaging Bruce's friends when they visited. "But I'd never ask what he could have done . . . There was no point in asking him if in hindsight he would have done this or that, because he did everything perfect," Bruce says with a laugh. "He won eight out of 13 times, and he was pissed the five times he lost. He was very competitive, so he was probably wondering, *What the hell happened? We should have won those other five.*"

It wasn't always easy on Sheraton Drive in the years after Toe's retirement. Bruce was now an adult, preparing to step out into the world and from under the weight of his father's shadow, which was pegged to pragmatism borne of the Great Depression and World War II and enabled successes of a certain simplicity. Betty was often the referee inside the home, "the glue that kept us together; she kept the peace amid a lot of friction.

She could calm him down since she was one of the few people he would listen to."

But Betty's death marked the start of a tradition of tragedy for the Blakes.

• • •

The hard, dark days that followed Betty's death in July 1971 took their toll on Toe's relationship with Bruce, who moved out of the family home soon after. For the two male Blakes, it just wasn't working. Bruce had always been "Toe Blake's son," even if he sometimes wanted to scream, "I have a name, too!" They bickered, offering their opinions on matters they probably shouldn't have. Bruce, 21, had just lost his mother and did not need to hear how to run his life from someone who didn't want to listen to any advice himself. Toe had lost his wife and didn't want his brood to tell him how to do things. They never discovered their common point of loss: they had both lost Betty.

"It was a really tough time, a really hard time because Betty went through a lot for many, many years and it was very difficult for him. They were devoted to each other; they were very close. Toe was just devastated," says Margaret McKie. "It must have been terrible to watch her daily suffering because she had so many surgeries and at that time there wasn't much hope. They tried everything. If you knew him, you knew he was racked with pain. She was suffering so much, it was so long and protracted and she was in constant, terrible pain. To watch that must have been horrendous. Her sickness and subsequent death changed things in the family. It was life-altering for Toe. I think he was very lonely . . . From the time she died to the time he got sick—it was never the same."

Bruce, who had moved out of the Blake home, continued to support his father despite the brief estrangement, including appearing by his side on Toe Blake Night in December 1972, when the Canadiens honored the Old Lamplighter. The team wanted to pay homage to their former leader, the inspirational heart and soul of the franchise. Blake was choked up by the time he emerged onto center ice, surrounded by his family, and after receiving an ovation for several minutes, he struggled to put into words his emotions.

"When the ovation went up, it brought back memories of the great days. There were too many of them to recall," Blake said, alternating between English and French in his address to 16,009 supporters from the Forum ice. "Hockey has been my life. I never had the opportunity of getting one of those million-dollar contracts, but hockey was worth more than $1 million to me in plenty of ways."

"I always admired his sentimentality and his emotional side, in defeat and in victory; I've seen him shed tears in both," said Beliveau, who had remained a close friend to Blake after retirement. "He gave so much of himself. Created a feeling of fraternity between us. He gave everything for us. He always loved his privacy. This was one of the toughest jobs I had to do with him, to convince him to accept this party. Toe was nervous about this night for the last month."

One picture from that night features Toe, beaming with happiness, surrounded by his three children. The white-haired Blake cradles a replica Stanley Cup bowl with an easy, comfortable smile conveying the joy he feels for a moment that has combined his own family with his hockey one. But some other photographs of that same moment look like they tell a different story. Only Joan smiles as Bruce, Toe and Mary Jane look to the cameras with dour expressions that convey the Blakes' everyday reality.

Approximately 300 guests attended the ceremony and the reception before the game, with Maurice Richard the only high-profile absentee. Richard's long-running feud with Pollock and the Canadiens, for what he perceived as post-playing-career snub, continued. "I'm sorry, Toe," Richard wrote in his newspaper column, to which Blake was sympathetic. "Maybe if some things had happened in another way, I might have shown up. But I don't want to make anything of it." The banquet at the Hotel Champlain featured plates of shrimp and cold cuts around a centerpiece block of ice carved into the *CH* logo of the Canadiens. Blake welcomed a cigar from John Ferguson as he exchanged stories with Beliveau, Elmer Lach, Doug Harvey, Tom Johnson, Dickie Moore, Butch Bouchard and others. "We used to tell him, 'You're lucky you have us to win all these Stanley Cups'," Jean-Guy Talbot remembers.

He huddled with old friends and, sucking on stogies, they reminisced about years gone by and provided obvious solutions for current dilemmas. The barrier the coach had erected with his former players was gone. These were now all just former players mingling, even if the majority saw Blake as an elder statesman rather than a peer. He may not have said much, but his words carried weight. The boiling personality and tenacity had softened. He finally seemed like the "Uncle Oscar" that former captain Butch Bouchard used to call him because "he walked a little bit like an old man."

"This man loves to win, eh? He communicates this . . . this . . . pride in winning. Some guys can communicate, some guys can't, eh? Toe can," Gump Worsley said. "He has a way, like an earnestness, of making you feel that since the idea of this game is to win, you've got to give it your best shot—every game."

Toe recognized his time had passed. "(I) wish perhaps they wouldn't shoot it in from outside the blue line as much as they do. I think that in many situations they would be better off making the play," said Blake, who had a habit of following up any words that could be construed as criticism with positive ones respectful of the game. "But when the style was to make the play, we used to say they should shoot it in more, so there you go. Anyway, they skate as well today as they used to, and they shoot better."

Blake had already turned down the opportunity to coach Canada at September's Canada-Russia summit, stating simply: "If I was going to come back, it wouldn't be with anybody but the Canadiens."

In June of 1975, Toe was taken to hospital, complaining of chest pains. By October of that same year, he was back at the Montreal General Hospital after suffering from a gall bladder attack. Back surgery would follow. He began taking better care of himself, performing daily exercises that included push-ups and sit-ups. He regretted not taking better care of himself during his coaching years. "I feel better now than I did 10 years ago because I do a few exercises. It's changed my whole life around. I could hardly walk down the street before."

Blake asked for his duties with the Canadiens to be reduced. The road trips and daily appearances were taxing. Eventually, he would come and go as he pleased. He spent more time with his grandchildren on Missisquoi Bay, laughing with his guests while barbequing chickens over charcoal with a beer in hand. As his grandkids grew older, Toe did his best to meet their requests for tickets to games, letting his granddaughter Judy take his seats in the reds while he sat above in the blues. Judy never had a problem finding a date for the game—all the boys idolized Toe. He was just Popeye to her as she looked up toward him for their ritual wave after the anthems were performed. He always welcomed his grandkids and their friends into his home—and they got a kick in meeting a hockey legend. Rather than leaving the tickets at the box office, Toe insisted that the kids come to the Sheraton Drive home to pick them up—he never wanted any of them to go unused. He'd sign autographs for these friends and anyone else who stopped him to ask—he always seemed to have a black Sharpie at the ready. He'd bring a stack of portrait pictures to sign if he was going somewhere with a crowd.

"He was a private man but a generous one, too. He was always giving," Bruce says. "As a grandfather, you saw a different side of him, a softer side that took a long time coming." Toe and Bruce slowly reconciled over the years, with Toe asking Bruce to return to their home on Sheraton Drive. Bruce told his father it was best for their relationship if he didn't, leaving him with Mrs. Salter, who was good company. Family visits became a little more frequent, with Bruce and Joan visiting to play cards, while Mary Jane would come on her own with the kids.

"He always had determination, which showed in everything he did," remembers Mary Jane's son Kenny Blake. "Even when he was older, and we'd be out in the driveway, horsing around taking shots on goal, we'd ask him to join in and show us his shot. He'd take the stick and really take his time, examine the net and line up his shot and rip it into the top corner. The shot was so hard it would force the net back and down to the ground!"

Toe was pleased with the club's fortunes under Scotty Bowman, who continued Blake's great winning legacy by propelling the Canadiens to another extended period of success. Montreal won five Stanley Cups between Bowman's appointment in 1971 and his exit in 1979. Bowman's departure for Buffalo saw Blake promoted to vice-president of hockey (again) as general manager Irving Grundman turned toward a club legend to help steady the uncertain waters.

"I feel better today than the day I retired 12 years ago," said the 67-year-old Blake, who took three weeks to mull over the offer before shaking on the deal. "It was a deal I couldn't refuse."

Much of the role consisted of Blake filling in for Grundman when the GM was unavailable, including on the road. Red Fisher remembered one instance that season when Serge Savard was late for the bus, holding up Toe, the team and coach Bernie Geoffrion for 20 minutes. To Blake, looking down repeatedly at his wristwatch, one player holding up the team was unacceptable. "He liked it even less that Geoffrion didn't bring it to the attention of Savard. 'That's the beginning of the end of Geoffrion,' Blake grunted." By December, Geoffrion had quit.

Blake, bothered by leg and back problems, continued to travel with the team until the close of the 1980–81 season, when he had seen enough.

"I will never accept that a team like ours accepts such a defeat," Blake said from Edmonton following a 6–2 loss to the Wayne Gretzky–led Oilers, who swept the Canadiens 3–0 out of the playoffs. "I don't understand it, especially how our guys couldn't compete with a team that finished 14th in the standings and that doesn't deserve to be in the playoffs. It proves one thing: that our team is not as good as we think."

Toe's decision was as much down to the on-ice play as it was to the company he kept. Floyd Curry was no longer traveling, which meant Blake found himself alone much of the time with younger club personalities such as Howard Grundman, 40 years Toe's junior, who was unable to penetrate the legend's guarded personality.

"Floyd idolized him, so he helped Toe a lot being there; he arranged a lot. He and Toe were like two peas in a pod; they were fun," recalled Howard Grundman, who often had to drive the pair home from Dorval Airport after the team plane landed. "What was most interesting was to be around him and to listen when he did talk. He would be disappointed in a player's performance and it was hard for him to understand. Toe would get upset with how the guys were then. But he wasn't the most boisterous fella."

"He was there as support if needed," says Jean Perron who coached the Canadiens to their 23rd Stanley Cup in 1986. "The players respected him. He brought to the atmosphere the tradition and history of winning. You weren't bringing a loser with you! He was an example of a hard-nosed, excellent hockey player and a demanding, no-nonsense coach. He was a serious, quiet guy, and very private. He never really talked about himself or his family."

Perron drew on Blake's practice of having the team stay outside the city during the 1986 Stanley Cup run, sequestering them at a South Shore site the players affectionately coined

Alcatraz. Perron remembers Blake making an impact in the postseason, too. "In the playoffs, I was impressed to see all the old-timers . . . What a tremendous motivation you are given . . . Toe was in Calgary, he was with us all the way through. But never in his life would he have accepted (the role of speaking to the players). He never came into the dressing room—never. Toe wouldn't go out of his way to speak to the team, he would just be there. And the players would go and talk with Toe. It was a real family atmosphere."

During these later years, Blake often went to visit Dr. Mulder with any medical issues he had, bringing a bottle of Chivas Regal as a thank-you gift. The bags under his eyes grew heavier, his face gaunt, his hair completely white. He pulled out reading glasses when needed. Despite his advancing age, he hung on to his opinions. When Plante was inducted into the Hockey Hall of Fame, for example, he said, "I still see goals scored that probably are scored because the goalie did not get a proper view of the puck . . . But, hey, I think the mask has prolonged their careers. A goalkeeper used to get hurt so often his nerves just wouldn't take it."

He also continued collecting accolades, including being awarded the Order of Canada in June 1982 for unequalled prominence as a coach. He received a life-size bust of himself—its current location is unknown—that same year. He had often been commended for his razor-sharp recollection of details, but his memory started to slip after the Canadiens' 1986 Stanley Cup triumph. Kenny remembers one visit to his grandfather's when Toe served him a Shirley Temple after Kenny ordered a Manhattan. Blake soon began confusing people and reverting to French in conversations.

> He would confuse my wife, Mary, with my mother, Mary Jane. He would tell me to take care of her; "You know, she's my daughter," he would say. Toward the end he would sign autographs

> "Hec-Toe" rather than "Hector." You could see he was troubled with this disease; his precise signature was turning into a scribble. Toward the end you'd be talking to him and he'd suddenly go into a rant in French, say he was very proud to be French. We figure that his mind started to lose focus once the tavern closed. He lost his livelihood—he was at the tavern every day despite his duties with the Canadiens—and maybe that's when he started to lose focus and slip.

Blake was diagnosed with Alzheimer's in 1987. He continued to live alone with Mrs. Salter's aid in the enormous four-storey home on Sheraton despite grappling with the day-to-day pains of the disease. His children preferred to keep their distance, as Blake's temper often overcame him when they interceded on his behalf. There was no chance he would go into a nursing home willingly. Then there was a car accident when Toe was driving without a license. Beliveau interceded—his son was a police officer at Precinct 25. They took Toe's car away. Floyd Curry's dedication to Blake—which would endure right up to his death in 1995—became even more clear as he drove Toe to appointments and the Forum and spent time with his former teammate. When Curry was unavailable, Beliveau or a driver sent by the Canadiens took him where he needed to go, including the occasional visit to the Forum. But after settling into his office, Blake often called on colleagues before 10 a.m. to lunch with him. And these visits to the Texan were filled with fitful episodes, not respectful conversation, as Blake's hard, unforgiving and mean traits bubbled over, leading to uncomfortable and sometimes intimidating moments in public.

December 18, 1989, proved to be the turning point in his battle with the disease. Joan discovered her father unconscious and bleeding at the foot of the stairs of his home. Blake had suffered severe head trauma in a late-night fall and was taken to the Montreal General Hospital. He was kept under observation in intensive care for days, but his life did not appear in danger. Toe spent Christmas in the hospital and remained there while Canadiens Nation honored Doug Harvey's life at the defenseman's funeral on December 29.

Blake never recovered from the fall. He would soon be moved to the Château sur le Lac nursing home on Gouin Boulevard, where Curry doted on him almost daily. Old friends like Maurice Richard, Red Fisher and Elmer Lach expressed their concern over his health, and all visited once but were then too overwhelmed by Blake's situation to return. Blake was wheelchair-bound and easily agitated when awoken or moved from a comfortable spot. But he never seemed to lose his appetite. Blake remained at the home until his death four years later, munching on cookies and staring vacantly into a television tuned into the Canadiens game. As with most sufferers of Alzheimer's, Blake's final years were a sad betrayal of his true character.

"He was one of the politest men but now his mood jumps suddenly against the nurses that are taking care of him. They obviously understand why, but . . ." said Curry, who had a clear response when asked why he doted on Blake. "Why wouldn't I? He was such a great guy," said Curry, a four-time Stanley Cup champion who not only shared Blake's No. 6 sweater but also ultimately succumbed to Alzheimer's.

Bruce received the call from his sister Joan in May 1995 signaling the end was near. He went to see his father one final time, to say goodbye. He descended the stairs to the lower floor, where they kept the patients whose final days neared. Most were out of their minds, screaming, frightening concerned family members who were there out of love. Bruce walked in to find his father, this mass of a man, bedridden and incapacitated. After the visit, Joan and Bruce decided to make funeral arrangements. Hector Joseph Blake, best known as Toe, died on May 17, 1995.

Hundreds gathered at St. Ignatius Loyola for the funeral three days later, including one Canadiens fan who snapped pictures of former players in suits with his Kodak Instamatic. A who's who of Canadiens royalty joined the Blakes in remembering Toe as Father David Fitzpatrick led the goodbyes in front of a Montreal Canadiens bouquet backdrop. Toe's youngest grandson, Brendan, couldn't attend. He was in the Montreal Children's Hospital, battling cancer.

"Now and then," Beliveau said during his eulogy, "somebody would make a great play and hit the post. He would tell that player: 'I've always told you to hit the inside of the post!'"

The sun shone on the pallbearers, who included former Canadiens trainer Hector Dubois, as they carried Toe's casket down the steps past an emotional Mary Jane and into the hearse. Everyone moved on to Mise au Jeu, the Forum restaurant, for the funeral reception, where a beautiful bouquet of roses was spread out in the Old Lamplighter's honor.

"People say he was stern and strict. I never saw that. I just saw my grandfather as someone who was always enjoying himself and having a good time. He always looked happy to me," remembers Kenny, who was one of the few family members to save mementos from Blake's home following his death.

A stroll through Kenny's house finds an official Montreal Canadiens china tea set in the entrance, while the basement walls are covered with pictures and clippings from Blake's time, including a large black-and-white print of Toe humorously holding up the Cup won in 1968 to a backdrop setting that would not look out of place on a Hollywood red carpet. Kenny has his choice of chairs from the Tavern to settle into—the contrast with Bruce's chest of mementos is obvious. "Bruce was more interested in taking things from the Missisquoi Bay cabin; they brought back happier memories for him. That was a beautiful cottage on an enormous piece of lakefront land. When they sold it, they didn't even take much out of it. Toe's fedoras were lined up high along the mantle and they were left there. Antique guns and swords, pictures—all was just left behind. Joan ripped all the NHL and Canadiens crests from his suits and donated them to Goodwill."

Bruce can't explain why he didn't take more. He wasn't thinking about the future and how nice it would have been to be able to give his children mementos. His mind was scrambled as Brendan lay in hospital, suffering from an aggressive form of cancer that would take his life just three months after Toe's.

Kenny's brother Doug Stuart also collected several valuable items, from the Lady Byng Trophy won in 1946 to a replica Prince of Wales Trophy to hockey sticks and life-size cut-outs of Toe. Those items were lost after Doug and his wife separated. Dougie, as he was known, battled drug addiction for years and ultimately took his own life by hanging in 1999.

"I think a lot of the family would see this stuff as a curse and not recognize the value of it," says Toe's grandson Kenny. "It sits there, and people fight over it. Even my mom's friend, a woman named Hellen, went into Toe's house after everyone and took things and sold them on. There were skates, equipment, hockey stuff, memorabilia, trophies and it was all left behind."

The tragedy did not end there.

• • •

Joan Blake hadn't spoken to Keith since he asked her for a divorce. They had remained under the same roof for at least a week since then, without exchanging words. Keith had been working relentlessly at his advertising business, including nights, which left her anxious and worried. Joan's friends had already noted the stress on their relationship and were concerned. Keith was now gone for several days at a time. They were already sleeping in separate bedrooms. Her two children—Judy and Blake—were out of the house, both living in Alberta. Joan was alone. Ativan alleviated some of the pain, but the half bottle of gin that accompanied her daily routine did little to steady the highs and lows.

Joan had been the public face of a social benefit to raise money for the Alzheimer Society of Montreal in honor of her father. In April 1994, she helped gather 16 corporate sponsors as her father sat inside an old-age residence, content with crackers and unable to recall his past due to the memory-destroying disease. A tiny woman—5-foot-4, 120 pounds—with a great smile, she launched the doubles tennis tournament alongside Toe's former Canadiens charge Dollard St. Laurent for her father and all the others grappling with this the disease:

> For those of us who remain in good health and have the capacity to function, there are never enough hours in a day, in a week or in a month as the days literally fly by. But for the victims of this terrible disease that has taken my father, time loses all significance: minutes slip away without apparent reason, leaving an interminable and incoherent existence devoid of all consciousness. My father and all victims of Alzheimer's are forced into a depressing and hopeless life sentence. This is, unfortunately, the sad reality I live with every time I visit my father. If by associating the name of my father to this event we can raise money to fight the disease, he would applaud and support such an initiative.

Toe passed soon after the fourth edition of the benefit. Her father's death had affected Joan more than most might have thought. The strains in their relationship were clear to everyone who knew them closely. There were great times during Toe's days as coach of the Canadiens, with the glamorous parties celebrating all those Stanley Cups. But Toe continued to side with Mary Jane, widening the already growing gulf between him and Joan. The strains were exacerbated by Betty's death. They may have lived just blocks apart, but Toe rarely ventured to Joan's and, when he did, he rarely lingered. It helped if Bruce was there. The three of them could play cards; peace was maintained and the conversation kept to a minimum. Just as in Toe's coaching days. Joan had practically grown up without a father; the one she had, when he wasn't on the road, was busy with hockey or working in the mines or tending to the leaky faucet in their apartment on St. Joseph Street. Little time was afforded to Joan, who was a woman by the time Toe took over the Canadiens. By then, Mary Jane and Bruce monopolized what time he had for his family.

With both of their parents now gone, Mary Jane was a stranger to Joan, and Bruce had his own family and his own worries following the death of his second child. Her kids were gone, and now her husband was about to leave. To Bruce and his wife, Julie, there was never any indication that Joan suffered from depression; she'd roll into their home for a drink and a laugh. She never revealed what was happening at home. But she had spoken of suicide before, even mentioning it to her children.

Joan roamed her home, smoking cigarette after cigarette, a pack per day, while often wearing the same clothes she had slept in. She wasn't eating. Her health was unimportant compared to the despondency she felt over Keith's preparations to leave. What should she do, she would ask her friends over the phone when they called to check up on her, before ending the conversation by announcing: "I am feeling very down, I don't want to talk."

Joan's friends decided to knock on her door at 448 Wolseley at 7:50 p.m. on Wednesday, October 22, 1997, since she hadn't answered the phone for days. No one answered, but a spare set of keys got them inside. They combed each floor of the McDonald home. The telephone was disconnected. In the basement, they noticed the garage door was closed. In the garage, they found her car idle with the windows covered in dark soot. Except the driver's side window, which was rolled down. They peered through to find Joan dressed in her pyjamas and bathrobe, her arms crossed and her head slouching toward the right, with a trickle of blood trailing across her right cheek. The key was in the ignition, the battery was dead. Joan had been in the garage for days—the odor of gas was no longer perceptible.

"Bruce, I've been to three funerals in a year, what's up with your family?" Bruce remembers one friend asking him. "There was a lot of tragedy in the family. I don't know how you put your finger on it."

CHAPTER 14

LEGACY

"I wanna win that championship, but I wanna win it clean. Old-time hockey! Like when I got started, you know. Toe Blake, Dit Clapper, Eddie Shore—those guys were the greats."

—PAUL NEWMAN IN THE FILM *SLAP SHOT*

WHEN HECTOR "TOE" BLAKE led the 75th anniversary Montreal "Dream Team" onto the Forum ice in 1985, it was hardly a stretch to think Montreal could soon go on to lift a 23rd Stanley Cup. Seeing Toe alongside Canadiens greats like Maurice "Rocket" Richard, Jean Beliveau, Dickie Moore, Doug Harvey, Larry Robinson and Jacques Plante, plus Aurel Joliat and Bob Gainey, it was hard not to feel this club held something distinct, something no other NHL team could claim. That feeling was there, alongside Toe, in the Calgary Saddledome on May 24, 1986, when the Canadiens won an unlikely Stanley Cup against the

Flames. Montreal was no favorite that season, but they were the Canadiens: winning was what they did.

"The Canadiens were more conscious of what it means to win," Gump Worsley once said. "To them, winning was the only thing."

The 1986 Stanley Cup triumph allowed Montreal to surpass the New York Yankees as the winningest professional sports franchise in North America. "What struck me about the Montreal Canadiens and the entire organization then was the embodied philosophy of winning," says Dr. David Mulder, who has been involved with the club since 1964. "I remember sitting between Rocket Richard, Ron Caron and Sam Pollock watching a junior game and they were so intense they would elbow you getting worked up."

The sheer joy of victory and the disdain of losing was what always drove Blake, who instilled that desire for triumph across the players and the organization from the time he laced up his skates in the Canadiens' red-white-and-blue uniform for the first time in 1936, to the beginning of his surrender to Alzheimer's disease in 1989.

"He hated to lose; it was incredible how he could hate losing to such a point. It seemed like he wanted to fight me whenever he lost a game of cards. But the next morning it was forgotten," remembered Canadiens publicist Camille Desroches. "He was a man of honor. He gave a lot to hockey. When he had the chance to make a living as a hockey player, he knew he had to give it everything, it was a chance to make his life."

Whether he had played in Montreal, Toronto, Detroit, Chicago or Boston, Blake would have gone on to become a symbol of the organization regardless of its colors. His life was hockey. Circumstances brought Blake to the Canadiens, where he helped kick-start a turnaround in club fortunes before helping to cement the Punch Line's place in hockey history and served as one of the steadiest captains in club history.

"He helped me score goals," the Rocket said. "We played six years (together). I loved his game. He worked so hard and assisted on a lot of my goals. His desire to win was certain."

So clear was that desire the *Chicago Tribune* noted it in 1940, a season in which last-place Montreal won just 10 times in a 48-game schedule: "Despite the fact that the Canadiens have spent most of the season furnishing themselves a more or less permanent place in the league basement, Blake continues to work as if every game is the deciding one for the Stanley Cup." That desire directly translated into the most successful coaching stint in Canadiens history. Desroches, a walking encyclopedia of Canadiens knowledge, felt Blake was even more valuable to a Canadiens team loaded with stars that won five straight Stanley Cups. "He was the one responsible for those five straight Cups. He completed that group. He knew what he was doing and what his players could do. I felt he could have stayed on as coach. But his wife, Betty, was nearly terminal with cancer and he wanted to be by her side."

"We loved him because he was always honest with his players. He was very respected," Beliveau said. "It wasn't always easy to lead a group of star players like we had. Toe had the capability to choose the right players in determining circumstances. And it's that instinct which guided us to several Stanley Cups."

"He always wanted the best, he set very high objectives for himself," said left winger Gilles Tremblay, who played for Blake from 1960 to '68. "A number one shouldn't finish number two, and a number two will never finish number one. Toe Blake always thought about finishing first, the championship and winning the Stanley Cup. This is how we were brought through the Canadiens system, and when we got to the team Toe would correct our faults or else it wouldn't work. He had one directive—my way or the highway. He was frank. It's a model that probably no longer remains."

Jean Perron remembers poring over newspapers and magazines for any nugget of information he could glean about Blake, his idol, while coaching the University of Moncton Blue Eagles before his jump to the NHL. "I wanted to be as successful as them," says Perron, who hangs a picture of himself with Blake on the walls of his restaurant, La Loge à Perron, in Gaspésie. "Toe was a master of putting his best players in the situation to make them win. It's easy to say, 'Oh, you have talent, and you should win with talent.' Work comes in first place. Work is more important for a hockey team than talent. This is what Toe did with his players. He had his team work hard, disciplined, and talent did the rest."

Lach spoke of the Punch Line as a collection of average players who excelled when brought together. In typical throwback fashion, Blake acknowledged the formidable task of accomplishing the five straight Cups in much the same way: "The challenge of competition is what motivates us. It's not a business you can relax in but that's what makes it interesting, that the challenge is omnipresent. When we are successful, we always want more. When we lose, we want to be done with it as quickly as possible and do our best to get back on the road to victory."

Ultimately, Blake was remembered by the people he valued and respected most—his players—exactly as he hoped: as not only a leader but a fellow player, one of the boys. "He meant a lot (to us). I had the same feeling when I found out Toe Blake had died as I did when I heard news (that) teammates like Claude Provost, Doug Harvey and Jacques Plante had passed," Henri Richard said. "He was a father who was very, very, very severe. And I loved him for that. He was severe but honest. We were scared of him; we didn't always agree with him, but he was almost always right."

Maurice Richard's name disappeared from the Stanley Cup in 2018: the 1959–60 team was on the last ring of champions' names retired to the Hockey Hall of Fame. Blake's name, meanwhile, will remain on Lord Stanley until 2031, when the band featuring championship-winning team from 1968 will be retired to the Hockey Hall of Fame. Toe's name will have featured on one of the most distinguished and oldest trophies in professional sport for nearly a century, since it first appeared in 1935. And yet there is little—tangible or not—for Montreal Canadiens fans to remember Blake by. Looking up into the Bell Centre rafters, it is surprising to see that Blake's No. 6 jersey does not hang alongside many of the men he played with and coached. There is but a bronze-plated plaque inside the Bell Centre to honor one of the organization's most revered and accomplished figures. "Certainly, something should be done for him," says Terry Harper. "He had a great playing career, too. I think a hell of a lot of him. He was the greatest thing to happen to me, getting to play for him."

Bruce Blake obviously feels the same way. He was chuffed by Gaston Legault's push to see Toe's No. 6 retired. Even Valleyfield—a team that Blake coached for less than five seasons and guided to one title—has honored Toe for exploits that happened nearly seven decades ago. "I just can't believe that the Montreal Canadiens haven't done anything," says Stephanie Blake. "I'm really disappointed with them; I can't believe this."

Perron believes Blake may not get his due because hockey coaches in Canada just aren't given credit. "Canada doesn't have the same respect for coaches as they do elsewhere. (Former Manchester United manager) Alex Ferguson is Sir Alex Ferguson. He was knighted by the queen! The coach is the most important person in team sport. He's the leader," Perron says. "The coach is the anchor of the hockey team, no question. Toe was the anchor of everybody. Everyone had so much respect for Toe. Toe said this, we do this, that's it. That was like the Ten Commandments."

The Canadiens have been quiet about jersey retirements since adding Guy Lapointe's name to the retired No. 5 jersey, first made famous by Bernie Geoffrion. "I don't know if there's going to be more in the future," Canadiens owner Geoff Molson said at the time of Lapointe's induction in 2014. "It is difficult, but as you dig deeper on a player like Guy Lapointe you learn that he really deserves it. You can't do them all at once and these things happen. The same thing happens in the Hall of Fame. Players get evaluated annually and this was his year."

Past and present players are hesitant about wading into the debate about Toe Blake. But the majority agree Blake's No. 6 merits a place in the rafters—not only for his playing career but because of everything he did for the Canadiens, from start to finish. Perhaps Toe's coaching success has ultimately—and mistakenly—overshadowed his playing legacy.

While Punch Line teammates Maurice Richard's and Elmer Lach's numbers hang high from the rafters over center ice to remind the current generation about the Canadiens' storied legacy and its Punch Line, Blake's No. 6 is available for any player to wear. Floyd Curry, Ralph Backstrom, Dale Hoganson, Russ Courtnall, Tom Kostopoulos, Greg Pateryn and current Canadiens captain Shea Weber are among the 17 players to don the number since Blake last wore it. When Blake retired prematurely to injury, he was a real threat to take over the NHL all-time scoring lead. Bringing Blake, Lach and Richard together was a stroke of genius, and coach Dick Irvin likely did not foresee the trio earning so many successes in such a relatively short time. And yet of the three members of the Punch Line, only Blake's No. 6 continues to be available for Canadiens players. While Richard's goal-scoring prowess set him apart, little separates Blake and Lach when you examine their career stats. Even when you compare Blake's achievements to famous Habs left winger Dickie Moore, there is little to differentiate the two:

	TOE BLAKE	ELMER LACH	DICKIE MOORE
NHL REGULAR-SEASON GAMES PLAYED	577	664	719
GOALS SCORED	235	215	261
ASSISTS	292	408	347
POINTS	527	623	608
POINTS-PER-GAME AVERAGE	0.91	0.94	0.85
NUMBER OF SEASONS SCORING 20+ GOALS	6 (1938–39, '42–43 to '46–47)	4 (1943–44, '44–45, '47–48, '50–51)	6 (1956–57 to 1960–61, 1962–63)
NHL PLAYOFF GAMES PLAYED	58	76	135
PLAYOFF GOALS SCORED	25	19	46
PLAYOFF ASSISTS	37	45	64
PLAYOFF POINTS	62	64	110
PLAYOFF PPG AVG.	1.07	0.84	0.81
STANLEY CUP–WINNING GOALS	2 (1944, '46)	1 (1953)	1 (1957)
HART TROPHY	1 (1939)	2 (1945)	0
SCORING TITLES	1 (1939)	2 (1945, '48)	2 (1958, '59)
LADY BYNG	1 (1946)	0	0
FIRST TEAM ALL-STAR	3 (1939, '40, '45)	3 (1945, '48, '52)	2 (1958, '59)
SECOND TEAM ALL-STAR	2 (1938, '46)	2 (1944, '46)	1 (1961)
HOCKEY HALL OF FAME	1966	1966	1974
STANLEY CUP	3 (1935, '44, '46)	3 (1944, '46, '53)	6 (1953, 1956–60)

In terms of point production during the regular season, Blake would rank sixth-most productive of the forwards who have had jerseys retired:

PLAYER	PPG—REGULAR SEASON
GUY LAFLEUR	1.20
JEAN BELIVEAU	1.08
MAURICE RICHARD	0.98
ELMER LACH	0.94
BERNARD GEOFFRION	0.93
TOE BLAKE	0.91
YVAN COURNOYER	0.89
HOWIE MORENZ	0.87
DICKIE MOORE	0.84
HENRI RICHARD	0.83
BOB GAINEY	0.43

But when we examine playoffs totals, only Jean Beliveau produced at a better rate:

PLAYER	PPG—PLAYOFFS
JEAN BELIVEAU	1.09
TOE BLAKE	1.07
GUY LAFLEUR	1.05
MAURICE RICHARD	0.95
BERNARD GEOFFRION	0.89
YVAN COURNOYER	0.86
ELMER LACH	0.84
DICKIE MOORE	0.81
HENRI RICHARD	0.72
HOWIE MORENZ	0.56
BOB GAINEY	0.40

Beliveau, Blake and Lafleur were also the only players who were more productive during the playoffs than the regular season. They featured during different periods but, for his time, Blake was one of the best players in club history. To Blake, that mattered most. When Toe was inducted into the Hockey Hall of Fame in 1966, he asked that his Hart Trophy triumph in 1938–39 be clearly noted, even at the expense of his Lady Byng Trophy win. Blake was proudest of winning the highest honor a player could receive for their ability on the ice. This leader of men, who emerged from an impoverished mining community with his sole purpose in life to play hockey, had achieved more than almost any hockey player could dream of, and had helped cement the legend that is the Montreal Canadiens franchise. Hector "Toe" Blake was a throwback to what the club was.

"He was a famous player. On the left wing, in my opinion, he was even better than Bob Gainey or Dickie Moore," Desroches said. "He was someone who got out of you what he wanted to get out of you by being honest with you. He was extremely honest with us and the players. I would say, 'Toe, you remind me of those old stories my mother used to read me with a knight in shining armor with a fair maiden to protect.'"

In 2017, to coincide with its 100th anniversary, the NHL released its list of 100 greatest players, and Toe was right there, "the embodiment of old-time hockey." And still, his jersey remains absent from the rafters above the ice at the Bell Centre.

APPENDIX: TOE BLAKE TIMELINE

1874 FEB. 15: Toe's father, Wilmer Blake, born to Eustache Blake and Christiana Osborne.

1877 JUL. 7: Toe's mother, Arzélie Filion, born to Francois Filion and Adeline D'Aoust.

1911 MAR. 5: Elizabeth "Betty" Marion Walters is born to Edward McKay Walters and Lena Bell Shepherd in Beamsville, Ontario.

1912 AUG. 21: Hector Joseph "Toe" Blake is born in Victoria Mines, Sudbury, to Wilmer Blake and Arzélie Filion.

1913: Blake family moves to Coniston.

1924:	Toe gets a job hitching horses to the milkman's delivery wagon before school. He eventually uses this money to buy his first pair of skates.
1929:	Aged 17, makes his team debut with Coniston Boy Scouts. Will go on to play junior hockey for various clubs in the regional Sudbury Nickel Belt League and the Northern Ontario League.
1931:	Aged 19, joins Sudbury Cub Wolves.
1932:	Wins Memorial Cup Final with Sudbury Wolves; Toronto Maple Leafs include him on NHL negotiating list.
1933:	Montreal Canadiens add him to negotiating list.
1932–35:	Plays nearly three seasons in Ontario Hockey League for Hamilton Tigers before signing with the NHL's Montreal Maroons.
1934 NOV. 24:	Marries Betty Walters in Winona, Ontario.
1935 FEB. 23:	Makes NHL debut for the Maroons in a 4–0 win at St. Louis Eagles. Plays eight regular season games and one playoff game as Maroons win Stanley Cup. Registers 0 points.
1935–36:	Maroons send Blake to Providence Reds of the Canadian–American League at start of season, where he registers 12 goals and 11 assists in 23 games; Canadiens receive Blake and Bill Miller for Lorne Chabot in Feb. '36 trade.

1936 FEB. 11: Makes Montreal Canadiens debut in 1–1 draw against the New York Rangers at the Montreal Forum.

1936 FEB. 22: Scores first NHL goal as Canadiens beat New York Americans 1–0 at the Forum. Finishes season with 3 points (1 goal, 2 assists) in 11 games played.

1936 JUL. 2: First child, Joan, is born at Moyer Nursing Home in Grimsby, Ontario.

1937: Finishes first full NHL season with 22 points (10 goals, 12 assists) in 43 games.

1938: Selected to NHL's Second All-Star Team after 33-point season (17 goals, 16 assists).

1939: Wins Hart Trophy after leading NHL in scoring with 47 points (24 goals, 23 assists); named Canadian Athlete of the Year; First Team All-Star.

1940: Named First Team All-Star after 38-point season (17 goals, 21 assists); Dick Irvin becomes Canadiens coach.

1940 OCT. 30: Irvin names Blake as Canadiens captain.

1943 DEC. 30: The "Punch Line" is born in 8–3 win over Red Wings.

1944 APR. 13: Scores Stanley Cup–winning goal as Montreal beats Chicago 5–4 in overtime for 4–0 series sweep. Sets NHL records with 18 points in nine playoff games and five assists in one playoff game (against Toronto).

1945: First Team All-Star; third in league scoring with 67 points (29 goals, 38 assists).

1945 DEC. 28: Mary Jane, second child, is born in Montreal.

1946 APR. 9: Scores Stanley Cup–winning goal win in 6–3 victory over Boston for 4–1 series victory; wins Lady Byng Trophy; named Second Team All-Star.

1948 JAN. 10: Fractures leg in third period of 1–1 tie against New York Rangers at the Forum. Retires with 527 career regular season points (235 goals, 292 assists).

1948 FEB.: Still on crutches, Toe is sent to Texas to coach Montreal affiliate team the Houston Huskies of United States Hockey League (USHL).

1948 APR. 15: Houston wins USHL's Loudon Trophy as league champion.

1948 AUG. 9: Toe announced as coach of affiliate team the Buffalo Bisons of the American Hockey League; also plays in 18 games, registering 1 goal and 3 assists.

1949 JAN. 18: Parts ways with Buffalo due to differences with owner Art Chapman.

1950: Wilmer Blake dies in Coniston.

1950 FEB. 10: Toe takes over as coach of Valleyfield Braves of Quebec Senior League; plays in 43 games over his first season, registering 12 goals and 15 assists.

1950 MAR. 11: Bruce, third child, is born in Montreal.

1951: Valleyfield wins Alexander Cup.

1952: Opens Toe Blake's Tavern. This marks his last season playing professional hockey as Toe features in one game for Valleyfield during 1951–52 season.

1954: Arzélie dies in Coniston.

1954 APR. 14: Detroit beats Montreal 3–1 in Game 7 to clinch Stanley Cup 4–3. Coach Dick Irvin's last game in charge of the Canadiens.

1954 AUG. 24: Toe announces he will not return to coach Valleyfield.

1955 JUN. 8: Toe named coach of the Montreal Canadiens.

1956 APR. 10: Wins first Stanley Cup as coach as Montreal takes series against Detroit 4–1. Montreal also wins the Prince of Wales Trophy.

1957 APR. 16: Wins second straight Stanley Cup as coach as Montreal beats Boston 4–1 in Stanley Cup Final.

1958 APR. 20: Wins third straight Stanley Cup as coach as Montreal beats Boston 4–2 in Final. Montreal wins Prince of Wales Trophy.

1958 MAY 17: Joan Blake marries Keith McDonald at St. Malachy's Church in Montreal.

1959 APR. 18: Wins record fourth straight Stanley Cup as coach as Montreal beats Toronto 4–1 in Final. Montreal wins Prince of Wales Trophy.

1960 APR. 14: Wins record fifth straight Stanley Cup as coach as Montreal sweeps Final series against Toronto 4–0. Montreal wins Prince of Wales Trophy.

1961 MAR. 26: Slugs referee Dalton McArthur in 2–1 overtime playoff loss at Chicago.

1961 APR. 4: Suffers first playoff series loss as coach when Montreal loses semifinal series 4–2 to Chicago. Montreal wins Prince of Wales Trophy.

1962 APR. 8: Montreal loses 2–0 to Chicago to lose semifinal series 4–2. Montreal wins Prince of Wales Trophy.

1962–63: Toe's worst season as coach; Montreal finishes third in standings and loses semifinal series to Toronto 4–1.

1963: Toe, Betty and Bruce move from duplex at 5259 Ponsard Street to spacious Montreal West home at 206 Sheraton Drive.

1964: Toe named coach of the year by the *Associated Press* and *The Hockey News* after guiding Montreal to the Prince of Wales Trophy.

1964: Toe loses first Game 7 of his career as player or coach as Toronto beats Montreal 3–1 for 4–3 semifinals series victory.

1965 MAY 1: Wins sixth Stanley Cup as coach as Montreal beats Chicago 4–0 for 4–3 Final series win.

1966 MAY 5: Toe earns seventh Stanley Cup as coach as Montreal beats Detroit 3–2 in overtime for 4–2 Final series win. Montreal wins Prince of Wales Trophy.

1966 AUG. 27: Inducted into Hockey Hall of Fame.

1967 MAY 2: Montreal loses to Toronto 3–1 to lose Stanley Cup Final series 4–2.

1967 NOV. 19: Toe reportedly attacks fan at Los Angeles Kings game.

1968 MAY 11: Toe retires after guiding Montreal to eighth Stanley Cup under his reign as Canadiens beat St. Louis 3–2 for 4–0 series sweep. Blake guides Montreal to a ninth Prince of Wales Trophy over his 13-year coaching tenure.

1971 JUL. 16: Betty Blake dies from cancer.

1975 JUN. 18: Toe taken to hospital suffering from chest pains.

1975 OCT. 28: Taken to hospital because of a gall bladder attack.

1982: Receives Order of Canada.

1983 JUN. 21: Inducted into Sudbury Kinsmen Sports Hall of Fame.

1983 NOV. 29: The Toe Blake Tavern closes.

1987: First symptoms of Alzheimer's appear.

1988: *The Hockey News* places Blake 66th on all-time player greats list.

1989 DEC. 18: Toe taken to hospital emergency after fall in his home.

1995 MAY 17: Toe Blake dies aged 82 in Montreal. Funeral is at St. Ignatius Loyola three days later.

1995 AUG. 8: Grandson Brendan dies from cancer nine days before eighth birthday.

1997 OCT. 22: Daughter Joan dies by suicide.

1999 JUN. 7: Grandson Douglas Stuart dies by suicide.

2010 JUL. 31: Daughter Mary Jane dies.

2017: NHL includes Blake in list of 100 greatest all-time players.